WARS

AND RUMORS OF WARS

When I consider the short duration of my life, swallowed up in the
eternity that went before me and the eternity that comes after, the small
extent of space I fill, the narrow limits of my field of view, swallowed
up as I am in the infinite immensities of space, which I do not
know, and which know not me, I am terrified and astonished
to find myself here rather than there. For there is no reason whatever why I should be here rather than there, why now rather
than then. Who put me here? By whose order and direction have
this place and this time been assigned to me?

Blaise Pascal

In peace and war I have found that frequently, naked and unashamed,
one has to go down into what one most fears and in that process,
from somewhere beyond all conscious expectation, comes a saving
flicker of light and energy that, even if it does not produce the
courage of a hero, at any rate enables
a trembling mortal to take one step further.

Laurens van der Post

And when you hear of wars and rumors of wars, do not be alarmed;
this must take place, but the end is not yet.

Mark 13:7

ROGER LINCOLN SHINN

WARS

AND RUMORS OF WARS

ABINGDON PRESS
NASHVILLE & NEW YORK

To Reinhold Niebuhr (1892-1971)—
teacher, colleague, friend

CONTENTS

FOREWORD

I belong to a generation familiar with war. Born during World War I, soldiers in World War II, my contemporaries are living through a period when war has become endemic in human history. It is not the first such period. It may be the last for the portentous reason that war now, as never in the known past, can destroy life and end history.

This book begins in personal history and reaches out into the history and thoughts of others. In the closing days of World War II, I was released from a German prison camp, returned to the United States, and granted the leave the Army gave to all ex-prisoners of war for rest and recuperation before reassignment. Mostly during those days I exulted in freedom and restoration to family and friends. But during part of each day I stole off to write out a record, based on a slim penciled diary, of my later days in the war. I wrote for myself and shared the result with my family and one trusted teacher and friend. The friend, David E. Roberts, urged me to publish the record, but I had no desire to do so. I did publish a few miscellaneous memories and one small book of reflections on the war, but this record was personal. I wrote it as an act of cleansing, then filed it away and never re-read it during twenty-five years.

Then my students and some other young men, both soldiers and civilians, drove me to think further about war, to write down some of my thoughts, to testify in court. I found myself picking up my yellowing record of the past and exploring what that younger man—myself and yet not *my* self—had thought and done. I found myself reading and writing some more.

One result is this book, so unlike any other book I have written. Part I is that record written in 1945. I have cleaned up the spelling, moved around the commas, and clarified some of the hastily written sentences. But I have resisted the temptation to make it seem more mature than it was. The story is there in its immediacy and naïveté. At a few points, when I have wanted to add an afterthought or correct an error or fill in historical information that I have learned in the interim, I have added a footnote rather than disturb the text. All the footnotes come from the present, not the original record.

I have asked myself why I now want to publish what I once preferred to keep in silence. I guess that part of the reason is that time has brought a little serenity to a mind once timid about self-exposure. Another reason lies in the changing course of cultural history. One current theory, which I reject, is that the only true philosophy and theology are autobiography. A theory with more to be said for it is that an autobiographical prolegomenon is appropriate to all human reflection. I'm not sure of that. But I will settle for Sören Kierkegaard's criticism of the heresy that separates thought from the thinker. So I start with myself at a time when the world, more than in the recent past, regards such a starting point as an act of candor rather than of exhibitionism.

Part II of the book is different, yet intimately related to

Part I. It is a reflective analysis of some of the ethical, political, and personal issues involved in war and man's propensity for war. Because the thinking was done under the impact of persons and events, it too had to be written in the first person. I hope that parts of it make sense in any context; I know that parts of it draw their meaning from the older record of Part I.

To put in print a book like this is to make oneself vulnerable. But to live in our time is to be vulnerable. Or, more precisely, to live in our time is to be aware that life in all times is vulnerable. Since that is so, it is good to know it.

Roger L. Shinn

November, 1971

PART I
171 DAYS
A FRAGMENT OF
AUTOBIOGRAPHY

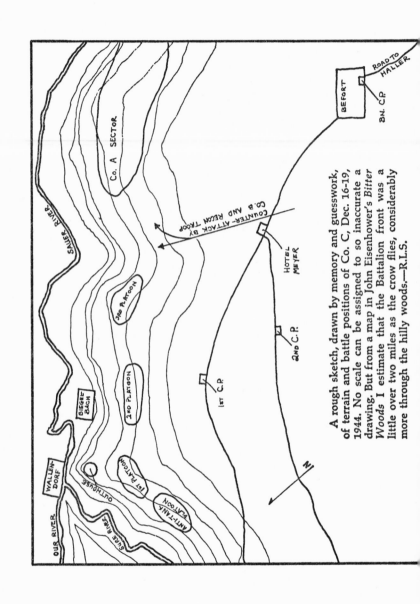

A rough sketch, drawn by memory and guesswork, of terrain and battle positions of Co. C, Dec. 16-19, 1944. No scale can be assigned to so inaccurate a drawing. But from a map in John Eisenhower's *Bitter Woods* I estimate that the Battalion front was a little over two miles as the crow flies, considerably more through the hilly woods.—R.L.S.

CO. A SECTOR.

SAUER RIVER

COUNTER-ATTACK BY CO. B AND RECON TROOP

HOTEL MEYER

2ND C.P.

1ST C.P.

N

BEFORT

ROAD TO HALLER

BN. C.P.

SIEGEL BACH

2ND PLATOON

3RD PLATOON

WALLEN-DORF

OUTHOUSE

1ST PLATOON

ANTI-TANK PLATOON

OUR RIVER

BLUEE RIVER

1. BATTLE

December 15, 1944, was pretty much like any other day. From our positions in the hills and woods of Luxembourg, we could look across the Our and Sauer Rivers into the Siegfried Line and occasionally see a Jerry or two walking about. They were beyond rifle or machine gun range, but if several stuck their heads out at once, the artillery observers might call for a few rounds on them. We had evidence that the famed Siegfried Line was formidable; I had inspected it from the air and had been inside some of its captured pillboxes farther north. But here both sides were taking it easy, satisfied to save their strength because they were pouring it out extravagantly to the north, where the First Army had recently taken Aachen in a rough and wearing siege and was now grinding painfully and bloodily through the Hürtgen Forest.

We knew our positions well. Company C of the 60th Armored Infantry Battalion (Ninth Armored Division) had occupied this ground for about ten days and had been in this same position for a week during November. We were spread out too far, we knew; as Company Commander I was responsible for a front that a battalion or even a regiment might hold adequately. That meant that there were big gaps which no one covered. Platoons and sometimes even squads kept contact by telephone. The anti-tank platoon on the left sent regular patrols to the 109th Infantry Regiment of the 28th Division, uncomfortably far away on our north.

But we were not worried. We had been assured many times that the Germans were spread out even more thinly. It was a little like the "phony war" of several years before. The Jerries sent out a few patrols, and we sent out a few. They occasionally dropped a few rounds of artillery in our area, and we sent back ten times as much. Both sides were rationed on ammunition, but we had more than they. We reported, for evaluation by intelligence officers up the line, every movement of lights at night and every sound that might indicate truck movements; but there was never much. Only two nights before, I had taken a patrol out onto a cliff overlooking the river and the German town of Wallendorf. Our mortar had fired flares across the river. We stared down into the ghostly, half-destroyed town but discerned no sign of enemy activity. Everything was quiet.*

The 15th of December, like other days, started out cold and gradually warmed up. The fog, which often filled the

---

* Our "tissue-thin front," as General Bradley later described it, was part of a calculated risk. General Eisenhower was to write about it: "Through late November and early December the badly stretched condition of our troops caused concern, particularly on Bradley's front. In order to maintain the two attacks that we then considered important we had to concentrate available forces in the vicinity of the Roer dams on the north and bordering the Saar on the south. This weakened the static, or protective, force in the Ardennes region. For a period we had a total of only three divisions on a front of some seventy-five miles between Trier and Monschau and were never able to place more than four in that region." The Generals expected a German counterattack—and actually wanted it, since they thought it would weaken the opposition with less cost to our armies than the hard attacks over difficult terrain, but they assumed that the counterattack would come farther north. See Dwight D. Eisenhower, *Crusade in Europe* (Garden City, N.Y.: Doubleday, 1948), pp. 337-41; Omar N. Bradley, *A Soldier's Story* (New York: Henry Holt and Company, 1951), pp. 437-38, 451-56.

river valley and hid each side from the other, lifted in the afternoon. I toured the company positions, partly in jeep and partly on foot. (The armored forces always talked of peeps rather than jeeps, but I'll use the common term in this record.) During the afternoon, I stopped for information at the Battalion Command Post, located in a large, well-built hotel in the town of Befort. Then I returned to my company C.P.— an abandoned house in the company sector, which we had moved into a few days before, because it was dryer and more convenient than the dugout we had been using. Soldiers in combat grasp for little luxuries. Battalion in the late afternoon sent out an ambulance, conspicuously identified by a huge red cross, which picked up a guide from the company and went down to the river bank to bring back the body of an American soldier, who had been found there by one of our patrols. He had been killed weeks before, when the Americans reached the river and pressed toward Trier at the high tide of the swift sweep through France. To recover his body now was an act of piety, functionally useless, but serious. The hard facts of logistics had stalled that great drive, and in this sector our army had pulled back to settle down on the river banks, while the attack went on at reduced speed, in areas that higher commands decided were more important.

Before dusk three shells fell in the company area. No damage. That was the total for the day. About normal. Chow went out by half-track and jeep to the platoons. Final details of co-ordination were sent out to the patrols scheduled to work that night. And December 15, like any other day, ended.

(December 16)

December 16 was like no other day, before or since. I woke early with plaster falling in my face. The C.P. was shaking. Shells crashed fast and furiously; our bewildered senses could not estimate their directions or numbers. Everyone was awake, and the headquarters crew went into action. I ordered the outdoor guards to report every bit of information they could get on the barrages, locations, duration, etc. Soon they brought in a hunk of twisted metal, found in a hole a hundred yards from the house, and we could see without doubt that it was big stuff. A sergeant came in from his night patrol of the river bank and reported strange sounds a few hours before; we noted his observations and sent him back to his platoon to prepare to fight. Telephone messages were coming in from all the platoons. Each had the same story. Artillery, lots of it, was coming down on the whole front.

I took the phone and called "Comfort 6," the Battalion Commander. ("Comfort" was the Battalion code name—and produced its quota of cynical wisecracks in that chill rainy autumn.) Lt. Colonel Kenneth Collins said that his hotel had been shelled hard and that he was moving into the basement. The reserve company's billets in town had been blasted, with some casualties. I reported our situation and rang off.

Messages continued to come in from the platoons. But there were long interruptions, as the big shells tore up telephone wires. Quickly the wire crews went into action and restored communication; that was the one thing we *had* to have, scattered as we were. The shelling continued as daylight increased. But as we became accustomed to it, we took advantage of the lulls. For though the crash of the artillery never ceased, it could not land everywhere at once. So our men kept eyes and ears alert, spliced wire, and made ready for the expected enemy assault. When the shells came in, they crouched in their foxholes, and casualties were few.

Still no report of enemy troops. But Co. A, on our right,

was fighting off an attack. I got the word over the phone and warned Lt. McCarthy, my right platoon leader, to watch his right flank. The gap between his men and Co. A was big, and a platoon of Jerries might march through the wooded valley before either company would see it. While we waited and prepared, we wondered. What was Jerry up to? A reconnaissance in force was our favorite guess. Could it be a major attack? Doubtful, but if so, we would fight as hard as we could.

By mid-morning the German skirmishers were hitting McCarthy's platoon. One at a time they ran across the front of his platoon, working their way from Able Company's sector into ours. Mac's riflemen, posted on the cliffs, picked them off as fast as they came. It was more serious when they started coming in through the woods on his right. Able was in a bad way—in danger of being surrounded by the Jerries penetrating between the two companies. And if enough got through, our right flank would fold up. I sent the tiny company reserve (about a squad of men) to help Mac build up his right flank. He not only strengthened his line, but managed to push his troops into the woods a short distance, to fire on the Jerries and perhaps relieve the pressure on Able. With a little more strength, we might be able to squeeze out the enemy penetration. But the Germans kept coming, and the situation looked bad.

I called Comfort 6. "Hello, Ken. This is Moe." (As a security device, we neglected military courtesy and used code names or nicknames over the phone.) "There are more Jerries over on the right than Mac can handle. He has killed a number, but they keep filtering through. With a little more strength, he might drive them out. But now he can only hold them off. We'd like to get them out before night."

It was the first major battle for the Colonel, as it was for all of us. But his voice was cool. He was a crisp and competent West Pointer. "Can you get your mortars on them?"

"The woods are too thick to do much with the mortars. And if we overshoot, we'll hit Able. Have you committed Baker?"

"Baker is starting to counterattack between you and Able. Let your men know so there'll be no mix-ups."

"Good. I'm going over to Mac's platoon, since all the activity is there. Ike [the motor officer] will be at the C.P. and can reach me by phone if you want me," I reported.

"Go ahead, if you think you should, but don't get out of communication."

I made another quick check by phone to see that none of the company except the right platoon was engaged, then headed off in the jeep. My driver dodged the shell holes which were frequent by this time. The barrages were still going on. The enemy artillery never stopped, but hunted out one place after another. We saw huge trees blown out of the ground. I spotted a stretch of 100 yards of our telephone wire chewed up by the shells. It had been relaid like other stretches of wire all through the company sector.

In the third platoon area I jumped out of the jeep and ran through the woods to tough and determined Mac. He led me first to the artillery observation post, where I could look far out ahead and to the right. We saw the Jerries across the river, but their crossing place was hidden. Our artillery was keeping them fairly well scattered. But the Germans had a big artillery superiority, and American troops were not in the habit of fighting that way.

Then we moved around to the right where the woods grew thick and the Jerries were infiltrating. We saw some dead ones. They had come in close before Mac had pushed out on his right. So far, Mac had had few casualties, and our medics were keeping up with their job. His platoon must have killed quite a number of the enemy.

On that right flank Americans and Germans fired at each other from close range. As long as men lay still, using trees or rocks or foxholes or little gullies as cover, they were hard to hit. Neither side fired often. Neither side could advance, or the hidden opposition would slaughter them. The stalemate might continue until dark. But there were still several hours, and perhaps the reserve company, Baker, could swing it our way. Our men were doing a good job in their first big fight. I knew them well. I had trained this company and had led it overseas. Now I was encouraged to see their confidence under fire. There was the mail clerk from company headquarters, carrying ammunition up to the riflemen. He was a conscientious clerk, a headquarters humorist, older than most infantrymen, and I had never thought of him as a combat soldier. How he got up here with a rifle platoon, I didn't know, but he vigorously ran the ammunition up, exposing himself to more danger than the concealed riflemen. A crash of artillery burst in on us. We hugged the ground and watched the shells knock the tops out of the trees. None of us was hit, but one or two Jerries might have caught it from their own artillery.

A runner came up, threw himself on the ground beside me, and breathlessly reported: "Telephone message, sir. The outhouse is captured." Tough news! The "outhouse" was a squad of men in an outpost far out on the company's left front. Their telephone wire, several hundred yards long, had been blasted out early in the morning, and the break had not been found. Their short-range radio had not been coming through either, and there had been no word from them since the regular night contact patrols. With trouble on both ends of the company front, I returned to the C.P. where I had the best chance of communication with the entire company. There I got the story of the "outhouse." The left platoon had seen a bunch of Jerries attack it from the rear, and after a short fight, move in on the isolated squad. That was all.

I waited anxiously during the next couple hours for word from McCarthy of some contact with Baker company, which should be near him in its counterattack. None came. Then through Battalion came news that Baker was finding rough going as it moved up through the woods. The afternoon was disturbed with repeated artillery blasts, though we no longer noticed any except the close ones. Communications went out with the first platoon on the left. Now came word that there were Jerries in the second (center) platoon's area, that the platoon leader had not been seen since early morning. I sent back word for the sergeant to hold the ground as best he could, and if Germans penetrated, to keep contact with the right platoon at all costs, so that he would not be cut off from all help. Messengers came from the first platoon. Jerries were infiltrating up the draw on their right and might cut them off from the rest of the company.

We were deciding that we didn't like our C.P. A shell hit would send the roof crashing in on us. So we moved outside and started looking for another place. I was standing ten yards in front of the house. First Sergeant Long had gone back inside to get some records. We heard the long whine of the Jerry shells, and the barrage came in on us. It was perfect. One of the first shells hit the house, and I felt the debris falling on me as I groveled into the ground. Another hit close on the side, and the man next to me cried. I tried to yell above the noise. "Are you hit?"

"Yes."

"Hold on till it lets up, and we'll take care of you."

The explosions kept rocking the earth and twisting the air.

It was the famous German "screaming meemie," a shell whose shrill whine always gave notice that it was coming. That whine was as terrifying as an explosion ten yards away. It was a whine that rasped on everyone's nerves. Its few seconds' duration seemed forever. In the distance every scream of the screaming meemie seemed to be coming straight toward us. It came louder and louder until perhaps it passed over, and we gasped for a new breath of air as we felt safe from *this* one. Or the scream crescendoed until it pierced our eardrums and the shell crashed close by. This barrage was registered exactly. It was like giant fingers reaching, reaching, sure to find us soon. Every shell was close enough to terrify us. It was relentless, and we were helpless. We could not fight back. Nothing to do but lie there for one, two, or five minutes— whatever the schedule was for the gunner on the other side of the river who, without seeing us or knowing he was hitting anyone, thus put us on the edge of eternity. Not a one of us would have given a nickel for his life.

Then it stopped. I jumped up, started looking for the damage. A civilian woman, hysterical with bleeding face, ran screaming down the road. Our wounded were only two, and the medical sergeant fixed them and sent them by jeep into the aid station in town. The First Sergeant shouted from inside the house. He was lying under a table that held off the falling roof, but was pinned to the floor by debris. A few men got him out. More were trapped in the basement, where they had tried to escape the shells. We tugged away the rubble and got them out, miraculously unhurt.

It was hard to believe that only two were wounded. The reason was that the screaming meemie was not as dangerous as it seemed. Its whine made it the most terrifying of all artillery, and its size (it was about an 8-inch shell) made a reverberating explosion. But it was designed for demolition and was most effective against buildings. Against personnel, the heavy shell case did not throw many fragments and hence killed men only when it came very close. But soldiers could never believe that when they heard the awful whine or felt its concussion.

Five hundred yards away we found an empty house with a basement that looked secure. Quickly the C.P. went in there. It would give artillery protection and black-out during the night. As dusk settled, we were a bedraggled headquarters, in communication with no one.* The late afternoon's artillery concentrations had broken every wire that tied us in with our men or the headquarters above us. While the wire crews worked, I drove in to the Battalion C.P. to learn what I could. The picture was dismal everywhere. "Able" company was hard-pressed. "Baker" company, counterattacking, had not been heard from for two or three hours. In "Charlie," McCarthy, out of communication with me, had got a message to Battalion H.Q., via the mortar battery's wire, that he was now almost surrounded and needed ammunition and medical supplies. There was some hope for reinforcements in the morning, but nothing sure.

"What about the rest of the front?" I asked. There were only vague reports. It appeared that the Germans were attacking in strength to our north. To the south of us, nothing was known. (Though it would be a long time before a picture emerged from the confusion, this information was essentially

---

* Unknown to us, the top command was at that time getting its first information on the German attack. That day General Bradley, driving because the weather was too bad to fly, left Eagle Tac (his forward tactical headquarters) in Luxembourg City to our south for a conference with General Eisenhower at Versailles. In the late afternoon ("at dusk" according to John Eisenhower's account) the conference was interrupted with news of five attacks on the First Army. See Omar N. Bradley, *A Soldier's Story*, pp. 449-50; and John S. D. Eisenhower, *The Bitter Woods* (New York: Putnam's, 1969), pp. 214-16.

right. We were at the south edge of what was to become the famous "bulge." But we could not know this now, and to us, as to all troops attacked by a stronger enemy, it seemed that our sector *must* be the focal point of everything. That night, as through the next few days, we could not understand in our desperation why Corps did not throw in all its reserves where we were. That, of course, would be the sure way to lose a war.)

I returned to my C.P. H.Q. men, a frightened family, and the local gendarme were huddled in the cellar. Remnants of the company's disintegrated center platoon had drifted back there. Some of the platoon, they said, had joined forces with the right platoon; others, unable to find out how they fitted into the company plan, had come to the C.P. I put them to guarding the C.P. until we could get them back into the fight.

There was no sleep that night. Communications were still out. I decided to visit the left platoon, if possible. With the communications sergeant, I started out in the dark. By this time, the platoon might be completely surrounded; so we moved carefully, but we got through without difficulty. Biegel-bach—the little town that lay at the foot of the first platoon's hill, between them and the river—was in flames. The Jerries were well established in the town, I learned. Huge searchlights were shining on the German side of the river. Evidently they were working fast over there, so confident that they were not afraid to use lights. Crouched in the platoon leader's dugout, I learned his situation. They had been shelled hard, but few of the dug-in men had been hurt. The Jerries had yet made no actual assault on the position, and the platoon (reinforced with the anti-tank platoon) had an all-round defense. We had got ammunition to it during the day, and it could hold out unless the pressure got considerably heavier. The communications sergeant made plans to get the wire back in, and we returned to the C.P.

Now there was the third platoon. One messenger from the platoon had got back to the C.P. without interference from the Jerries. Good. He could guide a patrol back via the same route. Ike, the motor officer, could lead the patrol—though that was not his specialty. The remnants of the second platoon, which had filtered back to my C.P., could all go up, loaded down with ammunition for McCarthy's men. Once up there, the platoon sergeant could reorganize the second platoon and push back as far as possible into their old area, without losing contact with McCarthy. The orders were issued. The patrol set out. It never got through. Too many Jerries.

(December 17)

There were still a few hours till daylight. A guard reported flares overhead. A quick look showed that they were not American flares. A German patrol in the woods 500 yards left of the C.P. was popping flares like kids playing Fourth of July. They must have got around the flank of the first and anti-tank platoons. A 60 mm. mortar would have broken up their party without revealing our position. But Company H.Q. had no mortars, and we didn't have enough men to ambush the Jerries. They didn't now know we were there, but in daylight they could bother us. Maybe our little headquarters crew could lick them, but we couldn't do the company much good if we were tied up in a fight ourselves.

So we moved to our third C.P. It was half a mile down the road directly behind the third platoon's position. The Hotel Meyer was a strong stone building, with a well protected cellar. On the edge of Befort, it had been a tourist resort hotel in peacetime. Despite heavy shelling that day, it was in good shape. We moved in and set up communications with

Battalion. It was some comfort to have a phone where I didn't have to duck every time a shell landed in the area.

The first message on the phone was an order to report to the Battalion C.P. There the Colonel quickly gave me plans for a counterattack at dawn. A reconnaissance company, in light armored cars, would drive through the same territory where Baker had attacked yesterday and would aim to restore our lines. Then he explained his improvised Battalion reserve—a minor work of genius. He had collected the three medium tanks of the three artillery forward observers working with us, added the one uncommitted platoon of Baker Company, and put the works in charge of Capt. John Hall of H.Q. Co. Hall would play fireman all day, running to any spot in the Battalion area where a little help might do a lot of good.

The recon counterattack shoved off from a place near my hotel. It had rough going through heavy woods under fire, but made progress. There was no chance of getting a wire through to McCarthy unless the Recon troop could push through, but meanwhile we could try to run a wire to the first platoon. We got a late start because of snipers bothering us. Scattered in the woods to the rear of the hotel, they might have been from the patrol that had forced us to move the night before. All hands joined in the fight and seemed to enjoy it. Combat has moments like that. Excitement was high, and danger somehow seemed little. We put snipers in the windows of a few houses around the hotel. They could see well and had some protection. Whenever a bit of Jerry uniform showed, it drew fire, and after a couple hours the enemy sniping stopped. Yet all day we were annoyed by little groups of Germans filtering through toward us, and we never felt quite safe outdoors. The enemy artillery, too, was still going strong. But shells landed everywhere, and this was the strongest building around, so we stuck with it.

Late in the morning, when the snipers were quiet, we put four men and some wire in a jeep and sent them out to the first platoon. A few hundred yards down the road they drew fire. The communications sergeant was wounded in the leg and had to be evacuated. The sniper was located in a house. It would be a long job routing him out; if done carelessly it might cost several men. So John Hall's tanks went into action and knocked the house down. Again the jeep set out with wire. This time it got through, but on the way back a rifle barked, and the jeep careened into a ditch. It never left the ditch. The men in it got back with minor wounds.

By midafternoon the recon troop had battled its way up to McCarthy's platoon. The medics' jeep went through and pulled out some of Mac's casualties. They were fired on coming back, and it was doubtful another jeep could make it. But Mac had to have ammunition. We loaded a half-track with ammunition, put a machine-gunner and a few riflemen, and sent it through. It drew some fire, but made the trip and returned. Good. We could put on some food and send it through again. The men were ending their second day with no food except their emergency chocolate bars.

But the half-track never got started. Our hands were full. The recon troop had pulled out, after losing some of its vehicles, and the Jerries were again filtering through. A group of two or three would run across a field. Someone would report a patrol working up a draw nearby. Snipers would fire somewhere. When we could, we ignored them. When we had to, we fought them. It had been this way all day, but it was getting worse. Captain Harder of Baker Company passed with two half-tracks and a truck, the first I had seen him since the battle started. He was trying to get chow up to his men, but soon had to turn back.

The sun came out in the late afternoon, for the first time,

and we saw a few P-38s and P-47s fly over. They dived on targets over the river. Heavy flack from the Siegfried Line burst around them. They cheered us, but soon were gone.

I called Battalion and reported half a dozen spots in the neighborhood where little groups of enemy were spotted. I didn't have the men to root them out. Battalion promised some help, but it had little enough to spare. We waited, and the situation looked worse.

Dusk drew near. A few men from H.Q. and Baker companies, separated and bewildered, turned up. I made plans for a defense of the hotel, if that should be necessary. We spotted men in the upper stories of surrounding houses. Machine guns were quickly dug in around the building. Everybody outside was ordered to fire from the outside positions, then to retire into the hotel if necessary. The stone building would make a fortress.

(Siege)

The relentless screaming meemies had pounded the hotel intermittently all day. I was doubtful how much more it could stand. Stepping outside, I looked around for other possible shelters for the night. While I looked, I could see a few Jerry riflemen on both flanks. Maybe it was too late to move.

Another artillery barrage came in. At the first whine of the shells, I got inside. The hotel trembled, but again it held. Then, looking out the windows, I could see the Jerries moving in on the flanks. In seconds, we were surrounded.

The fight started. We had a fortress, ammunition, and a few men—some cooks and mechanics, two or three company headquarters men, a scattering of individuals from the second platoon and wanderers from other companies. The wire to

Battalion had gone out in the last barrage, so we were on our own. Someone was posted near every door and window. The Jerries had us outnumbered and soon were firing from all sides. On the second floor I could move about and look out the windows in any direction. In the dusk, the German figures were barely distinguishable. They were a noisy bunch. Most of their bullets hit the brick walls and did no damage. But they worked in closer and soon were hurling grenades through the windows. Our men near the windows ducked behind cover whenever a grenade came in, then jumped up ready to fire if a Jerry soldier should follow the grenade.

A jeep parked in front of the building was afire, and in the eerie light the German figures were visible. I stuck my carbine out a window, and fired. One man dropped. I had probably killed a German, and he was probably the first man I had ever killed directly. While I watched, a burst of machine gun bullets splattered against the brick beside the window. I was lucky that time. But firing from windows would be dangerous now. The flash of our rifles would draw a machine-gun response. So we switched to hand grenades. We could hurl these from a window. A few men kept grenades popping from twenty windows. Once in awhile something called for a rifle or a carbine. Then we fired and ducked under the window sill and didn't mind when the Jerry bullets whizzed back through the window.

Downstairs the front door was somehow open. A German machine gun poured long bursts into the hallway. Our men kept to the sides of the hall and were not hurt. After one stream of machine gun fire came a German soldier. He was quickly taken care of. Another long burst and another German soldier. The same thing. More fire, but no more German soldiers.

We were holding our own.

"What are you going to do? We can't hold out forever." It was the motor officer.

"Keep fighting," was the only answer I could think of. Somehow, I was not much worried. If I tried to be reasonable, I could not see how we could expect to leave the hotel alive. The Germans outnumbered us and could eventually force an entrance. At the very least, they could hold us inside, and it seemed only a matter of time, in the present course of battle, until a German company or battalion would be there. But this fight was exciting. It was not like absorbing artillery. We could fight back, match wits and strength with the enemy. Our men were exhilarated and fought brilliantly. We were killing Germans, so far at low cost to ourselves. In years gone by I had wondered with some moral agony how I would feel about killing men. Now I wasn't thinking about that.

My one real worry was fire. The Jerries were using some white phosphorus grenades. So far these grenades had only bounced off the stone hotel front. Stupid troops! There was a barn attached to the rear of the hotel. An incendiary grenade would easily send it up in flames, and the hotel might go along. But they seemed not to notice.

So we fought and they fought. I don't know if it was an hour or two hours. A lot of lead and a good many grenades came through the doors and windows. But no more men. We sent a lot of stuff back and occasionally heard a scream of pain.

Now the half-track in front of the hotel was burning. That was dangerous. There were nearly 60 gallons of gasoline in the tank, and that might fire the hotel.

But soon there was no more noise of German firing. Listening, I could hear a radio working, and a few sounds in guttural German. Then a shuffling about, and a bunch of Jerries marched off noisily.

Why should they be so obvious about leaving us? I couldn't decide. Possibly they had radioed for artillery and would form for a last assault after the barrage. Or perhaps they hoped to lure us out into an ambush. Something had to be cooking.

We waited. Nothing happened. In the quiet I grew more nervous. Obviously we were goners if we stayed here till morning. But I doubted that we could get out now. The Germans would be on the watch for that above all else.

Several minutes passed. This waiting was too much. We would try to get out. I passed the word around. "We'll get out. Watch for the ambush. Try to stay hidden. Go in groups of two or three. Rallying point—the old castle, near the Battalion C.P." (That was a mile or two away, on the other side of the town.)

We would use the back entrance where we could stay out of the light of the burning half-track. I rather fancied it was my duty to stay until all others were out. But they were reluctant to leave. I was more afraid to stay than to leave, but for some the present danger of leaving was worse than the future danger of staying. All right. I would go ahead. I stepped through a window, flattened myself on the ground and crawled away. I thought two others were following me. I soon found it was a half a dozen, and didn't have the heart to chase them off, though I thought smaller groups would be safer. We crawled several hundred yards. There were Jerries in the neighborhood, but apparently no organized ambush. Though we kept out of the way of the Germans, they were always between us and our rallying point. We traveled several miles trying to get around them, much of it on our bellies.

We kept direction by watching the hotel. Half an hour after we left, it was a blazing beacon. In the distance we could see silhouettes against the flame—the German soldiers were there. Some of our unused ammunition was exploding in the flame.

We crawled near a German bivouac. I never stopped being amazed at what poor soldiers some of the Germans were in an army so marvelously trained on the whole. They were eating in the bivouac, shouting and flashing lights. We could easily have shot a few—at the cost of more important objectives. We were partly past the bivouac when I decided to get up and walk. I felt in a hurry to get to the Battalion C.P., and it didn't seem very dangerous. We walked on past and into Befort.

Now we could either take an hour slinking through backyards or walk quickly down the streets. There were certainly some Germans in town by now, but probably not many. I was beginning to disdain the stupidity of some of these troops, so I decided we would do it the quick way. Acting as if we owned the town, we marched through. There was no one at the rallying point, then, but about half the men in the hotel turned up elsewhere later. Jerry apparently got the rest, or maybe they temporarily joined other American units.

I approached the Battalion C.P. steathily. I didn't want to walk in on some Germans. The C.P. was deserted. Since H.Q. would not move toward the enemy, there was only one road they could have taken out of town. We headed down that road. A mile or so, and we found our supporting artillery, starting to move back. The artillery Colonel gave us a ride back to his C.P., talking on the way about how hopeless the artillery battle with the Germans had been.

At his new C.P. in a farmhouse I sat down. I asked him to radio my C.O. He offered me a drink of Scotch. I wasn't much interested, but this was the first social amenity of two bruising days, so I took a swallow. I ate a can of "C" ration —the first food all day. Then, waiting for the radio message, I dropped asleep on the floor.

Half an hour later someone shook me. "They want you at your Battalion C.P. A truck is outside to take you." I went.

2. COUNTERATTACK

A guide led me through woods so dark that I couldn't see the Colonel's black-out tent until I bumped into it. Inside were the Colonel, two or three of his staff, and a few maps.

"Glad to see you," he said. "I didn't expect to."

"I didn't expect that you would," I told him.

"I sent a patrol to inform you when we moved the C.P.," he said. "They told me you were surrounded."

Then we got down to business. Combat Command "A" of the 9th Armored Division had now been made responsible for the Battalion sector, and some reinforcements were available. At dawn, a counterattack would be made through the Battalion area by a task force including a company of medium tanks, a platoon of light tanks, and one or two platoons of engineers operating as infantry. It would aim to drive through to the front, cover the withdrawal of the troops up there, and permit them to pull back to a new defensive position.

"Do you think it can work?" the Colonel asked.

"It should have a good chance. There are a lot of Germans up there, but they are disorganized," I told him.

"Of course, we *aren't*." He was not cynical, just realistic.

A major from the tank outfit would command the task force. Captain Harder (Co. B) and I would go along, as passengers. When we reached our troops we would take charge of them and get them out. Capt. Schalles of Co. A hadn't been heard from for a long time.

The route forward was over unfamiliar terrain, and my maps were gone. I studied the Battalion maps as best I could. My tired eyes didn't focus well. "Better take some of this benzedrine," said the Colonel. "That's all we're going on."

The tanks were lining up in the predawn dark. I reported to the major in charge, then hunted a place to ride. Everyone was a little scared. We were on the edge of nervous exhaustion, and there were a few snipers around, though we were a couple miles back from "the front," if there was any such thing anymore.

The present Battalion C.P. was located in the former Battalion motor park. That meant there were plenty of half-tracks around and enough drivers to give some security. Some of my company half-tracks were to carry the engineers in the attack, so I threw on a carton of emergency ration chocolate bars to help out the men up front who must be mighty hungry now.

Daylight came, and the snipers got in a few more licks. There was about an hour's delay while they were cleaned out. I saw one dead German well inside our security area. The tanks were still moving around, getting ready for the take-off. One of them, in the middle of the column, was struck by a German bazooka. Two of the crew were seriously wounded. Someone got them out to the aid station. The tank would still operate, but its radio was ruined. I climbed in that tank in the place of one of the injured crewmen.

The tanks started forward along a trail. Everyone was a little confused. The column stopped for no evident reason. Then we heard that two light tanks at the head of the column had been hit by bazookas and were out of action. It was a bad start—three tanks hit before the attack began.

We moved on. The trail left the woods and moved out into open ground on the forward slope of a large hill. We could look down into the woods below and far out toward the river. But the Germans somewhere could see a long way too, and they brought down artillery on us. The engineers were ahead of the tanks, approaching the woods at the foot of the hill. German fire came out of the woods. Our tanks fired over the engineers' heads into the enemy positions. The Jerry artillery was hitting the engineers hard. Inside the armor of the tanks we were a little safer; a few of the tanks were knocked out of action, but casualties were light. Our tank 76 mm. guns tore up the woods, set afire a house. The German artillery churned up the ground in front of us. Cattle were grazing in the fields. Sometimes a horse or cow jumped into the air as a shell landed, then fell to the ground, legs thrashing the air, until it sank down and never moved again. From the hill top it was like a movie of a war, but terribly real and close. The engineers kept moving up. I felt as if I was with them, because I was really a doughboy, not a tanker. Some of them dropped. The medics worked through the shelling and pulled the wounded out in jeeps.

One of the medical jeeps carried Capt. John Hall with a leg wound. Headquarters Co. was getting hit hard. Lt. Ruder had been killed reconnoitering that trail the night before. Hall shouted at me going past. It was only a flesh wound, I hoped.

The battle moved slowly. We waited until our artillery got the range and poured in on the German infantry a while. Then the Jerry artillery began to slacken. The German infantry began coming out of the woods, hands over their heads or waving white rags. They surrendered by squads and platoons.

Between a hundred and two hundred straggled back, a few of our walking wounded guarding them all. They were a miserable looking bunch, most of them decrepit and bedraggled. That was the way we had often found it in our sector—second rate soldiers, but so many of them and so much artillery that they kept coming, through us and around us, until we were swamped. Sometimes, too, we would find a few of their better troops, who were stubborn fighters. But now it was the poor soldiers, surrendering fast.

The woods was pretty well cleaned out, and we moved forward. The engineers, leaving a lot of casualties behind, got back in their half tracks. I don't know where the light tanks were. The mediums now led out. With our broken radio, I couldn't tell what was happening, but the platoon I was in moved out first. I was in the second tank. Apparently the lead platoon had lost too many tanks.

We plunged down the hillside, following the trail that led into the woods. What lurked in the woods was unknown, and it was more frightening to a tanker than to a doughboy. A tank can't easily hide. In we went, past the flaming house that our tanks had fired, down the winding trail. Tankers are prodigal of ammunition, compared to the infantryman who has to carry all he uses, and they sprayed every suspicious spot with machine guns.

We crossed a large clearing, then another woods. Again the trail widened out into a clearing. Just at this point I saw a single German soldier beside the trail, taking aim at our lead tank with his panzerfaust, the one-man German anti-tank weapon, comparable to our bazooka. He had guts. He let the tank come within ten yards before he rose up and fired. The lieutenant in the tank saw him too, and dropped a hand grenade on him. But the panzerfaust had gone off and hit the tank in the rear. The hand grenade wounded the German, but the tank was on fire. With desperate speed the crew tried to get out. And as they got out, German rifle fire picked them off. One of the four lived, badly wounded. (That was the tank that I had started to ride before the bazooka fire early that morning got two of the men in the next tank and made a place for me there.) From our tank 25 yards behind we hurled machine gun fire into the woods where the Jerries seemed to be. The engineers were soon forward and deployed. The tank I rode soon threw a track and couldn't maneuver, so I joined the engineers' firing line. In a few minutes the Germans were coming out, surrendering again. While they were being rounded up, I looked at a few of our wounded, gave them a little help, and told them to stay near the trail where the aid vehicles would pick them up. As we pushed on, I jumped on a half-track. We crossed the wide clearing and entered the woods again. Once more there were a few Germans, but we quickly killed them or drove them off.

Here the trail ended. I had no map and didn't know where we were. We must have been close to the front and to my platoons. The major in charge wasn't sure. While he studied his maps, I saw extensive German telephone wire spread out on the ground. That was a bad sign; it meant that the Jerries had established a communications net, *behind* my men. I cut some of the wires, as a sort of spare time activity, hoping to cause the enemy as much trouble as broken communications had made us.

It was getting close to dark. I had not realized that the battle had gone so long. The major had lost nearly half his tanks and couldn't let the rest get caught at night. He gave orders to go back. It made me sick. My men were still somewhere ahead. But maybe it was all he could do.

We rolled back, past the flaming tank that the panzerfaust had hit. Its ammunition was exploding now. On into the

woods and another clearing behind. I was riding on the outside of a tank when a mortar barrage came in on us. A shell
landed right side of the tank and splattered me with mud. I
jumped off and into a hole, where I waited until the barrage
was over. My face stung and was numb, but there was no
blood. The tanks rolled on, as mortars would not hurt them.
There was neither the whine nor the terrific explosion of the
screaming meemies, but mortars throw a lot of shrapnel and
were probably more dangerous to infantrymen.

As I got up again, I saw two wounded men. They were some
of the same that I had left behind in our earlier advance.
No medical vehicles had come along for them, and they had
started to drag themselves painfully back to the aid station.
I looked around. Some of the half-tracks had not yet entered
the clearing on their way back. I told the wounded to stay
put, and ran back to the half-tracks. The men in them found
other places to ride, and two of the empty vehicles came up
to pick up the wounded. The mortar shelling might start
again, so we worked quickly. The wounded were loaded, and
we moved on.

Side of the trail lay a couple abandoned German 81 mm.
mortars. Good. Our own mortar platoon had lost its mortars in
an ambush the day before; they could use these. (The same
ammunition fits both.) So we loaded them on and headed back.

I reported to the Colonel on the failure. With him and the
S-3 (Operations Officer), I crouched in a deep foxhole so
that we would not have to interrupt the conversation whenever a shell came near, because the screaming meemies were
still busy. "I have authority now," he said, "to withdraw those
men by infiltration tonight. I'm trying to get the message
through to McCarthy on the field artillery radio. We've had
communication today, but can't get through now."

"How are they up there?" I asked.

"They're holding out pretty well. If the radio doesn't work, what chance do you think a small patrol would have to get through?"

"About 50-50. The Jerries are thick up there, but there are gaps in their positions."

"See if you can find some men to go."

I thought a minute. The handful of drivers and cooks available, along with the few soldiers who had turned up after the hotel fight, were not the best soldiers of the company.

"I think I'd better go," I said.

"Why don't you send M?" the Colonel asked. "There are a lot of other things you can be doing."

"He doesn't have the guts. He wanted to surrender back at the Hotel Meyer."*

"It's your decision," said the Colonel.

I decided to go. Capt. Harder of Company B decided to do the same thing. Each of us would head for his own company. If he got through, he would then try to reach the other company.

I found one sergeant who wanted to go along. He was not in good physical condition (who was?), but he was a reliable non-com. Looking further, the only men I saw would weaken the patrol instead of strengthening it. So it would be a twosome.

While daylight remained, we poured over the map and picked our route. We ate a K ration meal. I was weak from lack of food, but excitement kept me from noticing it. We gulped a few Benzedrine pills and put chocolate rations in our pockets.

The Chaplain of Combat Command "A" was there. He wondered how the men were doing. "They're doing a grand

* Years later, I regret that statement. As a military judgment, it was right; but it was personally too harsh. He died in battle; I didn't.

41

job," I told him. I was proud of the way they had reacted to this unexpected and overwhelming attack.*

I remember saying one other thing to him. "It's strange how much men want to live."

I took off my heavy outergarments, and got everything bulky or noisy out of my pockets. I turned over my glasses and a few odds and ends to a headquarters sergeant. Then Sergeant Ziringer and I took off.

As we walked up the road, I told him everything I knew about the situation. "If either of us is wounded," I said, "the other will have to go on and get the message through. If we're challenged, I'll try to talk German to the guard for a minute or so, and you try to get away. If they surround us and grab us, we'll look for a chance to make a break for it in the dark."

On the way forward we passed several friendly sentry posts of tank destroyer and recon outfits. We were challenged sharply and had to give evidence that we were friendly. The Americans were on the ball that night. In the little town of Haller we found the C.P. of the recon troop occupying the town. From the C.O. we learned that the group had started in the morning with orders to retake Befort. (The Jerries had

---

* Many years later John Eisenhower, in his detailed reconstruction of the Battle of the Bulge, wrote of our Battalion: "Collins' battalion was hit by nearly a whole volksgrenadier division, the 276th. With two companies on the line, Collins' men were able to exact a fearsome toll." That complimentary judgment may be justified. But Eisenhower was too flattering when he went on to say that by the end of the first day of battle, with the help of tank reinforcements, "the 60th Armored Infantry Battallion had restored the front along the Sure River with three companies abreast." (See John S. D. Eisenhower, *The Bitter Woods*, p. 211; cf. p. 263.) Even at the end of the third day we had not accomplished that. What we did achieve was a sufficient spoiling of the attack that a shoulder could be established from which General Patton's army on our south could soon (December 22) start its dramatic drive northward for the relief of Bastogne on December 26.

finished occupying the town after I had passed through the night before.) The recon troop had attacked and failed, and now were defending Haller. The Jerries were on the edge of town.

Then, surprisingly, I found two soldiers of my first platoon in that C.P. They had got out that day. Using the artillery field observer's jeep, they had made a run for it. They were volunteers and had made it on sheer guts under heavy fire. Both were badly wounded. The platoon was still holding out, they said.

With the Jerries' line so far advanced we had to change our plans. Sgt. Ziringer and I restudied the map and picked a new route. I was not confident of it; too much of the terrain was strange. But it was the best we could do.

We headed for the edge of town. The outposts showed us where the Germans were, a couple hundred yards down the road. We left the road and crossed the fields. There was a little firing from the Jerries, but it was not aimed at us. We headed for a big draw that we had picked on the map, and followed it about a mile. Somewhere we had to cross that draw, and it was deep. The sides were almost cliff, but there were occasional shelves with trees growing on them. From one shelf we could reach the tops of trees on the shelf below, and so, climbing down tree after tree, we reached the bottom. Then it was a hunt for a place to get up the other side. It was luck that we didn't fall and break a leg in the dark. Across the ravine we advanced by compass and a few visible stars. We were past Befort and not far from our own troops. It seemed that the roughest part of our job was done. But we were exhausted. Our eyes, half-way through the third night with no sleep (or half an hour, to be exact) refused to focus. The sky was cloudy, and in the dim moonlight we could see little. Sometimes the landscape seemed to swim. Any object, if we looked at it long enough, appeared to move. Haystacks looked like men.

It was past midnight. I decided that we had to hurry. We would abandon our slow movement, our careful investigation of every object. We would stand up, walk ahead, and hope for luck. We were well into enemy territory, but perhaps that would make us less suspect.

So we moved ahead. Now we covered ground faster, and we were encouraged. Then there was a grunt that sounded something like a "Halt." In the split second that I had to make a decision, I could not tell whether it was an American or German voice. So I simply halted. My eyes struggled to see. There was a rifle barrel sticking out of a hole in the ground. Another grunt, and other men came running toward us. Closing in from the sides, they grabbed our weapons and quickly searched us. Then they marched us off into the darkness. We were prisoners of war.

3. INSIDE
THE THIRD REICH

The guards moved us into Befort, the town that had recently been "ours." Twice we were challenged by sentries on the street, and the guards replied with the password. We moved into a house that was perhaps a company C.P. A Sergeant took charge of us. He looked us over and was delighted to see that he had an American officer. He emptied our pockets. In mine he found a hand grenade that the guards had missed, a few pieces of chocolate, and a wallet. He stuffed one piece of chocolate in my mouth and kept the rest. Then he searched through the wallet for some identification of my unit. I knew he wouldn't find it.

I looked at him. His uniform was the same that we had been fighting in the woods and from the hotel. On his belt buckle I saw the old phrase, "Gott mit Uns." I was surprised. That was in my mind the symbol of the old Kaiser's army. I didn't know that Hitler's army had kept it. The Sergeant spoke in good English. We told him name, rank, and serial number (as required by the Geneva Convention), but nothing more. He asked a few other questions. Where were we going? What troops were in the area? What organization were we from? We said we didn't know. He produced a map and asked a few questions about locations. Again we didn't know. He paused, and we said nothing. I was afraid. I expected threats, but he made none. He gave the guards a few instructions, and we marched out of the house.

The night was still dark. The guards pushed us down into the street. I recognized the place and knew exactly what part of town it was. If I could break loose and get into a backyard, I could probably work my way out of town. But the guards knew their business. There were two prisoners and two guards. They kept directly behind us, close enough that a shot could not miss, far enough that we could not turn and disarm them.

We moved to the ancient castle near our former Battalion C.P. It was now a German headquarters. Down in the basement we went. A German officer lay in a bedroll on the floor. Barely awake, he was talking over a field telephone. He paid no attention to us. We were given a corner of the next room and a guard, and we went to sleep.

At daylight (it was December 19) we were roused. I had scarcely dozed, though I was exhausted. Nervousness was too much. I didn't regard myself as really a prisoner yet. There should still be a chance to break away. There had to be, I thought. The guard led us outside where we joined about twenty other Americans. Most of them I recognized. A few had been in the hotel fight with me. There were my Mess Sergeant, two battalion medics, a few men from Able, Baker, and Headquarters Companies. But nobody gave any signs of recognition. No use giving away free information.

They marched us out of town, toward Germany. We walked down the road that had marked the left flank of Able Co. I spotted the German field wire. It looked as if they had an elaborate communications net. There were few troops around. Obviously they considered this area well in their rear. But right in this area there were at least small pockets of Co.

A's men—unless they had withdrawn or had all been killed.

Dense woods and hilly ground pressed in on the roadside. Give me a twenty-second start, I thought, and I can vanish into those woods. From there I'd get back somehow. But I was the only officer in the group, and they kept a special guard with me. I couldn't have got a five-second start.

We moved down to the bank of the Our.* There were some scattered German corpses. We passed close to them. Our guards said nothing, and we wondered what they thought. I had a guilty feeling—not the guilt of doing wrong, but the guilt of getting caught at it. There was nothing ferocious about these dead Germans now. They looked pitifully helpless. Their eyelids were still open, and their eyeballs had a deathlike vacant stare.

There was a delay on the river bank. Then a boat took us across. The river was strangely unwarlike. If the Americans had attacked across that river, there would now be a pontoon and perhaps steel bridges. Trucks would be rolling forward with supplies; everything would be activity. I marveled at the German ability to fight with little equipment and almost no activity in their rear.

We were rowed across the river, and we stepped out in Germany. The rugged hills of the Siegfried Line loomed before us. A new group of guards took over, and we started climbing into those rocks and woods.

Now I was depressed. Now for the first time I felt like a prisoner. A terrible weight came with that feeling. So far I had worried—about those surrounded platoons, about what the Colonel was thinking when I didn't show up, about plans for escape. But now I was in Hitler's Germany. Every inch was foreign ground. There was a river between us and my duty. I felt helpless.

* I think I should have said the Sauer.

We climbed slowly. The ground was rough and steep. We grew tired. So did the guards, and they let us rest. Then up and deeper into Germany we went. Artillery noises reverberated through the hills, but somehow seemed remote. In the dense forest we sometimes saw pillboxes. It could be awful to attack over this ground.

We reached a headquarters. It was located in a shell-proof pillbox of several rooms. An officer came out and looked us over. We were searched once again, then sent inside. The enlisted men were crowded in a dark room. They had to stand; there was water on the floor, and not enough room to sit anyway.

A rule in handling prisoners is to keep officers separated from enlisted men, and I was pushed into a corridor near the H.Q. switchboard. I sat down on a box.

The pair of Germans operating the switchboard paid no attention to me. I just sat. Hours went past. One of the operators got out a hunk of black bread and cut off a slice. I watched him eat it. I was hungry. I tried to think what I had eaten during the battle. I recalled one "C" ration (a meal in two little cans), and one "K" ration (an emergency concentrated meal in a small box), and a chocolate ration bar in three days. Nothing today. The German soldier cut off another slice. I asked him for some bread. I didn't know then how slim was his bread ration. But he gave me a slice. It was black and soggy. I tasted it. It was bitter. Hungry as I was, I could hardly swallow it. I ate half the slice, and stuffed the rest in my pocket. I could not then have believed that I should some day see American officers trade watches or wedding rings for a loaf of this sour bread. The German glanced over and thought I had eaten all the bread. He cut another slice. This one he covered with a slightly sweet spread (beet-butter) and gave it to me. I gave him a "danke schön" and tested it. Now I could eat it, and my stomach felt better.

More time went past. Guards came and ushered us out into the dusk. We got in a truck and moved off. There were a few stars in the sky, and I watched our direction. It was north and east. After awhile we got out and walked. This was better—not so cold, but hard on empty stomachs. Occasionally we passed a few horse-drawn carts moving west. They carried ammunition and military supplies, sometimes covered with straw, sometimes not. This was the only sign of a supply system that we saw. Again I thought of the roads in the American rear area, choked with supply vehicles, and marveled at this German army. As I learned later, Tiger tanks and heavy equipment were used farther north at the center of the bulge. But here Jerry had staged a major infantry and artillery offensive, with almost no visible supply system backing it up.

There was an hour or two of walking. We approached a little town. One house in it was a sort of military police headquarters. We filed in. I was shown a room with a little straw on the floor. I went in, sank down, and fell asleep.

I spent perhaps three days in that house. Another batch of prisoners came in. There was Lt. Robert from Co. B. He had been reported dead. And Lt. Hardy and some of the men from his anti-tank platoon. We wanted to talk, but waited until we were sure we were not overheard. Then we eagerly compared notes. Word to withdraw had got through to McCarthy by radio the day after I had failed. A patrol had brought it over to the first platoon and to Lt. Hardy's AT platoon. The move was to start at dusk. But just at that time, a German attack cut off and captured Lt. Hardy and his men —those who had not been killed. Perhaps Penrose had got out with his first platoon.

The German Feldwebel (a staff sergeant) who ran the station was friendly and treated us as well as he could. Perhaps it was he who first spoke the common slogan, "For you the war is over." The three officers were kept strictly separated from the men. Except for cramped space, almost no food, and the filthy outhouses, it was not bad. We talked what German we could to the Feldwebel. He explained that we would soon go to a stalag, where there would be sports, cinema, and music. That was about all he knew.

Then another German NCO came in for a full day. He took a room and called in the men, one at a time, for interrogation. Finally he called the officers. My turn came, and I went in. He was middle-aged and spoke English well. Again I gave name, rank, serial number. He asked my organization. I refused to tell him. His approach was "sweetly reasonable."

"After all," he said, "we know all this anyway. For instance, I know that you are the commanding officer of Co. C, 60th Armored Infantry Battalion."

I didn't bat an eye. But I saw a copy of the company roster on his desk. The Germans must have captured the company field desk. I thought it had burned up in the flaming half-track in front of the Hotel Meyer. But I told him nothing. He made a few more attempts to get information, then said he was finished.

The interrogation finished, I was able to talk to my enlisted men. I told them what I could about what they might expect. I gave them what I knew about the battle and let them know that I had been proud of the company's stand. They wanted to know what the whole battle meant. I told them that it looked like a big German drive, and I reminded them of Ludendorff's final offensive in 1918. That was about all. From one of the soldiers, I learned that the interrogating NCO had revealed that the Germans thought the Hotel Meyer was perhaps a Division C.P. The bad guess was flattering and amusing. If the Hotel Meyer was a Division Command Post, I was a Major General. But that status did me no good now. The next afternoon we were put on trucks and sent away. Toward evening we went into a city. I don't know its name. There was a high stone building that looked like a penitentiary. We went in. Another searching and hasty questioning from an officer. Then Hardy and Robert and I were ushered up into a frigid room for the night. The guard, who was ancient and decrepit enough to be my grandfather, grinned and said in a friendly way, "Sing Sing." That was the limit of his English.

A large batch of prisoners came in that night. They were from the 28th Division, which had been directly on our North. We compared notes and began to get an idea of the extent of the battle.

We spent a day in the prison. Then we got a "three day travel ration"—a loaf of bread and hunk of baloney—and marched off to the railroad station. At night our guards loaded us on boxcars. We were crowded. There wasn't room to lie down and the cold was bitter. I ate the three day's baloney and gnawed on the bread. The train moved a little, stood still a lot.

In the morning we heard that the tracks ahead had been bombed and that we would have to walk. That suited me better than freezing in the boxcar. We lined up in column and started marching. There were perhaps a couple hundred of us, including about 30 officers, in charge of a German Corporal and his guards. They took us into a little town and left us standing in the village square while he tried to get some information.

It was Sunday morning, and the Volksturm was gathering for drill. They were a completely unmilitary crowd, and they looked at us with curiosity. I was not feeling very friendly toward Germans, but I felt only pity at the idea of these men ever facing our army. They looked like some of the good simple Germans I had known as a boy in Indianapolis. A few were carrying rifles, but most of them were armed with shovels. All wore their farmers' or laborers' clothes.

In the square was one very different figure. He seemed to be the local party leader. Fat and pompous, he wore a yellow-green uniform and a swastika armband. He barked out orders and swaggered about, happy at the chance to strut in front of captured Americans. When our senior American officer, a Major, tried to ask him a question, he barked back and almost spit in his face. He provoked hate in every American there.

This, we supposed, told us something about Germany. On the one hand, the simple, bewildered people, doing as they were told without much idea why. On the other, the strutting offensive party leader—the type who made Nazism flourish.

After awhile our Corporal showed up again and started us marching. At first, we had no idea where we were. Then we struck a highway beside a river and found out we were moving up the Moselle Valley toward Koblenz. On the steep hillsides on either side of the river were the arbors of grapes— source of the famous Moselle wines. This Moselle Valley was supposed to be one of the possible approaches to the fortress of the Reich. It did not look very favorable here. The road was good, but the hills on the sides were high, and weapons might have been hidden anywhere among the grapes.

A couple of planes flew overhead. We winced, then saw the swastikas on them and with some astonishment felt safe. I realized that we needed a new set of conditioned reflexes in Germany. We were quickly learning to dread the American air force.

At Koblenz we crossed the Moselle and the Rhine. The

bridges were battered, and repair crews worked on them as we crossed. In happier days I would have been thrilled by this first sight of the legendary Rhine. As it was I hummed a few bars of Heine's song about the Lorelei, but was too miserable to get much fun out of it. The city of Koblenz was a ruins. The few people on its desolate streets looked dreary, and the air breathed hostility. The shell of a city was still there. Some life went on. Dug into the sides of a huge rock hill was the headquarters of the military commandant of the city. Around the railroad depot the damage was worst. Here absolutely no buildings stood. There were only the tracks, and men were working on them now, trying to keep these life-lines usable.

Even as we left the city, we heard the air raid sirens. In a few minutes the area was covered with an artificial fog. Now we understood the big tanks that lined the roads. They re-leased the fog that blanketed the city and hid the rail targets from the planes.

We marched on. Soon the bombers were overhead. Our guards were more afraid than we. Probably they knew better than we. They had seen the American air force operate. They made us take cover in the ditches. Flak burst around the planes. Soon a few German fighters attacked. We heard the machine guns overhead, then the Jerry planes turned and ran. Any one of us might easily have run away from our guards then. But there was no place to go. No one knew how to cross the Rhine and the Moselle.

We walked farther. After awhile there was a railroad sta-tion, a wait, and another train ride. About dark we got off the train at the town of Limburg. It had taken about 24 hours to travel perhaps 30 or 40 miles. That was the way German transportation functioned near the western front. Our captors had had even less faith in it; they had given us a three-day ration for the trip. It was probably the only time in the war that the Germans gave out too big a ration to their prisoners.

On Christmas Eve, just after dark, we marched in the gates of Stalag XIIA. There was an oppressive feeling of utter defeat as the gates opened and we passed through the barbed wire. The stalag looked cold and cruel. We learned later that it was a reception center for prisoners from the western front. An American sergeant greeted us and initiated us into the mysteries of life in a stalag. The officers' quarters, we learned, had been destroyed in an air raid the night before. The RAF had attacked the rail yards at Limburg, and a stray bomb or two had fallen in the stalag. Most of the officers had been killed, the rest wounded. There was a brave attempt to bring Christmas into the prison. Crepe decorations were hung in the barracks—gifts from the YMCA. And a little American coffee, from the Red Cross, had been saved from other weeks so that there would be more on Christmas week.

I was in the stalag several days. It was cold and dreary. All day long we shivered in overcoats. At night we slept two together and still were cold. If the sun came out, we took walks in the yard. Twice a day we stood a roll call formation. That was all there was to do. A very few books were around, and we read when we could get them. We heard that our permanent stalag would probably be better, and we hoped that we would move there soon.

Here we made our acquaintance with the prisoner-of-war ration. In the morning, a sixth of a loaf of sour black bread and a cup of coffee—sometimes ersatz and rarely American (Red Cross) with real sugar and milk (powdered). I didn't believe that coffee could taste so good. Dinner and supper were a miserable soup, drunk from a German mess cup, filthy with grease because there was no warm water to clean it. The soup was mostly an ugly brown liquid, with a few dehydrated vegetables in it. "Grass soup," it was called.

Occasionally as a luxury, there was barley soup, and it always brought a general shout of joy. The soup had the virtue of warming us up for a few minutes of each day. Beyond that we couldn't say much for it. Each day a few Red Cross treasures were distributed—cigarettes, a little chocolate, or cheese, or some crackers. But Red Cross supplies were skimpy at Limburg and didn't go far.

Cigarettes became a currency—an international one, because there were many races at Limburg, and all liked cigarettes. Partly because there was nothing else to do, bargaining went on all day. I bought a mirror with cigarettes. Sometimes one could buy bread or some other bit of food. It was an advantage to a PW not to smoke. The cigarette ration was about five a day, so the ardent smokers pined and gave away their valuables for cigarettes. One absolute rule governed bargaining. It was immoral to buy food from a fellow American with cigarettes. That would be exploiting his weakness and hurting him.

Limburg was a wretched place. But it had its blessings. We were registered as prisoners of war; the information would go to Geneva and then to our own government. We were allowed to send home a postcard (mine was written Christmas Day and got home March 6, the first word after the Army's missing-in-action notification). A few razors were scattered among us, and we were given some soap.

The most interesting thing at Limburg was the Indian prisoners. They were permanently stationed at Limburg, whereas the Americans only moved through the camp. The Indians were professional soldiers in the British Army. Many had been prisoners for years, taken in Africa or Italy. They wore turbans on their heads and looked not at all like soldiers from this war. They were marvelously clean, for such a home as Limburg, and extremely friendly. We liked to watch them crouch around their tiny fires in the yard and cook. Because of the various dietary rules of the Indian religions, their Red Cross supplies included no meat, but were strong in grains, so the Indians cooked and cooked and cooked.

News filtered into Limburg slowly or not at all. New prisoners were always greeted with a request for news. Sometimes something came by the grapevine, usually from the Indians who occasionally got it from a German guard. It was about as accurate as one might expect. We got the rumor of the fall of Cologne while we were there; it was about three months premature.

I met a few other men from the 60th Armored Infantry Battalion at Limburg—my supply sergeant and some others. Each had a different story of his capture. All of us were gloomy. Our only hope was that the German attack might force a decision in the war. But we were not cheerful.

Sgt. Ziringer was there—the last I saw him. Months later back in America, I heard that he had escaped from Limburg, but how or when I never learned.

Nearly everyone got at least a little sick in changing to the German diet. Diarrhea was the most common ailment. There was a hospital in the camp, if you could call it such. It was a barracks, like the rest, gloomy and frigid. The patients were mostly the wounded. The doctor was a British captain and a wonderful man. It was said that he might have gone to an officers' camp, but volunteered to stay there. His job was enough to break a doctor's heart. Medical supplies consisted of aspirin and a few bandages. His hospital, so far as I could see, had less equipment than our company aid men— privates—carried with them in battle. His only help for diarrhea was a recommendation to lay off German bread and liquids—and these were practically the whole of our diet.

The Americans at Limburg lived in the hope of moving on. Maybe, we thought, the next place will be as bad. But moving, and the end of the war, were the only cheerful prospects. So I was glad when my name was called to leave Limburg for interrogation.

4. INTERROGATION

It was New Year's Eve. High in a medieval castle, I listened to the melody of the famous hymn, from Beethoven's Ninth Symphony, floating up from the town of Diesz in the valley below. I stood on my bed, to see out of the tiny window high in my cell wall. There in the dim evening light was a little winding river, surrounded by hills. On one of the hills, this castle stood. Lying between the hill and the river was the town. The sight was peaceful. It had been just as peaceful three days before when I had walked through it in the afternoon and watched the Christmas tree lights through the windows of the homes. Too small to be bothered by bombers, the town seemed almost unaware what men were doing to men as they approached this year of our Lord 1945.

I had walked perhaps two miles from Limburg, climbed the hill to the castle, entered through the thick stone walls, and come up the narrow stairs and down the dark hall to this room. Behind me the guard clanked the heavy bolt, and I was in solitary confinement in this cramped room. My eyes ran around the room. Good, there was a radiator with a little heat in it—unaccustomed luxury. The rest of the furniture was a cot with a straw mattress. No chair, but a box that would answer for a small table.

(*Solitude*)

Now I was to learn how long a 24-hour day, which had often seemed a breathlessly short time, could be. There was nothing to read. The room wasn't large enough to allow that reputed pastime of prisoners—pacing the floor. When it was dark I slept—and sometimes when it was light. Events were few. Once a day a Russian prisoner came in and swept out the room. (In between times I could hear the German guards ranting at him—his name was Nicholas—and I got my first impression of German treatment of the Russians.) Once a day the guard let me out to walk down the hall and wash in a pan of cold water. Three times a day the guard came with food—the Limburg diet. He opened the door and called "Zoup. Kom, kom, kom."

When I needed to, I could knock on the door. A guard might or might not show up. If he did, I would say "Latrine," and he would let me go down the hall to the bucket that served for a toilet. If someone else was out of his room, the guard would grunt "Kamerad," and I would understand that I must wait. Only one prisoner could leave his room at a time, because there must be no communication among us.

Next door a prisoner was painfully sick with diarrhea. Each day I could hear him try to explain to the German guard that he needed a doctor. It never did any good.

Most of my predecessors in this room had left their mark on the walls. They were covered with signatures and dates. I read every one a hundred times. Most of them were officers. (Only a selected sample of prisoners were taken to these interrogation centers.) From the dates I could tell that they spent from five days to two weeks here. That was useful information. Some had listed the daily menus on the wall, but I knew all I wanted to know about the food. Others had put their home towns. There were two or three British signatures among the American. Over the door someone had penciled in large letters: "Greta Garbo's Paradise." I thought of the lovely, mysterious Swedish actress and her famous saying, "I want to be alone." Over my bed was an aviator's signature and his verse: "I crashed my plane, I know not where. When I awoke, there were Jerries there." On the door was the 91st Psalm:

He that dwelleth in the secret place of the most High shall abide in the shadow of the Almighty.

I will say of the Lord, He is my refuge and my fortress; my God, in him will I trust.

Surely he shall deliver thee from the snare of the fowler, and from the noisome pestilence.

He shall cover thee with his feathers, and under his wings shalt thou trust: his truth shall be thy shield and buckler.

Thou shalt not be afraid for the terror by night; nor for the arrow that flieth by day:

Nor for the pestilence that walketh in darkness; nor for the destruction that wasteth at noonday.

A thousand shall fall at thy side, and ten thousand at thy right hand; but it shall not come nigh thee.

Only with thine eyes shalt thou behold and see the reward of the wicked.

Because thou hast made the Lord, which is my refuge, even the most High, thy habitation;

There shall no evil befall thee, neither shall any plague come nigh thy dwelling.

For he shall give his angels charge over thee, to keep thee in all thy ways.

They shall bear thee up in their hands, lest thou dash thy foot against a stone.

Thou shalt tread upon the lion and adder; the young lion and the dragon shalt thou trample under foot.

Because he hath set his love upon me, therefore will I deliver him; I will set him on high, because he hath known my name.

He shall call upon me, and I will answer him: I will be with him in trouble; I will deliver him, and honor him.

With long life will I satisfy him, and show my salvation.

(KJV)

An Ohio corporal had printed it there, and recommended that anyone who saw it learn it. I did. I wondered what it meant to him. I wondered exactly what it meant to me. I was grateful to read it and memorize it.

In this lonely cell the transformation from soldier to prisoner became complete. Here *nothing happened*. I had moved all the way from battle—where activity was feverish and men drove themselves to the limit of human possibilities—to solitary confinement—where a man was alone and did nothing.*

A psychologist might have learned a great deal in this experience. But I was no psychologist—only a perplexed human being. It was a strange sensation—this slowing down of the human mind, this lifting it out of a world of action and setting it in a vacuum. The mind had been an anvil with the world pounding upon it, a living anvil that could pound back. Now it was nothing. It seemed as isolated and unreal as a bottled and preserved specimen of life in a biological laboratory—separated from the associations and interplay with other life that make people alive.

The dominant impression was the *lifting of responsibility*. And with the *lifting of responsibility* the mind became empty, because responsibility had been the biggest thing in that mind during the days that had wrought so deep an impression

---

* Years later I was to think of that experience when I read Sören Kierkegaard's comment that our age knows so little the value of solitude that we can only use it as a punishment for condemned prisoners.

61

there. For a week after capture, that mind had dreamed every night of responsibility. It had gone on patrol again. It had tried desperately, over and over again, to get through to the surrounded men and get them out. Now it had finally learned, even in its subconscious depths, the lesson of failure. It still dreamed, but now its dreams were of escape. Escape was the living thought in the empty mind. But even escape could not discharge that responsibility. So the mind felt defeated, futile—and relieved of responsibility.

Thousands of miles and, it seemed, thousands of years away that mind had wondered whether it could ever be the mind of a competent military officer. It knew then that it would never have the sparkling audacity or the power of unerring instantaneous decision of the military genius. But it thought itself capable of enough normal intelligence and judgment, and enough determination and power, to do its job of leadership. And it had pretty much unconsciously set up a criterion by which it could judge success or failure when the test came. It was not the standard of correct decisions in battle—there was too much luck there. Nor was it the standard of general competence in the confused crises of combat—it was reasonably sure of itself there. The criterion, though it had never been phrased or even formally thought, might be put in a question: will this mind in the danger and excitement of battle, in its conscious thought and its subconscious reactions, be dominated by *responsibility* rather than personal hope or fear? In battle the criterion had been forgotten; the mind had been too busy for self-judgment. Now in the cell, the old thought suggested itself. The mind knew that it had met its own criterion. It had passed. And it was, to that extent, happy. There were men in the company, it knew, who must have felt that their commander let them down, that he failed to get food, ammunition, information, and orders to them in their terrible need. They didn't know, of course, that he had been fighting as desperately as they. But the mind knew, to some extent, itself. Even now it could not judge how many of its combat orders and decisions had been correct, how many inadequate or mistaken. But it felt that it had done the thing it had always hoped it could do.

In its solitariness, the mind began to roam. It had been emptied by that lifting of responsibility, and it started to explore its world like a child's mind reaching out for the first time. Strangely, most of its thoughts were concerned with memories, but somehow they were new. The mind roamed, and stopped one place or another. It might stop on a problem of theology that it had studied a hundred times. But it was as if it were the first time, and the thoughts were fresh. Out of this appalling emptiness came a new vigor. The mind became intensely grateful—grateful for home, for memories, for the fact that life, now seen as never before, had been so grand, so wonderfully worth living. It leapt into a distant civilian future. It forgot the boredom of solitary confinement. It thought of learning and doing. It saw visions, made plans, and prayed.

The hours moved by. There was the yell of "Zoup" at the door, and the monotony became appalling. Now there were worries. A wife and an unborn baby. Fortunately the "Missing in Action" notice could not get home before Christmas. But it would be coming soon. Then how long would it be until some further news got there? The mind had no information to go on. It could only wonder and worry.

Thoughts miscellaneous and unrelated crowded in. What was happening to friends in the war? Where was a brother who must have been in the path of the German offensive farther north? Friends here and there, characters whom the mind had not thought of for months or years visited it and prompted recollection and speculation. Every song, hymn, ditty, chantey, or symphonic melody that had ever brushed against that mind came crowding through those solitary days. With them and between them came Lincoln's Gettysburg Address, the Lord's Prayer, a sonnet of Wordsworth's ("The world is too much with us"), many snatches of Shakespeare from roles once enacted in *Hamlet* and *Julius Caesar*. Three years before, doing guard duty on a California bridge, the mind had memorized Poe's "Raven" and never thought of it since. Now those rhythmic words of another introspective mind came rushing in. At first, only a verse here and there. Then through the days, by that curiously oblique process of memory where the mind grasps a thought or word precisely at those moments when it is not hunting them, the whole long poem came back. Then more various thoughts and anticipations. Times Square a few nights before embarkation. The unexpected bravery of some men in battle, the failures of others. That delightful family in the village of Kehlen, Luxembourg—had the attack harmed them? A professor known years ago. The last election campaign in America. The delight in America of coming from a day with the army to the cheap Louisiana rooms that, despite the roaches, were a home and there sitting down in the kitchen with *my* wife. And with that *my*, the mind was again a person. For minds, when they meet other minds and most of all when they love, become persons.

So I passed the time of my solitariness, now a mind, now a person. I don't know which of this multitude of unrelated thoughts was holding my attention on that New Year's Eve as I heard the Beethoven hymn. But I remember the hymn perplexed me. It was too beautiful, too peaceful. It didn't belong in this world. Its strains should have stopped at the window of this ugly cell. There was no rational problem; the ideas of the conflict and mingling of beauty and brutality, of loveliness and ugly war, were a commonplace in the dialectical theology I had learned. But still it perplexed me. Not my mind, but my whole self, was incapable of adjusting the conflict. It tried, and then gave up. The music stopped, but the cell remained.

(Interruption)

I didn't go to sleep easily; I had slept too much in the afternoon. I dozed a little, then woke up when the door of the cell opened. A guard grunted, "Kom, Offizier." I vaguely gathered that a German officer wanted me. I glanced at my watch. It was 5:00 A.M. So I had been asleep after all. I pulled on my shoes and followed the guard out. I supposed the interrogation was about to start. My sleepy wits pulled themselves together, and as I stumbled down the hall, I repeated to myself, "Name, rank, serial number. Name, rank, serial number."

The guard took me outdoors along a balcony, then into a tower of the castle. Up two or three flights of stairs he indicated that I should enter a room. I walked in. A German Feldwebel, speaking English, offered me a chair. I sat there and scarcely noticed when someone entered the room behind me.

"You are in the presence of a German officer," the Feldwebel said.

I stood at attention and faced about. There was a fat, middle-aged fellow, carelessly dressed in officer's uniform but with no insignia.

"Sit down," he said. I sat, and he took a seat across the table from me.

"Is that the way to sit before a superior officer?" he growled.

I had relaxed. In the American army, "Sit down," usually means "at ease." I straightened up.

"That's better." He put his elbows on the table and leaned forward toward me. The smell of liquor on his breath was oppressive. "What is your name and rank?"

I told him.

"Are you married?"

"I can't answer that, sir." I aimed not to yield at all, but to be militarily correct.

"What do you mean, you can't answer? That's not military information."

I could only repeat, "I can't answer, sir."

"Oh, you're going to be a tough guy," he said, with a voice full of sarcasm. "Look, there's no chance to be a hero now. There's nobody around here who knows you. And I aim to make you talk. Do you understand?"

He knew, and I was fast learning, that courage draws strength from a sustaining community. To be alone, perhaps to be annihilated with no human being to know that there was a moral reason, is a real threat to courage. We understood this as he waited for an answer. Finally I said, "Yes, sir."

"Are you married?"

"I can't answer, sir." He acted surprised. Probably I would have been smarter to say something else. At this late stage in the game, I had no tactical information that I might let slip. It was not a front line interrogation. And I could talk without giving anything away. But his attitude only made me more stubborn.

He bellowed back. "Listen, you 90-day wonder. You're talking to a Major in the German Army. I'm a professional soldier. If you think you're as tough as I am, you're crazy. I'll beat your head in. How old are you?"

"I'm sorry, sir. I can't answer."

He was becoming furious. He yelled and snorted, threatened and bullied. His language was full of American slang and profanity. "See that window," he shouted. "It's fifty feet down to solid concrete. I can throw you out of there and no one will ever know it. I can beat your head in." He held up a club menacingly. It looked like the leg of a heavy chair. "I have thumb screws. I can torture you until you will talk. They all do. But it's easier if you do it now. Will you answer my questions?"

"I'm sorry, sir. I can't."

He emptied my pockets. He took the watch off my arm, looked at it, and hurled it across the room and into the wall. My wallet had never been returned from my first quick interrogation, but I had my official officer's identification card. He looked at it. It would give my age and branch of service, no more. Then he found a picture of my wife and myself, mounted in a leather folder. It was obviously a husband and wife picture. "Oh, your wife," he grunted, and tore the picture from its mounting—ostensibly to see if anything was concealed. He threw this on the floor. Then he returned to his questions, and I stuck to the same answers.

He piled threat upon threat. "Your President Roosevelt," he said, "has personally promised to look after me if he ever gets a chance. So I can be as rough as I want." His rantings began to make me angry. What had been a reasoned determination to give no information now became a stubborn desire not to yield to threats. He knew now that I was 27 and married. But I wouldn't tell him even this, not simply because my Army forbade me, but because I didn't like his threats.

A few more angry questions. More cursing and yelling. And he strode out of the room.

The Feldwebel tried a friendlier approach. "We don't want to hurt you," he said. "Why don't you answer the Major's questions? He's not asking for military information."

"I'm under orders. That's all," I told him.

"But you're not just a soldier. You're an officer, who is supposed to use discretion in carrying out orders. If the Major had asked for military information, I could understand. But he hasn't."

"An American officer obeys his orders." I thought that answer might satisfy him. After all, the German army was supposed to know something about military discipline.

"But some of your officers are not so stubborn." His voice was still friendly and respectful.

"I obey my orders."

"I can't understand you Americans," he went on. "Why do you come clear over here to fight?"

I tried the same answer. "I am an officer and I obey my orders."

"But that is no explanation," he said. "Our soldiers know why they are fighting. You Americans never do."

He seemed to be intelligent, and I might have enjoyed talking to him under other circumstances. He and I both knew that he had cleverly trapped me. It is an American cliché that our soldiers have initiative and can think for themselves, whereas German soldiers follow orders in stolid obedience. He had turned the tables on me. My pride prodded me to give him an answer. But his tactic was to lure me into an ideological discussion that would soon turn into areas of military information. So I stifled my pride and simply said, "I obey my orders."

"Is it because of the Geneva Convention?" he said. "Of

course, we know that you are really only required to give
your name, rank, and serial number. But you must remember"—he spoke slowly and respectfully—"since that was
signed, you Americans have started an entirely new type of
warfare. Your bombing of our cities and destruction of helpless civilians is not fair warfare. So we cannot worry about
the Geneva Convention anymore."

He sounded as if he believed what he was saying. I wondered (and would wonder many times again in Germany) if
these people had utterly forgotten who initiated the world
to total warfare and the bombing of cities. But I said nothing.
He returned to his question: "Why don't you answer our
questions?"

The same answer—it was getting boring even to me—"I
obey my orders."

"But you are no professional soldier," he said. "Or are
you?"

I wouldn't answer that one.

"I am not a professional soldier," said the Feldwebel. "I am
fighting to defend my country and our culture. Do you really
mean that as an officer you simply obey your orders without
trying to understand why you fight?"

"I follow my orders."

"Then," he said, "and you will pardon my speaking so to
an officer, I can only say that you are not an intelligent
leader."

"I'll leave that for my men to judge."

"You know, I am sure, that we have found the British
officers much more capable than the Americans."

That, no doubt, was an old stunt, designed to make
Americans rally to the cause and loosen their tongues, so I
said nothing. There was a little more amiable chatter from
the Sergeant, and then the Major came back in.

"Well, are you still determined to be the tough guy?" he greeted me.

"I can't give you any information, sir," I said.

"I suppose they taught you that at Ft. Benning," he jeered. He leaned over the table at me and shouted. "Well, I'm telling you now, you'll never see the light of day until you talk. You'll never leave this room until I get all the information I want. Do you understand?"

"Yes, sir."

"Are you going to talk?"

"No, sir."

He picked up the club. "Are you going to talk?"

"No, sir."

I did not quite expect him to hit me, yet I was not greatly surprised when he did. The blow fell between my shoulder and neck and stunned me.

He repeated his question. I repeated my answer. He struck again. And again. I could tell now that he knew his job. He was striking me at a point that would pain and frighten me, but he was not intending to disable me. So I felt a little relieved. But he was half drunk and might miss. A two-inch miss would land squarely on my spine. I was worried.

As the club fell, my body began to shake. After perhaps a dozen blows, a hard one knocked me off the chair and on to the floor. He jerked me up, propped me on the chair again, and started all over. Another half dozen blows and he quit. He sat down opposite me again.

"Look," he said. "I've been easy on you because I'm an officer and you're an officer. But I've got a bunch of boys outside who would love to give you the works. Now would you prefer to talk to me as a gentleman, or shall I leave and send in the boys?"

I was really afraid, and didn't know what to answer.

"Which do you want?" he roared.

"I'm your prisoner and it's up to you," I said.

"Which do you want?" he snapped again.

"I'm your prisoner," was all I could think to say.

"Will you talk to me?"

"I can't give you any information."

"You'll never leave the room."

He stood up. "I'll leave you to think it over for five minutes," he said. "When I come back, you'll talk to me or I'll send in the boys. And they'll have guns."

He stalked out. I still did not think he would dare to shoot me, but I wasn't sure. I wondered about my behavior. Was I insane? So far, I had refused to tell him only one thing that he already knew: that I was married. He knew much more, from the captured Company C field desk. Why was I accepting abuse and unknown risks for refusing to tell him what he knew? * But I realized also that sooner or later he would ask other questions. Possibly it was better to refuse answers from the beginning. However, my thoughts were not strictly rational. I was angry enough that, though he threatened to shoot me, I would still refuse to talk—guessing, but not knowing, that his threat was a bluff.

The Feldwebel talked some more. Again he tried to be friendly. He asked several questions, toying with a pencil and notebook as he talked. He was apparently a sort of secretary, prepared to take notes on what I might tell. Again and again he returned to the question, "Why are you fighting?"

---

* In later years many debates have centered on the question of orders to our captured soldiers, especially in connection with the Korean war, when prisoners suffered brutality far beyond anything I endured. General Eisenhower himself wrote that "any enemy worthy of the name quickly learns through front-line contacts the identity of all units opposing him." (*Crusade in Europe*, p. 301.) Yet the soldier is forbidden to disclose his unit, even when he wears its insignia.

More than once I was to find the Germans fascinated by this question. Why did the Americans, with everything they needed at home, come to Europe to fight? In different circumstances I would have welcomed that question. But I gave the Sergeant no answers.

The Major returned, and I saw the Sergeant give him a quick glance—no doubt a signal. The Major sat down again and pulled out some American cigarettes. "Do you smoke?" he asked.

"No, thank you," I said.

"Do you ever smoke?"

"No, sir."

He lighted a cigarette for himself. Apparently he was not going to say any more about "the boys."

"Have a drink," he said in as friendly a way as he could manage. He produced a bottle of prune brandy and two glasses.

Again I refused politely. I had no desire to drink, especially since I knew it as a part of interrogation technique. He insisted. I said no. He was angry and said I *would* drink. I picked up the glass, preferring his liquor to his beatings.

I would go slowly, I decided, and keep from getting drunk— at least keep my mind clear. Maybe I could keep him ahead of me on the drinking. This would be hard, since he obviously was an old hand at this game. But he had a good start on his evening's drinking already, so possibly I had a chance.

He gulped his glass and I sipped mine. He refilled his and saw mine only a third empty. "Drink the rest of it," he said.

I swallowed it as slowly as I thought he would let me. He refilled it. The same thing happened. Faster and faster we emptied the glasses.

"I can't drink any more," I told him.

"You will drink more," he said.

"But I can't," I told him. My throat was tight.

He picked up the club again. I didn't want him to beat me, drunk as he was getting now. I swallowed another half glass, then decided that I had been telling the truth when I said, "I can't."

He tilted my chair back, shoved my forehead until my face turned up, and poured the liquor down my throat. "I'll smash your face in." The club hung poised in his hand. "Swallow it, God damn you," he said. "If you vomit, I'll shove your face in it. You call yourself an officer but a German corporal can drink more." I gulped the best I could. He quit and sat down.

I was feeling the liquor. My head swam and my body, shaking from the beating, was unsteady. But I could still think straight. All right. It shouldn't be hard to act drunk, with the start I had. I'd let him think I was really soused. I'd let my tongue run loose, but I'd be too drunk to understand anything military or give him any information.

He let me alone for a few seconds. He picked up the picture of my wife and myself from the floor and looked at it. Then he got out some pictures from his pocket. Now he spoke quietly. "This is my wife, and son," he said. "She is an American girl."

I stared at the picture.

"What did you say your name was?" he said. He glanced at my identification card and went on: "Roger, do you know where my wife is?"

I shook my head.

"She's dead, Roger. She and my son were killed by American bombers."

"I'm sorry, sir," I told him in drunken sympathy.

"Don't call me sir," he said. "My name is Bill and we're brothers. Just call me Bill."

Then he did surprise me. The old hypocrite was crying. And he put on a good show. "Do you have a child?" he asked.

"No, Bill," I said.

"But you have a wife, and you know how I feel." Then he stood up and shakily moved around side of me. I stood, too, and he put his arm around my shoulder. "Roger," he said, "tell me the truth. Did you ever expect to see tears in the eyes of a German Major?"

I was flabbergasted, and said "No." The answer seemed both appropriate and true.

"Well, you see them now." He went on weeping. He called me "Roger," and "Brother," and we sympathized as only drunks can do. Maybe neither of us was fooling the other— I know he wasn't fooling me—but each of us seemed to accept the other.

"Roger," he said. "I'm a Major in the regular German Army—a professional soldier and officer. You're only a young fellow and a Captain. It is never necessary for me to apologize to you. But I do apologize. I'm sorry I hit you. It's just that whenever I think of my wife, I can't control myself." He burst out weeping anew.

I forgave him, of course, and he sat down again. He talked a little more about his wife, and that reminded him of his days in America. It had been back in Mayor Jimmy Walker's time, when Lindberg was flying the Atlantic, that Bill had lived in New Jersey and had known New York well. At first I didn't believe him. But he knew American slang perfectly. He knew the popular songs of that time, but none since. He knew about the penny chocolate machines in the New York subways, and a dozen details of that city. I decided that he really had lived in America.

Gradually he grew more cheerful as he reminisced about

things in the States. We were just a couple of drunks chattering to each other. Then he remembered the date and decided that we were having a New Year's Eve party. He proposed some drinks and didn't complain when I fell behind him on the drinking. "Do you want a whore?" he asked suddenly. I told him "No." I haven't the slightest idea whether he was ready to produce one. He reached in a closet and pulled out a high silk hat. He stuck it on his head and danced around the room. I laughed deliriously and told him it was just like Broadway.

After a little more New Year's whoopee, Bill excused himself for a minute. The Feldwebel, who had been required to witness all this corny performance without any liquor to make it easier, started questioning me again. But I simply dropped my head on the table, as if I were too drunk to talk, and ignored him.

The Major came back in, with another German officer and an American Second Lieutenant. I could see them out of the corner of my eye, but they couldn't tell it. The Lieutenant was evidently getting the same treatment I had been getting. He was refusing to answer their questions and they were threatening him. I must be a miserable looking figure, I thought, and my anger boiled that they should try to use me to make another officer weaken. They took him out.

The Major came back and started talking again. Another drunk walked in, a skinny fellow, wearing an old sweater. Bill introduced him as a Lieutenant. The two fools carried on a while. Bill's friend explained in his best drunken manner that he had lived in America too. In fact he had been a Lieutenant General in the American army and had wanted to fight the Japs. But when they tried to make him fight the Germans, he left America and came to Germany. "And," he boasted, "I would rather be a lowly Lieutenant in the German army than a Lieutenant General in the American army."

I didn't have the slightest idea whether I was supposed to believe such tommyrot, but no one seemed to mind. It was just a New Year's party now. The Feldwebel occasionally tried to slip in a question, but I ignored him and talked to the other two about nothing. After a while, they asked a few things about the army. I managed to pay no attention to their questions, but I didn't like them. So I got on my feet, to pay my respects to the "Lieutenant General." I felt shaky, and it was easy enough to fall over on the floor, as if I had passed out. They got some cold water and threw it in my face, then put me on the chair again and gave me some coffee.

The picture of my wife was still lying on the table. Absent-mindedly I picked it up and put it in my pocket. They seemed not to mind. I wanted to get my watch back without appearing too intelligent or sober. So after awhile I looked at my wrist, wondered what time it was, and asked for the watch. "Brother Bill" got it and gave it to me.

There was some more frivolity, but no more questions. I threw a word of German into the conversation now and then, and they laughed whenever I did. I laughed at everything they said.

Then the party was over. They led me down the hall and into another room. There was the American Lieutenant, still telling them nothing. I felt proud of him. Bill said, "Tell them that we are his friends, Roger." Again I was angry. One of the oldest tricks in interrogation is to make a man think that his superiors have talked. I said nothing and, when the Germans were looking another way, gritted my teeth and winked at the lieutenant. I hope he saw.

A guard took me away. As we crossed the outside balcony, it was getting light. I looked at my watch. It was eight o'clock.

Three hours for the whole performance. The guard took me up to my cell. Apparently this was old stuff to him. As I went through the door I turned and said, *"Ein fröhlich Neujahr."* He looked surprised. I sank down on the bed.

All day I worried about what might come next. I could not expect the Major to quit after one session. I dreaded seeing him again and wondered that I had ever been such a fool as to want to leave Limburg.

(*Matching Wits*)

Next time it was at ten o'clock at night. I had just gone to sleep when the guards called me. Again I went up to the same room. Only the Major was there. I went in and stood stiffly at attention. "Sit down, Roger," he said casually.

"Thank you, sir," I said correctly.

"I'm just Bill." Apparently he was going to try the friendly technique. He offered me coffee again. It was American coffee from a Red Cross parcel. I disliked this hypocrite, and he annoyed me by using Red Cross supplies in this way. But the coffee might make my stomach and head feel better, so I took some.

He started recalling the night before—kidding me about how drunk I had been. He said it had taken two men to carry me back to my room. I knew that was a lie, but there was no use starting an argument.

Then he pulled the prize one. Still cheerful and friendly, he pointed to a small scar on his cheek, and said, "Did you know that you did that?"

I insisted that I hadn't. But, still smiling, he explained that I had done it while I was drunk. It would have been silly to argue, so I simply repeated that I didn't see how I could have done any such thing and let it go at that.

77

"But I don't mind," he grinned. "After all, we're brothers and we have forgiven each other everything that happened." So that was his game. Striking a German officer would be a serious offense, and no doubt he could produce "witnesses" to confirm his lies. So I agreed that we were friends.

He pulled out a sheet of paper. "You won't mind writing down that you haven't been mistreated, will you?"

This was disgusting. I wanted to rebel. But his scrap of paper might save me trouble, and I had had enough trouble by now. It couldn't possibly reveal any information or do any harm to our Army. And I knew that it would be legally worthless to him if he should ever be called to account for his doings. So I scribbled something on the paper, and my name, in a deliberately distorted handwriting.

Now started a sort of battle of wits. In a way I enjoyed it, because I thought myself smarter than Bill. And, strangely, solitary confinement was oppressive enough that the sight of any human being was, in a way, a diversion. But the nervous strain of the game was not fun. Bill did most of the talking. I asked him questions often, to forestall his asking me. He talked about New York and America again and again, then slipped in a military reference. Usually I said I didn't know. He accepted the answer. Once or twice he looked suspicious, but he never again threatened. I often wondered how he could believe that anybody was as dumb as I, with my frequent "I don't know."

The truth, I suppose, is that he didn't believe my declarations of ignorance. Apparently he had gone as far with brutality as he was prepared to go. Perhaps we had come to a tacit agreement. He would not beat me, and I would not provoke his pride with outright refusal to say anything. To say, "I don't know," however incredible, did not affront his sense of command so much as to say, "I refuse to answer."

It was interesting to see what he would ask. He was after the American order of battle—the line-up of corps and divisions on the western front. He pulled out the chart of shoulder insignia of the various divisions and wondered which ones I had seen in France. I picked out four or five that were prominent in the Stalag at Limburg and that he was bound to know about; by dint of great thoughtfulness I recalled seeing them. He seemed disappointed.

He asked about several divisions—he didn't know whether they were in France or whether they existed. I knew nothing. He pulled out his printed information on American Armored divisions. My shoulder patch—the American army wore them in battle, except in highly secret operations—told him that I was in the 9th Armored Division. By my orders I was forbidden to tell him my organization, but he knew and didn't ask. His information correctly showed the activation of the division at Ft. Riley, but was incomplete. He had the wrong commander listed, and I did not enlighten him.

His knowledge of the American Army was sometimes amazing. But there were big gaps in it and funny misconceptions. Very rarely I tried to mislead him or deliberately lied. But this was dangerous. Some other prisoner in the same castle might tell him a different lie, or the truth, and I would be on the spot. He wondered about our replacements of casualties, our maintenance of vehicles, our equipment, our tactics. He tried to impress me with the German manual on American weapons and vehicles. It was a good book—probably as good as our manuals on the German army.

He asked about Russia. "Would you like to live there?"

"I like America," I told him.

"What do you think of the Russians as allies?"

Once again it was no time for an ideological argument, so I simply asked what he thought of the Japanese.

"Well, you know, Roger," he said, "to tell you the truth—just as one officer to another—he paused—"I don't care who wins that war. We don't even know how it is going. We can't believe what the Japanese say."

His most interesting exhibit was a printed intelligence map from West Front Headquarters, dated about Christmastime. I am sure it was authentic, and it gave me my first real news on the extent of "the bulge." The map showed the American units on the front and their locations. He showed it to me in the hope that I would reveal something further. Pointing out the German advances, Bill showed how he expected the drive to win the war. Other interrogating officers elsewhere, I learned from friends, said that the Germans were attacking, not for victory but for a peace. I studied the map as carefully as I could without seeming too interested. As far as I knew our disposition of troops, it was accurate. He showed me the 9th Armored Division, located at four widely scattered places, and asked if I could figure that out. I could; the division had been temporarily divided between two corps. And in one corps, it had been split between corps reserve for the north half and for the south half of a 30-mile front. But I acted puzzled and admitted nothing.

My interrogation took four sessions, including the New Year's Eve party. I don't suppose my lies ever did much damage to the German Army. But I am confident that I did not betray my own Army. In the last three meetings, Bill always tried the friendly approach. He was an interesting conversationalist and was fairly smart, though never quite sober. Sometimes I actually enjoyed listening to him. Once I enjoyed a few moments of remarkably beautiful music from Radio Berlin—music of the kind rarely broadcast in America except on Sunday.

On my last visit Bill gave me a Red Cross parcel and described the delights of living in an officers' prison camp. A train would be leaving that day from Limburg, and I would go on it. And Bill bade me farewell with the thought that he might see me in America someday. I said I hoped so, and thought to myself that such a meeting would not be very healthy for Bill.

He allowed me to write one letter to my wife. I figured that it was a trick and hardly thought it would be mailed. But I wrote it—a simple love letter with no information except that I was O.K. It actually reached America.

In later weeks I talked to a number of Americans who were interrogated at Diesz. Combining our information, we figured that there were probably four German officers doing the interrogating. Most of the Americans started by talking about anything except military information and avoided any rough treatment. Major Bill (or Wilhelm von Bohn) was the only one, it seemed, who handed out any beatings. He tried a different technique on one friend of mine. He undressed him and set him on a chair, then put a stove under the chair and heated it until my friend passed out. Then he threw him, still naked, out into the cold, where he passed out again. Bill never offered him liquor and never became a "brother." His only friendly gesture was the final Red Cross parcel that was given to every one at Diesz.

5. GERMANY
FROM A BOXCAR

Bill had, for a wonder, told the truth when he said that I would get on the train that day. He had been mistaken when he said it would leave; we sat on it twenty-four hours before it moved. And he had been wrong when he said we would ride in coaches. It was the familiar boxcar that I learned to know and dislike in Germany. Some of the German rolling stock had been stolen out of France, and I wondered for a minute whether I was in the right war when I approached the little car and saw on its sides the famous *"Hommes 40, Cheveaux 8."*

The legendary 40-and-8 boxcar had never had a reputation for comfort, but we wished that it had been loaded with the *Hommes 40*. It would have been less crowded. There were 24 American officers on it, but we had only between a third and a half of the space. A wire fence kept us in one end of the boxcar. The other end and the center door space was occupied by a half dozen guards. There was straw on the floor, but not nearly enough space for everyone to lie down. There was a bucket for sanitary purposes. Still we were lucky. Often prisoners were stacked in 60 to a car with locked doors for long trips.

The boxcar was our home for a week, though we got on

with no idea where we were going or how long it would take. Most of the time, it seemed, the train sat on sidings. We were always cheered when it moved.

Our guards were an interesting bunch, especially since I had seen little of German soldiers. An old Master Sergeant was in charge of us. He had the self-assurance of old Master Sergeants in all armies. The rest of the men were a little afraid of him. He kept a sort of dignity and attention to duty. He was slightly friendly but he kept his distance from us, except that when offered an American cigarette he would unbend. But it was unfair to judge him in the face of that greatest of all temptations for a German soldier. And despite all cigarettes, he never yielded to tell us our destination.

The Corporal, who managed the guard, was a short young fellow with a Hitler moustache, who obviously fancied that he looked something like *Der Führer*. He enjoyed striking poses. As a connoisseur, I rather thought his attitudes resembled Napoleon more than Hitler, but no doubt he knew more of Hitler than I. He enjoyed his authority and loved to order the guards around; it was an obvious thrill to him to be guarding officers. The first couple days we thoroughly disliked him. Then he began to amuse us, and we found out that he was human. He was another of these pitiful little Nazis—one of the small-town folk who in a different world might have lived a normal life but who responded to the phony grandeur of Nazism and must bear part of the responsibility for its terror unloosed on the world.

We were an unhappy bunch in the boxcar. The food was more pitifully small than at Limburg. A little bread and maybe some spread was doled out daily by the guard. The first day and the last day, as I recall, there was nothing. Cigarettes were few, and the tobacco addicts made themselves and everyone else miserable with their complaints.

Those who had come from Diesz had Red Cross parcels or remnants of them. The rest had none. Only a few were generous. The rest hoarded their food and tobacco, and everybody complained.

We got water only by grace of the guards, and the guards at first were not very gracious. Gradually a few cigarette donations melted them, and by the end of the trip they were a friendly bunch. They loaned us their knives to cut our bread and toasted it for us on their stove. (It was unusual luck for a PW car to have a stove.)

Every evening started a squabble for floor space that went on all night. After a few days, the guards got us a bench, and we worked out a scheme. If a third sat on the bench, the other two-thirds could lie down in two rows. Legs tangled with legs, but that was better than feet butting heads. It lacked some of the spaciousness of a sardine can, but it worked. By agreement, eight men lay down side by side, all on their right; after a while, by further agreement, all turned and slept on the left side. We divided the night into shifts, and everyone got some sleep.

But still each day grew worse. Nerves became jangled and tempers short. Sometimes we froze and sometimes we suffocated. Idle talk became arguments, and arguments became quarrels, and quarrels almost became fights. Human nature was about as petty and mean as I have ever thought it could be. In a boxcar much must be forgiven.

It was perhaps the third night when we pulled into the railyards of Berlin. The guards were more excited than we. They had never seen the capital city of the *Vaterland* and were somewhat more ambitious in that respect than we. Someone of us remarked that now we could say we had beaten Patton to Berlin, and we let it go at that. We saw nothing of the city. The railyards, to our disappointment, seemed in good shape.

There was no sign of bombing here. I learned later from other prisoners that Berlin itself was already largely destroyed at this time; but these yards, if they had been bombed, were in good repair. Our Master Sergeant left the car for awhile, then came back with good news. The German Red Cross would give us noodle soup. The pails of hot soup came up in the car. We filled whatever cans we happened to have and enjoyed it like a banquet.

We had thought that our camp might be in the neighborhood of Berlin, but our boxcars jerked on, day and night, as we became more weary and quarrelsome. We could tell little about where we were, as the doors of the boxcar were seldom open. But sometimes we could look out and perhaps catch the name of a station. The ground looked flat and desolate. It was covered with heavy snow. The names of the towns were different now, and we gradually realized that we were in Poland.

We held low hopes for our future home. But it was a tremendous relief to get off the boxcar. We marched through deep snow into a little town and out the other side, toward the prison camp. And this time, as we entered the barbed wire, there was less of the oppressed feeling of that first time at Limburg. Our morale must have been low, for it seemed almost less a prison than a haven.

6. OFLAG 64

It was a pleasure to shake off our shoes and step from the frigid air indoors. We crowded into a room where a peppy American Lieutenant greeted us. In a few minutes there was some coffee—the bitter German ersatz stuff that tasted bad but was warm. Then came a grunt or shout at the door, which we somehow understood to mean that we should stand at attention, and a German officer and NCO came in.

The officer was an Oberstleutnant (Lieutenant Colonel) and a handsome man. He was meticulously dressed and looked the aristocrat. His face lacked the hardness of the German Field Marshalls in *Time* Magazine, but in every other respect he was the picture of the Prussian Officer. The NCO introduced him as Oberstleutnant Loida, the assistant commandant of the camp. The officer gave us a short speech, interpreted by the Sergeant, in which he welcomed us, told us that everything possible would be done here for our comfort and enjoyment, and that we in turn must obey orders strictly.

He left, and food came.

No dinner, however elaborate or delicious, had ever tasted so good to me as that one. Everyone in the room said the same thing. It was a dish of oatmeal with a couple spoons of sugar. For the first time, I realized how hungry I was. It was the first good food in captivity. Cold and half-starved, in our eagerness we must have looked like baby robins welcoming mama home to the nest. Oatmeal I had always considered a common food; frequently I had passed it by in the mess line. Since that day, I have regarded it as a rare and delightful meal. The American Lieutenant explained that they had it seldom and were glad they could welcome us with it.

The oatmeal was barely finished when another delight came in. A Red Cross Christmas parcel for each of us. The American officers had generously saved them for arrivals like us. We looked at the canned chicken, the candy, and the plum pudding—delicacies unknown to prisoners except in Christmas parcels—and wondered that luxury could be so great.

As we pushed the food into our mouths, we turned a barrage of questions on the American Lieutenant. His name was Chappel, and he had been taken prisoner in Africa, where he had been a forward observor with the First Armored Division. He gave us our first information about life at the Oflag. (*Oflag* is the German contraction for *Offizier* and *Lager*.)

Oflag 64 was the camp for American ground force officers and reputedly one of the best of the German prison camps. It was located near Bromberg, Poland (between Posen or Poznan and Danzig) on the edge of the little town of Szubin. The Germans, when they conquered Poland, had changed the name of the town to Altbergund, so, of course, the Americans called it *Szubin* (or Schubin).

Chappel could talk almost as fast as a bridge club, and he poured out the answers to our dozens of questions. The climate was cold. There was a pretty good stock of Red Cross parcels, and "they" were now issuing them once a week. There were athletics in the summer, provided the parcels were coming; if not, there wasn't enough food to exercise much. The officers kept a garden to help on the food situation. The PW's called themselves Kriegies (short for *Kriegsgefangener*) and called the Germans "Goons," a title regarded as less friendly than "Jerries." German treatment was not too bad. After the attempt on Hitler's life the last summer the army had been Nazified and the captors got a little tougher; but as Germany came closer to losing the war, the jailers became a little more considerate. Chances to escape were no good. Everybody who tried got caught. The Americans ran the camp; the Germans only kept the guard and enforced regulations, most of which were annoying. There was a formation twice a day (called *Appel*) for roll call. News came from the German communications and the BBC, and it was put out in a camp newspaper. Right now, the Americans had stopped the German offensive and were squeezing in on the "bulge." So on and on.

We could not move into barracks until we were deloused, so we slept on the floor of that sort of administration building that night. The next morning we got a magnificent hot shower, and our clothes were baked to get the lice. The American doctors checked us and found three officers from our train (from a second boxcar) with scarlet fever. So we were quarantined and assigned to a barracks of our own—47 of us. We got razors, a towel, and a few items of American Army clothes from the Red Cross. We soon began to feel like men again.

Under the military caste system, recognized by the Geneva Convention, officer prisoners do not work. As a matter of fact, they do practically nothing and usually are extremely bored. It was especially so with us in our quarantine. We could not enter into the life of the Oflag. By the tolerance of the Germans and some noteworthy efforts of the Americans, the camp did some remarkable things. One was the school. In such a group of officers (close to 1,500) there are some good teachers, and courses were set up in languages, law, science, engineering, history, and a variety of subjects. The chief limitation was books and paper, but the courses followed the American pattern with examinations, and it was hoped that they might be recognized for credit later in America.

The library had some excellent books, most of them gifts from the International YMCA. The Y furnished books, musical instruments, athletic and recreational equipment. The Americans had a dramatic group and had put on several plays. Occasionally there was a movie, courtesy of the "Goons." The special Christmas issue of the American newspaper pictured a German actress as its choice for the Kriegies' pin-up girl.

All this life passed by our quarantine barracks, and we simply sat and talked and bored each other. The library sent down a bunch of books. The lights were poor, and I had been without glasses since I started on that night patrol, but I read all I dared. There were card games, and checkers and chess, because the Red Cross Christmas parcels contained games. We slept long hours and spent part of the day time in bed, because that was the warmest place in the always chilly barracks. Because of the quarantine, we could not even write letters, and we missed that most of all.

The biggest activity was cooking. The food issue was not much better than at Limburg, but Red Cross parcels made an immense difference. The daily bread ration was the same as at Limburg. There was ersatz coffee in the morning and soup at noon. The evening meal was a few (very few) boiled potatoes and meat (usually salmon or corned beef) from the Red Cross parcels. The kitchen, run entirely by Americans, opened the parcels and took out the main meat items. The parcels were then issued to us, at the rate of one a week at the time I was at the Oflag. I know no way to tell how much that eleven-pound package meant to a prisoner of war. The foods were common enough to Americans, but exactly what a Kriegie needed. The powdered milk, margarine, soluble coffee, cheese, sugar, prunes, and so on, were marvelously delicious to anyone living on the German diet. The parcel was a hobby, too, for Kriegies inevitably turned into cooks. It was amazing what combinations, what puddings and pies and stews, could be made from those simple items. Our group included one lieutenant who had formerly managed a Howard Johnson restaurant. He quickly became a man of invincible status, an oracle and counselor to all.

Our barracks had two stoves, made from oil drums. They were of slight value in heating the barracks on those frigid days. But their flat tops were wonderful ranges for cooking. All day long YMCA pans or skillets and our own tin cans sat on top of these stoves. When they became too crowded, we used little homemade stoves fashioned from tin cans and called either (1) smokeless burners or (2) smoky Joes. Title (1) was considered more dignified, title (2) more accurate.

Carving bread became a ritual and a pastime. The common ration was a loaf of bread per day for six men. We organized in groups of six, numbering off from one to six. No. 1 approached the bread with a knife, while the rest gathered around and gave advice. With dramatic deliberation he cut the loaf in six parts. Then No. 2 took his choice of the six pieces. The others chose in order, with No. 1 getting last choice and suffering the consequences of any inequity or lack of skill in his own cutting. The next day No. 2 became the cutter—and so on. The system guaranteed the optimum possible equity. Cheating was impossible, and error was self-punishing. On sparse days the ration might call for seven men to a loaf. Then groups were reorganized and the ritual became more meticulous because, as anybody knows, it is far more complicated to divide a loaf seven ways than six. In the absence of any theater, radio, or sports, the act of bread-cutting brought some drama into each day.

No one could cook or cut bread all the time—not without more food than we had. But anyone could talk. And talking became the chief occupation. If there was nothing to discuss, there was always something to argue. All day long and part of the night, hanging around the bunks or huddled near the stoves, people argued. We reformed the army, revised the system of pay and allowances, devised new tables of organization. We went into politics and religion, economics and the race problem. There were arguments on co-education, the best liquors, universal military training, styles, jobs after the war, and always *food*. Nothing could rival food as a subject for talk. Sometimes I felt unacculturated since I seemed to be the only man in the barracks who did not plan to become a restaurant operator or a farmer someday. Talk of the future brought us to the one topic that rivaled food in intensity (though not frequency) of discussion. That was the end of the war.

Old Kriegies were traditionally pessimists at Oflag 64; new ones were optimists. Among all there was more realism, or perhaps just more resignation, than back in the army. Still, you could hear all the theories here. A few months before, the then new Kriegies—anyone who had been captured since D-Day in Europe—were all in the "victory before Christmas" group. The old-timers—from Africa and Italy—were not so sure. The two groups had organized bets and put up hundreds of dollars, all in I.O.U.'s. Now Christmas was past, and our group should by precedent have been the optimists. But we had all been too much startled by the German Ardennes drive, and no one was sure of anything.

Anxiously we waited for the news each day. The "bulge" was shrinking. That was good. Then came the news of the

Russian drive. The Soviet tanks were moving. Here in Poland this took on a new importance. Daily our news report gave the mileage of the Soviets from Szubin or the Vistula nearby. We all knew and respected the power of Russian offensives. Would this one reach us? Excitement became feverish. Everywhere we heard the hope that we might be overtaken or surrounded.

Still in quarantine, we woke on the morning of January 19 and saw, through the window, the road clogged with westbound wagons. It could be only one thing—refugees. Every wagon was loaded. Chairs and bicycles stuck halfway out the back ends. We kept looking. All day long they rolled by. It must be mass evacuation.

Enthusiasm mounted. Somehow I couldn't quite imagine that the Germans would let us—most of the American ground force officers—be caught by the Russians. But there was a chance. And regardless of that, this was pushing the war closer to an end. So I too was enthusiastic.

We waited with extra eagerness for the news that day. It never came. Were the Russians drawing near, and our captors afraid to let us know the truth? That was the only answer we could see.

The morning of the twentieth we rushed to the windows again. There was the same picture. An endless stream of wagons, going slowly past. Something was bound to happen soon, we thought. It did. An order to be ready to move, at any time after 7:00 P.M., by rail or on foot.

That really touched off the excitement. Imaginations ran wild. By rail or by foot. Certainly they wouldn't try to get us out by foot, said someone who didn't know the Germans. But rail movement seemed even more unlikely. We had seen enough of their rail disorganization to know that German transportation was in a bad way. And near an active front, railroads could be used for more important things than prisoners of war.

Late afternoon. Now we are told to be ready to move in the morning. The commandant is trying to get boxcars, but doesn't know if he can. A Red Cross parcel is given to every man. We are cooking madly, eating up what is in the old parcels. There has been a physical examination by our American doctors of all who may be unable to walk. We have been told that a German doctor would examine the officers on the list, but he does not appear, and our doctors' list becomes final. All the reserve clothing has been passed out, but we still are in no shape to face this weather. Yet that won't keep us from leaving.

One of the old-timers says that there was some excitement once before when the Russians attacked, and nothing came of it. But the Reds must be close, with all this civilian evacuation. We are planning ways of carrying our blankets and parcels, tearing up mattress covers for straps or using them for bundles. We are organized, we hear, in platoons of 50 for the trip. Orders come from the Senior American Officer authorizing attempts to escape on the move, provided the platoon leader is notified. But escape is not recommended.

It gets dark outside. It gets late at night. Still we are cooking and eating. It has been a long, long time since anyone has eaten all he wanted, so tonight is the time. The week's ration of coal is burned in one night, and for the first time since I was captured, I sleep warm all night.

7. 350 MILES

The 21st of January. It was getting close to noon, and we were still standing outside the barracks, in groups of 50, more or less. Though we had been standing for three or four hours in the freezing weather, the Americans were in no hurry to move. We might as well let the Russians get as close as possible. So every time the German Adjutant went down the line to count us, he got a different number. Everybody seemed confused. The German Commandant had given us a speech that we couldn't hear, but we gathered that he had a destination a hundred miles or so away and hoped to get rail transportation somewhere between here and there.

Eventually the Germans decided that they had us counted or else gave up the attempt, and we started to march. We moved past the hospital, where the sick were staying back, and out the gate. Our column, stretched out on the road was a fantastic sight. We were perhaps 1,300 strong, all officers except for a platoon of enlisted men who had lived at the Oflag, working as K.P.'s or orderlies. There was every conceivable kind of uniform and pack. Some of the old-timers, who had accumulated more possessions and wisdom than the rest of us, were pulling sleds. I envied them. I needn't have. The sleds lasted no more than a day or two. My pack, improvised from a blue-checked pillow case, became uncomfortable in

94

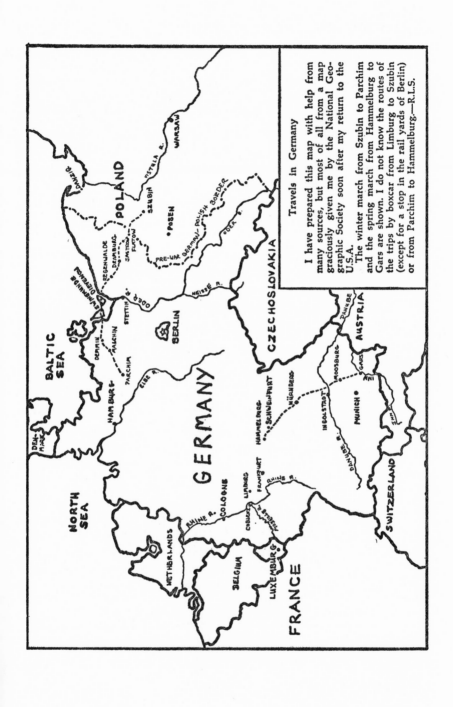

Travels in Germany

I have prepared this map with help from many sources, but most of all from a map graciously given me by the National Geographic Society soon after my return to the U.S.A.

The winter march from Szubin to Parchim and the spring march from Hammelburg to Gars are shown. I do not know the routes of the trips by boxcar from Limburg to Szubin (except for a stop in the rail yards of Berlin) or from Parchim to Hammelburg.—R.L.S.

the first hundred yards, though what made it heavy I never exactly figured out. Whenever I wanted something, it seemed that the pack had nothing. But whenever I lifted it, it felt like a portable hardware store. There were two blankets and a mattress cover, a razor and some soap, a couple cans and eating utensils, two paperback books from the Oflag library, and a little more than one Red Cross food parcel.

(*Marching*)

Oberst Schneider, the German Commandant, stood near the gate as we moved out. It was the first close look I ever had of him. He was old, fat, and pompous, and I knew I didn't like him. A few Polish civilians watched us move out; they gave us a friendly smile.

Again today the wagons of the refugees crowded the road. We walked on hour after hour, growing dreary and weary. Our column began to stretch out. Muscles unused to exercise grew sore, and the freezing weather helped to make them ache. Stragglers fell far behind. There were no longer any recognizable platoons, any military order. Now there was just a mass of men, moving slowly and painfully forward, strung out for miles. Sometimes they glutted the road, where there were no wagons. Sometimes they strung out single file, hugging the edge of the road and avoiding the horses.

The scenery, if anyone had an eye for it, was sometimes breathtaking. The white Polish plains stretched out as far as we could see, broken occasionally by evergreens whose branches barely showed through their coverings of snow. But we saw little of it. Our eyes were usually on the road in front of our feet. After the first hour there were no organized halts; if the head of the column stopped, the tail was too far away to know it. As each group of men got too tired to walk, they stopped awhile and then trudged on. The guards grumbled and protested, but were too tired themselves to really care. Horses of the refugees slipped and fell in their harnesses. They struggled to their feet and iron shoes pawed frantically at the icy road, trying to catch hold so they could move on. Sometimes an American fell, too, and strained to lift himself and his pack off the ground. Our spirits were low. But perhaps a cart would go past and we would hear a baby crying inside or see an aged woman trembling in the cold. Then self-pity would change to compassion.

It was just dark when our motley crew turned into a barn-yard. We stood in the cold for perhaps an hour, while the Germans tried to figure things out and give us orders. Then we moved into the barns and spread out our blankets in the straw or on the bins of grain. The lucky ones found places in stables, where the body heat of horses and cattle warmed the air. That night and on many a following night I thought of the Christian nativity story and wondered whether Mary and Joseph, if they had to live in a stable, were not grateful for the nearness of the warming beasts.

In the barns we dug into our Red Cross parcels. The Germans gave us no food that day. All day there had been no water, and the well in the barnyard was probably not pure, since it was obviously subject to seepage from animal wastes. But we had to drink, or thought we did, and trusted that the cold weather might prevent disease. We slept in pairs, to keep warm. And in that pile of straw, I slept warm all night for the second time since I was a prisoner of war.

(The Second Day)

Morning came too soon, and we piled out into the frigid barnyard, muscles stiff and aching. Men had straggled into the farm the previous night for two hours after the main group arrived. It was obvious that some of them could not make another day's march. Our doctors went to work and picked out about 150 to stay back. They returned to the barns. What would happen to them no one knew. Perhaps the Germans would find some transportation; perhaps the men would just stay there. Maybe the Russians would come along and liberate them; maybe there would be a battle in the town and they would get killed.

As the rest of us moved out, I tried to figure why yesterday's march had been so tiring and painful. It had been about 13 miles, short enough by American army standards.* Mainly, I suppose, it was undernourished bodies and muscles too long without exercise. Then there was the effort of lifting feet high to get through the snow, or the strain of keeping balance on the ice. And always, ill-adjusted packs tugged on shoulders or bent backs.

We moved out again across the endless plains. Today we had some sort of road priority over the evacuees, and progress was faster. The Poles along the way were extremely friendly and sometimes passed us bread out of their doors as we walked through their villages. About mid-day we crossed the Bromberg Canal, and saw the bridge already prepared for demolition. Near it we heard artillery—probably German batteries registering in on target areas. The sounds were hardly the firing of combat. But the guards seemed apprehensive today, and there was an air of expectancy. Three planes flew overhead that day. That was always the way on the eastern front. There were never the huge formations that

---

* The German roads that we traveled had frequent markers indicating the number of kilometers to the next town. Each day I noted these and transferred them into miles. Later verification from maps indicates that my estimates of distances throughout this record are fairly accurate.

we saw in the west. Only one or two planes at a time, and those very seldom. I never saw a Russian plane. The gigantic air battles of the west were as strange to this front as the massed tank corps rolling off the Russian steppe were to the fighters on the Siegfried Line.

Once, when we stopped for a ten-minute rest, a boy, eight or ten years old, approached and looked us over curiously. I said "Wie geht's" to him. "Sind Sie Volksturm?" he asked.

I laughed. "Nein, wir sind Amerikaner," I told him.

My German was apparently good enough for him to understand. He wasn't taken back in the slightest. "Mein Vater ist im Volksturm," he said in a casual and friendly way.

I looked at myself and at our column, and didn't wonder that a child might take us for Volksturm. We were ragged and polyglot enough for the worst of Germany's assortments of their "people's army." I wore mostly American clothes. But my overcoat was French, with the insignia of a cavalry regiment, as a French prisoner once explained to me. My cap was the undignified green wool-knit army cap, which most of our column had; in the American army it was worth a real chewing out, and sometimes a fine, to wear that cap anytime except under a helmet. The blue-checked pack "did something," as a department store clerk might say, for the costume. I had no gloves. But I had salvaged a few socks from a pile of discarded clothing. All of them had holes in them, but the holes weren't all in the same places. So by wearing four socks on each hand, I had a first-rate mitten.

As we trudged along, I decided to try my meager German on one of the guards. In an inexplicable burst of generosity, I offered him a prune from my Red Cross parcel. Then I started the conversation by saying "kalt." He answered with a "ja," and something about his feet. I found that he had been in the army about three years, was about 18 years old, and came from Vienna. "Oh," I said, "on the Danau."

He said yes, and mentioned a song about the Danube.

"Ja," I told him, "Johann Strauss."

He grinned.

The guard company was a conglomerate group, mostly of 4-F-ers unfit for combat duty. Many of them were from Austria or Poland and had no love for the Germans. Most of them were old, and some were physical wrecks. A number had been wounded in battle and assigned to this less rigorous duty. There were no more than two or three who had any enthusiasm for the war. Many of them became friendly with us before long.

In late afternoon we came to a town where we stopped for an hour while the German officers tried to puzzle out something or other. Civilians offered us ersatz coffee. It was hot and felt good. Then the German guards issued us some oleo— about a quarter pound per person. It was the only food issued us for two days of marching and we had nothing to put it on, but we were grateful for this first indication that our captors understood that the human body required food.

The march that day was about 16 miles to a little town near Wirsitz. When we pulled into the barns that night, I was exhausted. My left leg was so stiff I could only drag it, and I could scarcely climb up into the straw to find a bed. I soon slumped into the blankets, vaguely wondering whether the Germans would ever give us a meal. I doubted that I could march at the scheduled time of 7:30 the next morning, and went to sleep.

Sleeping was not easy that night, tired though I was. Snow came in through holes in the barn roof. The straw was wet, and I was cold and my muscles ached. But morning brought news startling enough to make us forget all our troubles.

(*Almost Free*)

We heard an American voice down at the barn door. "The German officers and guards have left," it said. "The Russians are supposed to be very close, but we have only rumors, and Col. Goode (our senior officer) orders that everyone stay where he is."

The news struck us like lightning. We were elated. Then we began to wonder. The more we thought, the more questions came up. Obviously the Russians were close if the Germans had fled without us. But was it a Russian reconnaissance element or a real attacking force? Naturally, we couldn't simply march out to meet them. We didn't know where they were. If we left, the Germans might catch us. If we did meet the Russians, that could be dangerous. A boy had mistaken us for the Volksturm yesterday, and the Russians, like most armies, would probably fire first and ask questions later. There were supposed to be officers in our column who could talk Russian; that might help. But suppose we made contact with the Russians, and found that they were a patrol, and that the army was twenty or fifty miles back. Col. Goode was right in wanting no hasty action.

An American organization quickly started to work. Col. Goode and his staff from the Oflag were efficient, and we soon had a hot thick pea soup. It seemed in our pride that American officers in this strange country could do better for food than the Germans who presumably ruled it.

Our group had slept the night before in several barnyards. Today we called them quadrangles, with the easy familiarity of a university campus, and each quadrangle had its commander who got orders from Col. Goode. American flags were made ready to identify us to the Russians. Civilians were questioned for information, and some of them went out to get us further news. Hauptmann Menner, the German Adjutant, was still with us—the only one of the Germans. He was a funny character, often confused, with a mincing, effeminate step that amused us. He was always friendly and helpful, and we liked him. If the Russians came, they would use tanks for the advance guard, he thought.

Excited though we were, the Polish family who lived on the farm outdid us in eagerness. Our "quadrangle commander" moved his headquarters into their house and called me in to be mess officer. The Polish farmer killed two hogs— the first, he gleefully told us, that he had killed for years without a German permit. We would have a wonderful stew before night. He had a stove in a shed where we could heat water for coffee. We settled down to wait and hope.

In the living room of the farmhouse the picture of Adolf Hitler glared at us from the wall. This family had lived in terror for years. They had to be correct, and they let Hitler watch them every day. But they hated that picture, I guessed, more than we.

From the family I got a few sheets of paper and started to keep a diary. Paper was scarce, but I could put down a few words each day. I jotted down the events of the two days before, then went to the kitchen to see how the evening stew was coming. The poor people were dragging potatoes and flour from their basement, offering us everything they had. They were simple, and their joy was real. From deep in the cellar the old man brought out a bottle of wine, and passed it around.

Then reality crashed in on us. It came in the form of the German Commandant. Oberst Schneider and the guard came back. Disillusion punctured our ecstatic excitement. Nerves felt the let-down. Orders came to march on at four o'clock— about an hour and a half. The rumors sounded reasonable—

that a Russian armored patrol had reached a nearby town, then withdrawn. The Russians were supposed to be on the far side of the Bromberg Canal in strength. If that were true, our friends in the hospital at Oflag 64 and those who stayed in the first night's barn were probably free! But no one knew.

In the Polish farmhouse, the people were in tears. They brought bushel baskets of apples from the basement and passed them out. By chance I was the last one out of the house. The column was already formed in the yard ready to move. But a girl of the household would not let me past. My pockets were bulging with apples, but she kept trying to find room for more. There were tears in her eyes. She threw herself in my arms, her head on my shoulder. Hitler watched grimly from the wall. I hugged her, then pushed her away and went out.

(Marching Again)

The column moved down the road. It was a little smaller. Some were attempting escape. We saw them move off across the fields. How many reached freedom, I don't know. It was not the guards who kept us from escaping in those days; we could easily have evaded them. But in the brutal weather, without food, a man might easily die. Certainly he would have to seek shelter. Few of us knew much Polish, German, or Russian. And meeting an invading army is always dangerous, the more so when we knew nothing of their language or tactics and little of their location. So most of us marched. But day after day we talked of that "liberation." Such a little had separated us from freedom. It was a bitter thought.

It was only about five miles that day to Charlottenburg. There was a huge, beautiful farm, like a palatial manor. Through Poland and Prussia the farms were large. There were many with barn space where a thousand men could sleep. We were reminded that Poland had been feudal till modern times, that the Prussian Junkers were still lords of vast estates. Now it was not serfs, but foreign slaves who worked the farms. The crumbling Third Reich was held together in those fateful days by the most conglomerate mixture of races that the world had seen.

At Charlottenburg, another group of sick were left back in the barns. But perhaps 30 hid back when we moved out, hoping to escape. A detachment of SS troops found them and returned them to the column. They lived under dire threats for a few days, then were forgotten. But Oberst Schneider had his temper aroused. He assembled us for a harangue of threats. The next morning when we moved again the barns were sprayed with machine-pistols (burp guns, we called them)—sufficient incentive for anyone to move on. I doubt that anyone escaped that time.

Many miscellaneous memories have stuck with me from those days. A group of Latvians joined our guard company for awhile. They were even less enthusiastic about their duties than the regular guards. Most of them did not even understand German, and the mix-ups of orders were amusing to us, who delighted in anything that made trouble for our guardians. The Polish people were always friendly. One town emptied its kitchens of bread and cheese for us. The officers of the local German garrison became angry at the civilians' friendliness. As a small boy passed a piece of bread to a prisoner, a German lieutenant yelled at him. The boy turned to run, and the officer struck him with a "potato masher" hand grenade. No wonder the Poles hated the Germans. They were enthusiastic for Americans. I often wondered how they regarded the Russians. I had no way of telling, but they seemed joyous as their German oppressors retreated.

(Bread and Rest)

On the fifth day we were given three-quarters of a loaf of bread per individual and a small piece of cheese. It was the German black bread that had once tasted so bad. Now it was most welcome, and its heaviness was a virtue. A loaf weighed about three pounds. We didn't know exactly what it was made of—rye, potatoes, and barley were the common guess—but it was filling, and we realized that bread in Germany was really the staff of life.

It was the same fifth day, as we marched toward Flatow, that the Russians again drew near. The artillery was intense behind us, and we heard some machine-gun fire. Again the breathless excitement. The German Hauptmann who led the column kept us on back roads, stopped apprehensively at every crossroads, and questioned the civilians along the way. But we moved on into Flatow without event. The Oberst must have got word that the military situation was in hand, because movement was not scheduled until two o'clock in the afternoon. Then at noon he announced that we would stay the rest of the day.

It was a good place to rest. We slept in an upstairs hayloft. The barnyard was crowded with refugee carts, but there was room to build fires. We huddled around them to keep warm, toasted our bread, and cooked if we had any food. On one wagon in the barnyard was the corpse of a Russian soldier. How it got there we didn't know. The Germans gave us a good cup of soup that day, and we felt a little better. But Oberst Schneider was determined we should not become cheerful. He announced, with obvious pleasure, that he had received news that Russia had recalled her ambassadors to the United States and Great Britain. "And," he said triumphantly, "some of your comrades who tried to escape may become the first American prisoners of the Russians!"

It was too fantastic to believe. Possibly, we thought, the ambassadors have been recalled for consultation. But a split among the Allies could not be possible. Yet, the relations with Russia were always enough of a question-mark that we could not be absolutely confident, and we were never quite sure until we learned of the Yalta conference.

The day's rest at Flatow gave us time to tape blistered feet and wash a little. Two boxcar loads of the physically unfit— 120 men, I think it was—left us that day. They probably went to the Leuchenwald Camp near Berlin. The next day another carload went. The number of sick was always large among us. The inadequate diet, the cold, and exposure were the main causes. My knee, once hurt in college football, was stiff, but there was never enough tape to help it. Medical equipment was painfully inadequate. Men with wounds that should have been dressed daily could get clean bandages once a week or so. Fortunately there was a little sulfa powder. Other medicines were almost unknown. Diarrhea was common, and usually there was no help for it.

A major cause of sickness was undoubtedly inadequate sanitation. In the U.S. Army sanitary discipline is rigorous. Even in the worst field conditions kitchens are meticulously inspected and messkits sterilized. In entering a bivouac the first chore is the digging of the latrines in carefully chosen locations. But none of this was part of our life. We could rarely sterilize the cans from which we ate. Arriving on a farm at night, we were simply too exhausted to dig latrines in the hard-frozen earth, even if we could have found enough tools. The barnyards were usually spotted with men crouching to defecate in the snow. If the women of the household were moving about the yard, both they and we took no more notice than when cattle did their comparable acts. It was not that we had lost a sense of human dignity; rather, dignity centered on more important issues.

From Flatow we marched to Jastrow. Again the roads were crowded with the wagons of evacuees. Farmers in that area traveled often in horse-drawn sleds, speeding across the snow; but the refugees went slowly in wagons. About five kilometers outside of Jastrow we crossed a small river. German soldiers in white snow-camouflage suits manned foxholes on the river banks—the first sign of an actual defense position that we had seen on our entire trip. The eastern front with its vast distances and fluid tactics was immensely different from the smaller western front with its mighty defensive works. Jastrow we found crowded with prisoners of war of all nations. All were on the road, like ourselves. We greeted one another in passing and learned that they had been marching about as long as we.

Each day we moved according to the Oberst's orders. He had no plan, no evident destination. It was simply a day-to-day proposition of keeping away from the Russians. Our directions varied from day to day, although, of course, we generally got farther west.

(Characters)

We were gradually learning to know our German commander. As a representative of the German character, which is so misunderstood in America, he fascinated me. I never liked him because he seemed too pompous. When angry—and that was not seldom—he stormed and snorted in an almost apoplectic fury. In some of his speeches to us, he seemed to hate to stop pouring out his anger long enough for his interpreter to translate. But he was not cruel. His punishments were always the lightest possible, his bark noisy and his bite easy. I don't think he was much of a Nazi, but he was loyal to *Vaterland*. He sometimes talked of his long military career, but much of it, after the first World War, had been spent on a farm. He had the pride and aloofness of the German officer class, and I never saw him jovial or friendly. I think he must have been convinced, during all the time I knew him, that Germany would lose the war. But his duty was to carry on as his army directed him, and he would not waver from that. He would still regard himself as superior to us. Yet he had an obligation to us, which he took seriously. His notion of what he should do for us in the way of food and shelter was not a very high one, but he would not fail in it. And all the while, perhaps with an eye fixed on the future when we would be conquerors and he a prisoner, he tried to impress us with the efforts he made on our behalf.

His protagonist, Col. Paul Goode, on that march became our hero. As far as we were concerned, he was our real commander, though the Germans had the only power of enforcement. Col. Goode's only status was Senior American Officer: he was recognized as such by the Germans, and they put out their orders through him. Whenever we received an order, we knew whether it was Col. Goode's order, a German order endorsed by him, or a German order simply passed on by him for our information. And our obedience varied accordingly. We admired Col. Goode because he was efficient and had courage. He stood up to Oberst Schneider in demanding our rights, and whenever given a chance, he ran things well, as he had done at Oflag 64. We admired him for the way he kept discipline among us. Morale and respect for rank grow low among prisoners, but Col. Goode demanded that we salute him and address him respectfully. I remember seeing a junior officer shrink when he said, "That's not the way a lieutenant talks to a colonel." He insisted that we shave and clean up as often as there was an opportunity. And though we complained, because shaving was painful in that weather, we respected him for it.

He was old, and the trip was hard on him. We wondered how he kept up when so many younger could not. Sometimes the Oberst gave him an opportunity to ride, but he seldom accepted it. He was an inspiring sight, striding out at the head of the column each day, carrying under his arm, of all things, a set of bagpipes—reportedly a gift of the YMCA.

Our odyssey was about as disorganized a thing as anybody can conceive. Usually we started in the morning with a direction, but no destination. As the column marched out, the Oberst would drive off on the road for that day. When he got as far as he thought we could march, he hunted a farm. There he made arrangements for us to stay. What we ate depended on what the farm happened to have. Sometimes it was nothing. Usually it was a bowl of soup cooked in hog vats on the farms. Potatoes, cabbage, and turnips were the mainstays of the soup. The meal was late at night because it had to be prepared after we arrived. Rarely there was gruel or thin soup for breakfast. Spread was issued when it was available. In the early part of our trip that was seldom. Gradually the Oberst made a few concessions to us. He acquired an old truck, which went ahead with him each day. Eventually he agreed to put on it an American officer and two cooks, who started working at supper before we arrived on the farm. Then sometimes, if we were lucky, we got a soup and some boiled potatoes for supper. We could carry the potatoes with us to eat on the next day's march, or, if we had oleo or grease and could build a fire, we could fry them.

Hunger was always a problem. We soon learned to pick up food around farms and to trade with the civilians. Usually we could find a few raw potatoes somewhere, or perhaps some that had been cooked for hogs. The guards were not efficient, and we would appropriate the food. Trading would sometimes get us bread, and bread was the ideal food for marching. We had left Oflag 64 with plenty of cigarettes, and these were better than dollar bills (or marks). We could have bought half of Germany for cigarettes. Food was not plentiful in Germany, but sometimes we did rather well. Every Kriegie in Germany learned to say "Cigaretten für Brot." We used to joke that if there were a Kriegie coat of arms, the scroll should read, "*Haben Sie Brot?*" Our guards, particularly, wanted cigarettes, and they would often secure bread for us. I sometimes wondered how many cigarettes it would take to buy Oberstleutnant Loida's coat with its ostentatious fur collar. But no one ever proposed that deal.

(*The Second Week*)

At Jastrow, Oberst Schneider ran into misfortune. His car broke down. We all got a wicked pleasure out of seeing him start out walking with us the next day. It was January 28, the eighth day of our march. This was one of our worst marches. The cold was bitter and the snowdrifts deep. Although we moved only about 11 miles, the march left us exhausted. But the old Oberst kept ahead of us. When we came to the town of Zippnow, he looked haggard. He had trouble finding quarters. Standing on the streets in the interminable wait while the German officers hunted billets, I noticed one of the guards with a badly frozen nose. I investigated mine. It was numb, but not frozen. The town had been evacuated, but other refugees occupied some of the homes. Eventually we found a place to sleep in a church. We hauled bales of straw from a barn and piled them between the pews to make beds. I felt sure God did not resent this use of his sanctuary.

110

The church was cold. We would have preferred a barn. But there were lights in it, and I read a little. That night, I recall, I started to memorize "Casey at the Bat" from a paperback book I carried. Before I fell asleep, I saw the Oberst step in the door to see if everything was all right. He was worn out, but his German sense of duty moved him.

The next day, we went only five miles. Again the drifts and the cold were cruel. I noted in my diary, "Never felt so bad after so short a march." We passed a few evacuees that day. One of them said in English, "Isn't there room for you in America that you have to come over here?" We felt that we'd be glad enough to go back, if that was what the Germans really wanted.

The German military seemed to be a little better. There was no sign of the Russians near, and more German troops were in sight than usual.

Our march ended in a vacated stalag, where we went into the barracks for the night. There was coal, and we built roaring fires in the stoves and reveled in the luxury of heat. We had a sauerkraut supper and slept hard. Next day we rested till noon, washed and shaved, and hoped that it would be a day of rest. But suddenly the Oberst ordered us to march. Rumor was that the Reds were in Jastrow (now about 16 miles away). Col. Goode argued in vain for more rest. We wished the Russians might catch up with us here; a stalag would be the safest place to be liberated, because they would scarcely fire on us by mistake. But we moved on.

Again the terrible cold and snowdrifts. I marveled that the Russians could attack in weather like this. Staying alive in this cold was bitter enough, let alone fighting. My knee was so stiff that every step was painful. My platoon was at the head of the column today, but by the first halt I had dropped to the rear. At the halt I caught up, and managed to stay there. We struggled eight or nine miles to the partially evacuated town of Machlin. Then for an hour or so, in probably the bitterest cold of the trip, we stood in the streets while the "Goons" decided where we could sleep. There were no barns, so we settled for a shed and slept well.

On the next day, in Templeburg, streets were crowded with German troops, prisoners of war, and refugees, moving in nearly every direction. When we stopped in the city, some of the women offered us hot ersatz coffee or water. We were grateful. Since leaving Poland, we had seen the natural change in the attitude of the people. Now they greeted our guards when we marched by; the Poles had greeted us. But the German women, through all our trip, were usually good to us. It was very seldom that they were unfriendly, and often they did us small favors.

One sight in Templeburg aroused us to real rage. It was a column of Russian prisoners or slave laborers. We had grown accustomed to see the men and women slave laborers working on the big German farms, without freedom or family life. But this was more cruel. Haggard and starved, the column shuffled along the road, slowly and painfully moving, as if they had iron weights on their feet. Some of them wore wooden shoes. The women straggled at the end of the column. The guards scolded brutally and threatened. It was a searing picture of miserable humanity.

There are odds and ends of memories for the next few days. The towns were now mostly inhabited, but the roads were still filled with people. At one place a woman said that the refugees had been streaming past for eight days. There were barns and more barns. We became filthy. Oberstleutnant Loida was the only man I ever saw who could walk through a muddy, dungfilled barnyard and look like an aristocrat. But he had the advantage of farmhouses and occasional baths. We had only barns. Straw makes good beds, far better than the beds in Oflag 64. But barns are not always convenient. I remember moving into barns when it was dark, trying to find a place to sleep when we couldn't see. Sleeping on top of a threshing machine, because there was no room any place else. Barns so crowded we began to wonder if we were in boxcars again. A night when a bunch of us had to move out of a barn so some horses could get in. A barn on a Sunday morning, when we paused for a moment while the Chaplain led us in the Lord's Prayer.

Just as I had been on the western front, I was amazed here at the German rear areas. Again there was so little of transportation and supply facilities. We saw rather few troops and very little equipment. On one day, near Falkenburg, we observed considerable military traffic. On foot, on bicycles, truck, and wagons, the men and equipment moved, both toward and away from the front. Nearly every truck that could run towed a broken down truck. Many a towed truck had no engine under the hood. Sometimes three or four trucks were pulled by one. And the one that ran would have been called a wreck in the American army. A typical American soldier, given such a vehicle, would have driven it into a ditch in order to get a new one. But here such trucks did the work of the war. I often wondered whether there was a single truck in Germany that would not have been deadlined in the American army. Some of them burned wood or charcoal. Often they were old American models, especially Fords built in Germany, modified to work without gasoline. This amazing German army, which had unleashed on the world mechanized and armored warfare, blitzkrieg, and the Luftwaffe, was now demonstrating to that world how to fight with nothing.

The most common word in the tottering Third Reich was "kaput." Two words every American prisoner learned quickly: "Brot" and "kaput." "Kaput" meant no good, busted, worthless, finished. Most of the German military equipment was kaput. Most of the army was now kaput. Morale was kaput. As we marched through Deutschland, our guards were as unhappy and discouraged as we. Sometimes we would hear them talking—"All' ist kaput in Deutschland." Much as I longed for the defeat of this country that had terrorized the world, I felt a little sad at that statement. It seemed too bad that anyone should have to say of his country, "All' ist kaput."

(A German Sergeant)

These days my feet were getting more painful. The stiff knee was getting better. But I had huge frostbite blisters. And for a long time the tendons at the back of my ankles had been bruised and bleeding. One day it seemed that I couldn't go on. I marched at the end of the column that day, with a group of perhaps twenty of the "sick, lame, and lazy," as the army always calls them.

A Feldwebel from the guard company was in charge of us. All the Americans knew him slightly because he spoke English and was given considerable responsibility by his superiors. We rather liked him, because he never bellowed and snorted in the manner of so many German non-coms, and he had been known to do small favors for the Americans.

I had talked to this Sergeant once. It had been on a day when the Russians were close and we were struggling through snowdrifts. He had started the conversation. "Well, when you get back to America, you can write an article for *The New York Times*, and call it "Between the Swastika and the —what is the other thing?"

"The hammer and sickle," I said.

"Yes," he said.

It interested me that he knew enough to talk of *The New York Times*. Few American sergeants knew the names of German newspapers. We had talked a little more that day, but I had not learned where the Sergeant learned his English.

Today we were grumbling about the march and the weather and one thing or another, as we often did on the march. And everyone in this cripples' department was walking with some real pain.

"You have been spared nothing," he said. "Weather, marches, clothes—all have been difficult." He talked in the rather formal, slightly British manner of many English-speaking Germans.

"It has been tough," I agreed.

We walked a little further. An officer slipped on the ice and fell, his pack emptying out on the road. The Feldwebel was side of him helping him up and gathering his possessions. I had never seen anything like that before. This Sergeant interested me.

A little farther. Then I asked him, "Where did you learn English, Feldwebel?"

"I have been in England," he said.

"In England! What did you do there?"

"I was a professional boxer," he said. "I boxed in England many times."

"Have you been in America?"

"No, but I know your Jack Dempsey. I met him in England."

"What did you think of him?"

"He was a great boxer. But I think your Gene Tunney was better. He was faster and more skillful."

115

"Yes, I think he was."

"But in America he was never so popular as Dempsey." This Sergeant knew us pretty well, it seemed.

"Well, he was not so colorful. Americans like the spectacular boxers," I explained.

"I suppose so," he said. "But Tunney was an educated man."

Several others were in the conversation now, and we momentarily forgot the difficulties of walking as we compared the points of Tunney and Dempsey.

"What do you think of Joe Louis?" someone asked.

"A real fighter. I remember how he beat Max Schmeling." The Feldwebel knew Schmeling rather well, it seemed.

"Was Schmeling killed in the war?" one of us asked.

"No. He was seriously wounded."

Someone asked the Sergeant his age. He was about 45, as I recall, but in his perfect physical condition did not look over 35. He was a veteran of the First World War. After that he had been a boxer. More recently he had been a physical education instructor in the schools and in the Hitler Youth. We asked a little about the Nazi educational system and the Hitler Youth. It was interesting to hear him talk. He spoke of the Hitler Youth about as an American might of the Boy Scouts, with no political feelings at all. We didn't ask him about the government or the Nazi movement, but it was obvious that he had little opinion about them. He was typical of a great many Germans, whose attitude toward their government was simply one of acceptance. The notion of responsibility for government seemed almost lacking in Germany. A few of the SS troops and their kind were fanatics, and another few resisters struggled against Nazism. But government, for a great many Germans, was simply one of the facts of life, like weather or geography. And almost without an opinion toward it, they simply conformed.

But the Feldwebel did not like war. "Two wars have almost ruined my life," he said. "I have nothing now except the clothes I am wearing."

"War is a dreadful thing," someone said.

"Yes," he agreed.

"Where is your home?" I asked.

"I have none. It used to be in the Rhineland, but it is destroyed. I brought my wife to Poland, but she had to leave at the same time we left." I thought again of the long processions of refugees that we had seen on the road so often. He went on, "We have two children. We are expecting another one. It should be coming right now."

It was not the only time that the troubles of some of these German soldiers made ours seem mild. But the Feldwebel's last comment awoke a poignant thought in me. Possibly my child was being born now in Ohio.

(*Turning North*)

Dramburg was the first normal looking German town that we saw. We reached it on February 4, the beginning of the third week. The snow had melted, and walking on the nearly dry roads was almost a pleasure, though still painful. Dramburg was not evacuated. The shop windows, like those all over Germany, were almost barren and revealed the severity of life. But this town, unlike the others, did not shout that the Russians were near.

The Russians, however, were still moving fast. Temporarily they were not on our heels. But a little south of us a long Red arm was reaching for Stettin. We knew more about this than our captors thought we knew, and sometimes more than they. Hidden in our column, divided among several officers on the march, was a radio. It was assembled whenever it seemed safe (almost every night) to pick up the BBC reports. Within our column, it was known as "the bird." Its reports were given to the platoon leaders, and they passed on the news to us. Now "the bird" told us that Marshall Zhukov's forces had reached the Oder River, within 45 miles of Berlin and that the Russians were 25 miles from Stettin.

As far as the Oberst had any goal, it seemed to be a vague purpose of getting us across the Oder. It was obvious that the Germans would make no real defense before that river. On the other side, he might be able to get us out of the clutches of the Russians. A glance at the map (there was one in the platoon) showed that Stettin was the obvious place to cross the Oder. This city stood at the point where the river widens out into a broad estuary that extends for miles before it reaches the Baltic Sea. But now the Russians were getting close to Stettin. They might reach it before we could, we hoped.

But the Oberst would not be stopped that easily. At Wangerin, not far beyond Dramburg, he turned us north and headed for the Baltic. Wangerin was feverish. Strange, when Dramburg had been so quiet. At Wangerin everyone seemed to be on the streets, moving hurriedly and confusedly. Road blocks were thrown up on the edges of town. It looked as though the people were preparing to evacuate.

For the next five days we moved toward the Baltic. A hundred and eighty more of the unfit were put on trains. Our column was getting smaller; less than half of its original strength was left. We saw many small PW enclosures, where British and French prisoners stayed at night, while they worked in daytime on the farms or in the bakeries of the towns. They were going on with their jobs and had no thought of evacuation. We envied them. They seemed to have food, and they didn't have to march. But at other times we saw endless columns of prisoners—Jugoslavians, French, British, Italians—moving on like us. Some seemed a little worse off than we, some better. Then sometimes there were Russians. And they were always in terrible shape. They passed us one day when we were halted. Haggard and starved, they begged for cigarettes. We still had some, carried from Oflag 64. But as someone handed a cigarette to a Russian, a German guard struck the Russian's hand with a rifle butt. The Germans hated the Russians. Even more, they feared them.

Once we stayed on a farm where Russian prisoners lived in a small stockade and worked the farm. These had not been treated so brutally, because a man must have some strength if he is to work. Word got around that the Russians were passing salt through the barbed wire. We Americans crowded around them. We craved the salt; we had none, and our soups were unseasoned. They gave it to us liberally and passed out other little items of food, though they must have been nearly as hungry as we. Though we could not talk, except for a few German words that both they and we might know, their friendliness was exuberant. We automatically pulled out our cigarettes to trade with them, but they wanted nothing in return. Seldom in my life have I seen such generous friendliness.

Our hunger in these days became worse. Hunger was more than a feeling; it was a haunting sensation. It never left us. This was a hunger we had never known before. It was the hunger of men who marched every day, who could never

119

fill their stomachs or find in food the energy they needed. We felt the weakness in our bodies and knew that we were getting thin. Sometimes we gnawed on "cow-beets" that we found in barns—a vegetable never grown for human consumption. Then we stopped because we theorized that they made us sick—a shaky theory, since we were sick much of the time anyhow. We could get up after ten hours of sleep and still feel tired—not just sleepy, but tired. Night after night we dreamed that we were eating. We told each other of dreams of our wives—always bringing us food.

Hour after hour on the march we talked of food. For food was our obsession. The Howard Johnson manager was still with us, and he led an endless seminar on food. My buddy on the trip, Willard Smith, had once been a soda jerker, and all of us joined him in concocting remembered and imaginary confections. We talked of installing soda fountains in our homes someday. We thought with envy of soup lines in America's depression. We made imaginary visits to grocery stores and spent imaginary budgets of twenty-five cents or a dollar, always starting with bread.

Our tastes changed. I had never much liked sardines; now, when they appeared in a Red Cross parcel, they were indescribably good. Those parcels sometimes included the emergency army chocolate ration, designed more for energy than for flavor. In combat we had never thought of that bar as tasty; now it was an unutterable delicacy.

We could not pass a bakery or food store without a pang in our stomachs. The smell of baking bread was almost too tantalizing to endure. Psychologists of some schools would have changed their theories if they had been with us. I am sure that if a group of aproned German *Hausfrauen* with bread in their arms had walked past us on the right, and a group of Minsky's chorus girls had danced past on the left, all eyes would have turned right. Conversations frequently noted that nobody had wet dreams.*

More than anything else, hunger made us bitter over our captivity. Our guards got better rations than we—not much better, but some. We resented that as a violation of the Geneva Convention. But mostly we simply resented hunger.

As we moved closer to the Baltic, the land was less bleak. The snow was about gone. Regenwalde, where we slept in the barracks of a German submarine school, was an attractive town with many stores. The stores didn't have much to sell, and everyone was poor. But the people were not so harrassed and the families were happier—except that there were few men. Here war was not immediate, and the townsfolk looked at us with curiosity when we passed through their villages.

The Russian armies were moving more slowly now. There were pockets in their rear areas to clean up. They had at least two brigades across the Oder, pointing toward Berlin, but were not expanding them. On the tenth of February, I wrote in my diary, "Russians with bridgeheads across the Oder seemed slowed more by logistics than by the Germans. But Germans show no sign of giving up." It was at this time that I got my first feeling of what "unconditional surrender" would mean. If the Germans had yielded this much territory and could see the Russians across the Oder, the last defense before Berlin, and had not moved toward surrender yet, perhaps they meant it when they said they would fight to the

---

* In 1948 I read of experiences conducted by clinical psychologists on the effect of semi-starvation on volunteers at the University of Minnesota. Many of the results were much like ours, with the major difference that we faced other simultaneous issues of survival and hope for freedom that motivated us powerfully. One of the subjects of the Minnesota experiment said, "I have no more sexual feeling than a sick oyster." After our experience of hunger, I have never understood why hungry India has so high a rate of reproduction.

end. The Western Allies would have to meet the Russians in central Germany before the end would come.

(Across the Oder Estuary)

Two large islands, Wollin and Usedom, almost block the Oder Estuary where it reaches the Baltic. Bridges and ferries, even railroads cross the estuary here. The islands were a farming, fishing, and resort area in peacetime, and even in war had a charming, peaceful atmosphere, though crowded with military establishments. On February 10, a beautiful, spring-like day, we approached the estuary and crossed the short bridge on to Wollin Island. Dievenow, the first town on the island, was a pleasant place, full of beautiful blond children. I remember sitting beside the road during a ten-minute break outside the town when a woman and her little girl walked past. I winked at the girl, and she smiled back.

We stayed that night in the barracks at a large Luftwaffe training school. A few land and seaplanes were based there, and the base was full of kids, both boys and girls. The boys were training, the girls working. Over the door of one barracks I saw a sign, "STALINGRAD." I was surprised and wondered whether I had read correctly. Yes, the next one said "TUNIS." And so on and on, each barracks named for a great battle that the Germans had *lost*.

Over another was a German motto which meant, "Who would live must fight." So that was it: the spirit of militant revenge dominated this school. We saw the youths march across the grounds in their snappy Luftwaffe uniforms. They were young—what we would call high-school age. Their morale was superb, their marching precise, their singing bois-terous. We looked at them and wondered. They had been sheltered from war and nourished on propaganda. Would the

Nazis be able to preserve these boys through the war so that they would never feel the despondency and disillusion that was blanketing the rest of the nation? Would they never know the horror and the morbid pessimism of war, especially of defeat in war, that was infecting the rest of the army and the civilians of Germany? If so, they might remain romantic fanatics in a country that was fast losing its desire for fanaticism. They might be a problem someday.

We crossed the hills and woods of Wollin Island. We celebrated Lincoln's birthday by marching our 200th mile and arriving at the famed Baltic naval base of Swinemünde. There had been a small cup of thin gruel for breakfast that morning. Then after a 15-mile march, there was nothing for supper. We stopped in a warm naval barracks, and took our clothes off for the first time all trip. It was a shock to see our naked bodies so thin and scrawny. It was hard to go to sleep so hungry.

Next day fortunately we rested till noon and ate boiled potatoes and gravy before we marched. As I walked out of the kitchen where we filled our eating cans, a window went up and a sailor stuck out some bread. Everyone in sight pressed against the sill. The sailor cut the loaves in half and did a brisk business for cigarettes. I suppose he was a K.P. who stole the bread out of the kitchen. I walked away clutching my half-loaf, grateful for his dishonesty.

A ferry took us across the channel to Usedom Island. On the Northwest tip of this island is the base of Peenemünde, where the secret V-1 and V-2 laboratories had been. But we followed the southern edge of the island. Many planes were concealed in the woods of the island, and many more dummy planes stood in the open, designed to fool our air force. On a farm on Usedom there was an evening with as many potatoes as we could eat. It was wonderful to get full. But a stomach not used to being filled gave me awful cramps that night. On St. Valentine's Day, 100 of the sick and weary got a train ride. Now there were only about 500 of us left. Each time we dropped a group, we figured it should be easier to find food for the rest of us. But it never was. There was a day of rest near the shore, a beautiful sunrise over the water the next morning. A few shoes were repaired, the first on the trip. On February 16 we crossed the bridge to the main-land. Now the Oberst had got us across the Oder, and we looked for some sign of his next aim. But there was no sign, only more walking.

(Food)

There was, however, something better than a destination. For several days there had been rumors of Red Cross parcels. Of course we were cynical, because the cynics were usually right in this game. But the first day on the mainland, the 28th day of our trek, as we came near the end of a 15-mile march, Oberst Schneider's car met us and the old Colonel popped out to announce, in an ingratiating speech, that we would get Red Cross parcels that night, and would start marching late the next day. Col. Goode asked that night that we rest the next day. The Oberst refused. But the farm was owned by a Countess whose son was a prisoner-of-war in America. Because his letters said that he was treated well in America, the Countess was very gracious to us and inter-ceded with the Oberst to get us our day off. All day we crouched around our fires, like a bunch of hoboes, cooking and eating. I recalled California, where I had seen the old hoboes, packs on their backs, walk down the roads, and stop at night under a bridge where they built their fires and cooked their meals. With my experience now, I thought, I could lead a luxurious life in California.

When we marched off this farm, the Countess stood at the gate, distinguished-looking and friendly, and saying in English, "Good-bye," to us as we passed. We felt 100 percent stronger now, with a few proteins working inside us.

Demmin was a modern looking town, as much like America as anything we had seen in Germany. It was not rich, but it had movies, restaurants, and modern buildings. Himmel! Here was another Red Cross parcel and another day's rest, just three days after the last. Col. Schneider massed us again —how he loved to make speeches!—and told us how he had gone to great effort to get the parcels. Then he announced that Berlin had promised him railroad transportation for us. It would be several days before the boxcars would be available, but somewhere in the future we would stop walking and start riding. We cooked some more, this time with some Canadian Red Cross parcels for variety, and marched again. Now our packs were heavier, but we felt strong enough to carry them. I never thought myself overburdened with food.

We observed Washington's birthday and our 300-mile mark. Beyond Malchin we again saw road blocks being constructed, the first since the Oder River. We moved on dirt and mud trails through the wooded Lake Country northwest of Berlin. On February 24 the "Bird" reported the news that thrilled us all: the First and Ninth Armies had attacked toward the Rhine. Was this the big drive aimed to end the war? We hoped so, and went on marching. Once more we saw the wagons of evacuees on the road—apparently from the region of Stettin. In one little town we found most of the people were evacuees from Berlin. The original population of the town had previously moved on. I wondered how many of these thousands of people shuffled so far through Germany would ever find their homes again.

A German General inspected our column. It struck me as surprising, in a way, that a nation so far in its death throes as Germany should pay this much attention to its prisoners. They didn't pay very much attention, it is true. But it was something that someone should send out a General to look us over. Maybe there was some conscience left somewhere in the high command. Or maybe a General found a way to keep busy and out of combat. I don't know.

It was the last of February when we arrived at the little town of Siggelkow, near the city of Parchim northwest of Berlin. There we settled down to wait for our rail transportation. We stayed there almost a week, while the First and Ninth Armies kept driving. Each night the "Bird" brought news. The original drive had started slowly, but when German resistance broke, the armies moved swiftly, and by the end of our week were well established on the Rhine.

Siggelkow was our favorite town in all Germany, the ideal place to vacation after our 350-mile march. We lived in barns which were actually in town, and no place so small had a more thriving black market. We were well supplied with cigarettes and soap from recent Red Cross parcels, and Siggelkow had a bakery. Some of the housewives would even part with sugar, jam, oatmeal, and flour, sometimes even eggs, for a little American soap. The Jerries gave us soup and boiled potatoes every day, and for a couple weeks we had been getting our daily sixth of a loaf of bread without fail. With another three-quarters of a Red Cross parcel issued at Siggelkow and the contributions of the town itself, we feasted. All day long, until blackout, we cooked, and enjoyed for the first time such delicacies as pancakes. There was a strict German order, covering the entire nation, that prisoners of war could not trade with civilians, and Col. Schneider repeated the order to us in Siggelkow. However, the German officers did not really care so long as we were not too obvious, and most of the guards did not care at all so long as they didn't get caught watching us trade. So trading thrived. A couple officers, faring well and desiring new worlds to conquer, took to trading in a nearby town. Success made them bold, and they were soon knocking on doors. All went well until a German soldier answered the door and hauled them in. Oberst Schneider was a little upset by this, and gave an extra noisy speech. It followed the usual pattern—that he had regarded us as gentlemen and had done his all for us, but that we had once again betrayed him. But he let the offenders off with a little solitary confinement.

From Siggelkow I wrote one postcard home. It was the first time I had been allowed to write since the letter I had turned over to "Bill" a day or two after New Year's.

On March 7 the train was ready. We marched the three or four miles to Parchim and boarded the usual boxcars with the hope that our Air Force would take it easy for a few days. Our destination was Hammelburg, in Bavaria. The trains were operating far more efficiently than we expected. We started the morning of March 7, rolled through Central Germany (Madgeburg, Halle, Weimar) and on the morning of March 9 were a few miles from Hammelburg. It took the rest of the day to get to Hammelburg, and on the next morning we got off the train.

8. LAGER HAMMELBURG

From the railroad to Lager Hammelburg was an hour's march across the beautiful rolling hills of Bavaria. So calm and peaceful was the scene that I forgot for the moment my dread of going back into prison. On a hilltop just outside the camp we moved into a mass, and Oberst Schneider appeared, to give us one more speech.

"We have had a long and hard trip," he said. "You have walked 350 miles and the weather was very difficult. At the beginning of the trip I promised that I would never leave you for a single day. I have kept that promise." (We thought of one day when the Russians were near and he *almost* forgot the promise.) "Now," he continued, "I turn you over to a new commander. A General commands this camp, and when you go through the gates, you will leave my command. I have thought of myself as your protector and have done all I could for you." (He is thinking that this war will soon be over and he had better stand in well with us, we thought.) "I wish you all good fortune and a happy return home." (Maybe, we thought, the old man has some sincerity after all.)

The Oberst had finished his job, and in some ways he had done well. He had walked with us in some of our worst marches. He had never failed to find some sort of place for us to sleep; it might be wet or windy or crowded, but he had always found something. He had never quite starved us, and we had to grant that sometimes food was hard to find. And despite his pompous angry speeches, he had been fair, I suppose, within the limits of the German military framework.

We did not know it then, but we found out later from Col. Goode that shortly before the Oberst addressed us, he had learned that the American armies' advance had engulfed his own home and that his wife was now one of the refugees making the aimless and hopeless movement away from the swift-striking conquerors of Germany.

The old feeling of oppression hit me again as we moved through the barbed wire into the camp. The commandant of the Lager, Major General von Goeckel, gave us a speech of welcome. We were searched in the usual manner. (I had nothing to hide except my diary. I hid it, slipping it through a tear in the lining of my coat—a probably unnecessary bit of melodrama.) We lost a lot of dirt in the delousing bath, which ended at three o'clock in the morning. We were grateful for that bath, because at Hammelburg the Germans could never spare fuel to heat water for anything less urgent than delousing.

The first afternoon at Hammelburg (March 10), even before the bath, was a big one. The news was abroad that the Americans had crossed the Rhine! It went breathlessly from man to man through the camp. This was the event that we had waited for week after week. This was the sign that victory was near. (Weeks later I was to learn that my old Division, the 9th Armored, had on March 7 seized the Ludendorff Bridge at Remagen and established the first Allied bridgehead across the Rhine.)

We met old friends at Hammelburg. Most of the American officers captured in the "bulge" were here. I had gone to Poland on the last or next to last train for Oflag 64. All the later ones came here. I found a number there from the 9th Armored Division, officers of battalions used farther north in the Battle of the Bulge. One Infantry Battalion must have lost most of its strength. Three company commanders were here, and a fourth had been killed. Battalion Commander and Executive Officer had been been captured. I hurried to meet them all again. Our greeting was always the same: "Glad to see you, but sorry it's here."

Almost the first look at the Hammelburg camp convinced us that we had been lucky. The officers here were weak and depressed. Their skins were pallid, sometimes yellow. Compared with them, we were healthy. Our march had been painful and hard to endure in its first weeks; but toward the end, when weather improved and food was more plentiful, it was better than living in a prison. We were thin, but healthy, and our spirits were good. At Hammelburg they were a miserable looking lot. They lived on the regular prisoners' diet, with half a Red Cross parcel every two weeks or so. Glad as I had been to see anyone I knew, I soon quit visiting old friends. The depression was too stifling. They sat listlessly, spirits almost dead. For awhile they would talk food. Then there was silence. Somebody would dimly hope that the war would soon be over. More silence. Then they would talk about food.

Spring and Col. Goode brought improvement. For weeks these officers had shivered all day long and had spent most of their hours in bed, the only warm place. Now the sun became warm, and on some days we could lie outside with clothes off. Col. Goode took hold with characteristic energy. He scheduled Saturday inspections when everyone had to be neat and dressed in his prison best. The camp became clean and shining. Letters went to the Red Cross and YMCA. Plans were set up for language classes, and the Colonel repeatedly went up to talk to the General. He never got much out of the General, but the fact that he was talking for us made us feel good.

Warm weather meant that we could do some laundry. A little soap was available, but no basins for soaking clothes. We wet our clothing from outdoor spigots and rubbed the soap on the cloth. Sometimes, longing for the luxury of an old-fashioned scrubboard, we used straw to rub the dirt out and found it tedious but moderately effective. Shaving, too, was easier in warm weather. Before each shave I examined my hoard of three or four aged blades and picked the least dull.

The library was skimpy at Hammelburg, but we read what we could. Lectures were scheduled once or twice every day. The subjects were agriculture, economic geography, insurance, psychology—anything that some officer could lecture about. We attended by hundreds. Every lecture or church service had a crowd, not so much because crowds were interested, but because there was nothing else to do. Having got there, we became interested. I remember a vigorous panel on socialized medicine. It almost ended in a fight between a doctor and an economist. I had not thought there was so much energy in Hammelburg.

But mental energy cannot lose its relation to food. And food was bad. Again we lost weight. The doctors worried. Once more we dreamed of eating and hoped our Air Force would slow up long enough for a carload of Red Cross parcels to get through from Switzerland. One Sunday a representative of the International Red Cross visited the camp. He said that our diet was the same as in all the stalags and that there was no violation of the Geneva Convention, because we had the same ration as German "depot troops." We could never decide exactly what these depot troops were, because our guards certainly ate better than we. We divided the few Red Cross parcels that Col. Goode ferreted out. The Germans annoyed us by dumping the food out of the cans before they let us have it, so we would have no food for escape.

The stalag had originally held Serbian officers. Now they occupied three of its four compounds. Americans and Serbs talked through the wire whenever they could find a common language. The Serbs were a wonderfully friendly and generous bunch. They were old prisoners, all of them, taken when Hitler overran Jugoslavia. They had given their extra clothing to the first Americans who arrived. Every Red Cross parcel that came to the Americans at Hammelburg before our arrival was from the Serbs. No parcels consigned to the Americans had yet arrived, and the Serbs shared what they had. We who were just arriving never got to know them well, but the officers who had been there longer constantly praised their generosity and friendliness. When a Serbian officer died, the Americans had a formation in his honor. And when an American officer was shot by a guard, for no good reason at all, representatives of the Serbs were honorary pallbearers.

Sometimes the Germans gave us sheets of the Munich *Beobachter* for toilet paper. They were a week or two old, but I enjoyed trying to read them. The front page of the newspaper always had the German military communique at the bottom. The rest of the page was entirely filled with propaganda feature stories. Usually they were built around a little war news. Uniformly they aimed to build up hatred and fear against the Allies. The most furious articles were directed against the Russian ground and the Allied air forces. Occasionally there was something about the cruelty of Eisenhower or the atrocities of his armies. But usually it was our "terror-bombers," as they were always called, and the Red armies. The Russians burned and pillaged every village, killed every one in sight, ravaged everything they conquered. So the stories went. The German people, subject to this propaganda, and nothing else, saw themselves as innocent, assaulted people.

Inside pages had book reviews (in the Nazi line), agricultural information (Bavaria should grow more potatoes to make up for the regions lost to Russia), explanations of the slow mail service, and long casualty lists. There was usually a paragraph on the Japanese war, quoting Tokyo communiques. Sometimes there was a little news of the U.S. or Britain, all propagandized. Every tightening of rations in the U.S. was mentioned. If any American politician talked about inadequate diet or civilian supplies, he was quoted. And there was a great to-do over the Senate squabble on confirmation of Wallace as Secretary of Commerce; it appeared that the government might fall apart at any minute.

Hammelburg lay due east of Frankfurt-am-Main. It was a wonderful and agonizing feeling to look out over the hills at sunset, knowing that in that direction freedom lay. I chafed at Hammelburg, as I never had before. Somehow this barbed wire had a spiritual quality of oppressiveness worse than I had known. I went to the lectures and tried to stir my brain. I read the New Testament clear through. I wrote a letter to my wife and a postcard to my mother and father, and waited for the opportunity to write more. Still I felt my spirit warped by this sensation of slavery here, freedom in the direction of the sunset.

Each day we received the German news communique. The Americans were punching away at their Remagen bridgehead, expanding it daily. Through the Serbs we got rumors, presumably based on BBC, but we were never sure of them. As one of our captains said, he never had seen such a bunch of rumor spreaders as the Serbs, except for the Americans.

The German communiques were usually accurate, though sometimes a little slow and technical. Explanations in terms of tiny place-names, which we could not find on our few maps, hid the significance of big events. Every day I waited anxiously for that communique, waited for something big. For, in the pattern of this World War, there would be a period of painful advance on this side of the Rhine; then things would break and the Allied Armies would shatter the German defenses and come racing through the Reich.

On March 25 we learned of an American Bridgehead south of Mainz. Perhaps this was it. It was close to us, and eager expectancy gripped our minds. That day we saw American P-47s overhead. Day after day we had seen the great formations of heavy bombers pass over; but these were the first fighter planes, and fighters meant that the lines were getting closer. Thoughts of freedom floated in our minds. Easter would be April 1. K-rations by Easter became a hope. Those K-rations, so tiresome in the American army, made our mouths water.

The next day rumors ran wild. There was a terrific air bombardment to the west. Hour after hour it lasted. We heard the rumble of bombs, saw some of the planes, and listened to our window panes shake with the vibrations. It was miles away, we did not know how many. But it sounded like tactical bombing, preparing the way for ground troops. Excitement rose to fever pitch. Would the Germans try to get us out again, as they had in Poland? Where would they take us now? Or would they leave us here? We went to bed that night with hopes and excited desires running wildly through our minds.

9. DECEPTIVE FREEDOM

March 27. Artillery noises helped us wake in the morning. For a week we had been arguing over whether the rumblings in the west were artillery or bombing. The last day or two some of them had come in the rhythmic pattern that convinced us we were hearing artillery. This morning it sounded closer than yesterday. The air tingled with suspense. Today the Serbs all wore their best clothes and calmly said that they had put them on for their liberation.

At mid-morning someone saw Col. Goode walk up to the gate where he met the General. A short conversation, and he came back. The news spread swiftly over the camp: Be prepared to leave at 5:00 A.M. tomorrow. There was a meeting of field officers, and more details came down. As on a day months before, a column was organized for the march. The kitchen was throwing all the rations on hand into the soup, and we would get a three-day bread ration. Once again we started figuring what we would carry with us and what sort of pack we would organize.

We drank our noon soup. The artillery was still pounding. Then came the new order: Leave at seven o'clock tonight! The Americans must be getting closer. The Germans are determined to get out. So ran our thoughts. The hours moved by, each hour bringing a new rumor. Americans were here, there, yonder—names of nearby towns were clicked off. The German driver who brought the bread truck from Wurzburg had rushed to escape the Americans, someone said. A Serb enlisted man, back from a work detail in the town of Hammelburg, reported the civilians hysterical, preparing to flee. Up and up the rumors piled, more fantastic all the time.

For once, no rumor was as fantastic as the facts.

It was late afternoon. Looking out in the direction of freedom, I saw German soldiers. They were moving northeast. By individuals and squads they came, sometimes running. They looked like soldiers retreating.

We heard machine gun firing. Probably guns being targeted. But could it be combat firing? Possibly.

There were Hauptmann Menner and Oberstleutnant Loida in the street talking to Col. Goode. Everyone was smiling. It looked like a reunion of old friends. We would be lucky to have our old guard company again. They had become pretty friendly on that last long trip.

There was more machine gun firing beyond the hills. Maybe that was why Col. Goode was smiling so. Still we couldn't figure it out. Time went past; the evening soup came. It was good, thick. We ate a little, went to the windows to listen to the noises, then ate some more. Machine guns were firing long bursts—the way tanks fire. Again we crowded the windows. An officer came out of the Administration Building across the street. He shouted jubilantly, "We don't move," and made a motion with his arms as though to tell us we were encircled.

Now anticipation became feverish. Some of us remembered a time when our German officers had fled and we expected that the Russians would free us, and we weren't so confident. But this was the American Army! It couldn't let us down.

There was Col. Goode outside again, talking to the General. He looked happy. Of all of us, he had the most right to be. With him was his right-hand man, Lt. Col. Gouler, the first American ground force officer captured in this war. He had been taken prisoner when he was an observer with the British in Africa. He too had a right to be happy, after all these years.

Soon came information and orders. The General had agreed that he would not defend the camp. We would put up white flags. Everyone would remain indoors. This might be a ticklish situation.

The flags went up on the roofs. The German guard came down from his tower. Were the Germans giving up control of the prison entirely? No, the guard returned to his post. The machine guns still barked not far away. The German soldiers outside still were moving back. Now all of them ran. It looked as if some Jerries were firing. That meant the Americans were close. Still no sign of them. A few bullets had whizzed into the camp, one small shell had landed. We obeyed the order to stay indoors.

There was a roaring fire in the stove, and we toasted bread on the top of it. There had been no fuel ration for a week or two, so today we burned the chairs. Strange creatures! The best way we knew to celebrate was to toast bread and eat it. We had a three-day ration—almost half a loaf—and now we would not need it. So we toasted and ate, ran to the windows, listened to the firing, went back and toasted some more.

Now the big haystack on top of the hill was afire. The flames leapt high into the air. It had been almost a legend in the camp that the Serbs would set that haystack on fire when they were liberated. Now they would be saved the trouble. Germans had been firing from near the base of the haystack; American shots replying had fired it.

We toasted and ate some more. Back to the windows.

137

Now the tanks rolled onto the hilltop. Sherman tanks. Their machine guns swept the hillside, down to the very edge of the camp. A few Jerries just outside the fence were firing back. The machine guns would quiet them soon. The big guns on the tanks fired. Their shells landed beyond the camp. Now a few machine gun bullets clattered in the street outside our barracks. Back from the windows and under the beds! Soon we were at the windows again. The doughboys were in sight. The silhouette of the American helmet on the hilltop was beautiful. The GIs looked wonderful. They deployed, fired, and advanced, in the tactics that we knew so well. It looked like a task force from an armored division. I wondered if it could be the Ninth.

Machine guns still rattled, shells exploded. One of the Serb barracks was on fire; a shell had landed there. It was curious to be a spectator in this fight. No fight had ever been more exciting to us, yet we could do nothing. So we watched. We saw planes in the sky, American fighters. There was an ancient German stuka, come out to do battle with a P-51. We watched the dogfight, saw the Stuka go down in flames. Now the Jerry fire outside had stopped. A tank started rolling down the hill. Lt. Col. Waters, the son-in-law of General Patton and a fine officer captured in Tunisia in 1943, walked out to meet it with the American flag. I, who had always hated parades and the dramatics of patriotism, thrilled when I saw that flag.

The tank was at the foot of the hill. It moved straight ahead, through the barbed wire, and up the street to the administration building across from our barracks. On its front was the "4" and the triangle that meant Fourth Armored Division. A lieutenant stuck out his head, climbed out of the tank. He was quickly surrounded. He shouted that we would leave the camp that night. A couple French officers ran up and kissed him; he didn't know these French and looked embarrassed. Someone whisked him off to see Col. Goode.

In a few minutes we were all outside, everyone carrying a blanket or some other thing—whatever he thought he might want with him. We moved down the street, out through the big gap in the barbed wire. The Serbs gave us a hearty cheer and a smile as we passed, then settled back to wait longer for their freedom. We started running up the hillside where the tanks and half-tracks sat. We felt emotion in our throats. It was not only the glorious hope of freedom. For with this, perhaps even more than this, was the feeling that someone had come after us, that after months when we had not mattered, someone cared enough to come and get *us*. It felt wonderful to be Americans.

Now it was dusk. The burning haystack lighted the hillside, and we scrambled on to the half-tracks and tanks. Someone shouted, "Hanau on Main. Hanau on Main. If anything happens your destination is Hanau on Main."

Half-tracks were jammed. They could never carry these loads. But hundreds of men were still coming up the hillside, milling about, trying to find a place to ride. What would happen to them?

It seemed an interminable time on that hillside near the flaming haystack. If there was German artillery within several miles, it could certainly destroy us here. Why didn't we move? Still the mad confusion. We questioned the crew on our half-track. They had done some tough fighting on the way to Hammelburg. They gave us a few "K" rations. We were eating them before our slogan-target of Easter. We gave the soldiers our treasured bread. They tasted it and spit it out.

Perhaps it was an hour of nervous delay on the hilltop. Then the vehicles moved. Off the skyline, out of the light of that haystack. A few hundred yards. Then a stop.

139

It had to happen. Someone came along ordering us off the half-tracks. They could not carry so many. I clambered off, with many others. And still there were hundreds who had never found a place.

The little road was filled with Americans running around, shouting questions, trying to learn what was going on. Gradually we got the answers, the answers which made it inevitable that this adventure would be a fiasco.

Friendly American forces were 60 miles away. They had information that about 300 American officers were imprisoned at Hammelburg. (There were many hundreds more than that.) An order had come, apparently from Third Army Headquarters, for a task force to strike for our camp. A company of tanks and a company of armored infantry, plus a few odd platoons, were organized. They had started 24 hours ago, hoping to reach us by morning. By sheer audacity and surprise they had thrust through weak German defenses, crossed bridges before they could be blown. But it had cost them. They were twelve hours behind schedule, and nearly half their men and vehicles were lost.

On the vehicles that were left, they could not nearly carry the three hundred they had expected, let alone the extra hundreds. Gasoline supplies were low, maybe enough to get back, maybe not. They did not know how they would return. They couldn't use the same route; the bridges were gone now. Yes, there was the Captain who commanded the task force, his map spread out in front of his jeep's headlights, as he looked for other roads.

The soldiers were not bitter. Combat was their job and they were used to risking their lives, as we had been a few months before. But to us, who had been outside that tension of combat for a while, this adventure seemed a terrible thing.

It was decided that only the few who had secured weapons

and could replace dead members of the crews of the vehicles would ride back. Only that way could the task force fight its way home. The rest of us? There were two possibilities. We could set out in groups of three or four and try to reach American lines. Or we could return to the prison camp.

The thought of prison made us shudder. Our imaginations tried to reckon with the possibilities of getting to American lines on foot. Sixty miles! Weak and half-starved as we were, we could never make it without food. I tried to get K rations from the half-tracks. There were none left. A few officers had two or three; perhaps they could make it on that. We did not know where American forces were. Hanau was a name, but not a place unless one had a map. "Go due west," someone said. But where was west? Clouds covered the stars, and no one could keep direction in these winding valleys. With food and a map it would be a dangerous job but worth the risk. Without them, it seemed hopeless.

I saw Col. Goode. He refused to give advice. "What are you doing, sir?"

"I'm going with the vehicles. I think I have done my duty."

"I think you have, sir," I said.

Some had already returned to camp. The rest milled around on the hillside, conscious that it was a dangerous place, yet hoping that something would happen. I saw one of the senior Lieutenant Colonels who had made the trip from Oflag 64 with us. He might have more information than the rest of us. No, he didn't, but he bitterly called the whole affair a "Buck Roger's stunt" and headed back for camp. I moved around a little longer, still hoping I might find some food, someone with a map. No luck. It was early morning, not yet light. Soon it would be too late to do anything. I turned drearily back, walked again through the oppressive barbed wire.

I could not feel sure that I was right. Circumstances, I believe, justified the decision. Even before the tanks left the hillside, some were hit by German panzerfausts and a few men killed. A few miles away they ran into a fight. Not a single vehicle from that task force got back to American lines. The hills were combed by German troops yet that morning, and the Americans rounded up and put on a train for Nürnberg. Col. Goode was among them. A few got farther away and were caught a day later. A few, I suppose, reached American lines; I never learned for sure, but some had food, and probabilities would favor a fraction getting through.

There were many arguments later about the mission of the task force. Generally it was considered an ill-conceived attempt. None of us could justify the deaths of American soldiers for such a mission. There was one other possibility: a commander might have wanted a diversion here to draw attention from a major attack farther north. If so, the task force was perhaps effective, because it certainly drew German troops into the area, and surprised the German commanders. If this was the purpose, it might have been worth the cost, reckoned by that cruel arithmetic in which combat losses must be figured. If not, some commander was guilty of a glaring and unjustifiable error in judgment and sacrifice of life.

Back in the prison camp, the Germans were again in control and rounded up a few hundred of us to march that night. I saw the Feldwebel (the boxer) I had known before. Col Schneider, he said, had been called to Berlin only a day or two before. Lt. Col. Loida commanded our column. We moved out while it was still dark, once more exchanging prison for the road.*

* Many years later this venture remains one of the most controversial episodes of the war. General Bradley called it "as brash a venture as Patton dared during the entire war" and "a story that began as a wild goose chase and ended in tragedy." General Patton

ordered the attack, against the objection of both the corps and division commanders who received his order. It was often said that Patton insisted on this unrealistic effort because his son-in-law, Lt. Col. Waters, was in the camp. Patton strenuously denied this charge. John Toland, two decades later, produced evidence that in his judgment proved the claim. I am not competent to adjudicate the case.

A task force of 293 troops (some say 307) and 50 vehicles made the attempt. A scattered few of them and of the liberated PW's got back. Most were killed or captured. All the vehicles were lost. Captain Baum, who commanded the task force, became a wounded prisoner in Hammelburg, and Col. Waters was severely wounded.

Patton himself wrote: "I can say this—that throughout the campaign in Europe, I know of no error I made except that of failing to send a combat command to take Hammelburg." The combat command—much more powerful than the task force—might have succeeded. But General Bradley insisted that so strong a force was not available within the tactical plans of the Army Group. (Incidentally, General Bradley dates the arrival of the task force Hammelburg March 28; other historians confirm my personal record of March 27.)

In one respect my record is erroneous and unfair. I was told by soldiers on the task force that they expected to find 300 American prisoners at Hammelburg. The accounts published since then state that the task force was sent with the intention of liberating perhaps 900 prisoners—we were actually about 1,200—and included enough half-tracks to bring back a few hundred (in the unlikely event that all the vehicles would complete the trip). Most of the task force were poorly informed about their mission. In repeating their misinformation, I exaggerated the magnitude of the very grave error in the whole episode.

The actions of the task force had some military effectiveness, insofar as they deceived the German armies as to the direction of the major American efforts at that time.

My sources for these comments, made long after I wrote my original record, are these: Omar N. Bradley, *A Soldier's Story*; George S. Patton, Jr., *War as I Knew It* (Boston: Houghton Mifflin, 1947); John Toland, *The Last 100 Days* (New York: Random House, 1966); Kenneth Koyen, "General Patton's Mistake," *The Saturday Evening Post*, May 1, 1948; W. L. White, *Report on the Germans* (New York: Harcourt Brace, 1947).

10. A WALKING TOUR OF BAVARIA IN THE SPRINGTIME

The early morning of March 28 was a pleasant time for walking. The bitter disappointment of the past night was a vivid memory, but life went on. In one small town on the way our captors gave us bread and a little German Army canned meat. This was an auspicious start for a trip. We walked nine miles, then pulled into a woods for the day. There we cooked some raw potatoes that the Germans gave us, and slept. At six o'clock in the evening, we walked again, this time only six miles to a little town where we slept in the barns. Next morning at seven o'clock we started once more.

Bavaria was enchanting. From the hilltops, we could look out for miles over the rolling landscape. Half a dozen towns were in sight. Everyone lived in town; there the farmer had his house and barn. The small farms were grouped around the edges of the towns, and as soon as the farms got too far from one town for convenience, there was another town. It was the season of ploughing and planting, and the air smelled good.

The picturesque scenes looked like color plates in the *National Geographic*. Old men puffed on elaborate long-

stemmed pipes. Every town had its churches and its *Gasthaus*.
Strange names these *Gasthausen* had—the Inn of the Golden
Angel, Inn of the Yellow Lion, Inn of the Lindens. There were
ancient, walled towns with their colorful houses in lavenders,
yellows, and blues. The women, too, wore colorful peasant
costumes. Sometimes, as we walked by, we saw women sob-
bing and wondered why. Did we remind them of sorrows in
their families?

Little roadside shrines, crucifixes, or statues of the saints
dotted the countryside. In the walls of many homes, too, was
a niche with a carved figure of Christ or the Virgin Mary.
Sometimes the air seemed to breathe the simple Catholic piety
of these people. They were strong, hard-working peasants;
we often saw women casually do jobs on the farm that would
have strained our strength. But their attitudes were gentle
and kindly.

Nowhere in Europe had war seemed so remote as on this
peaceful countryside. The sight of a German uniform, which
we sometimes saw in the town, seemed strangely out of harmony. The American Air Force was often overhead, and near
industrial Schweinfurt (an important ball-bearing center)
many of the towns had been bombed. But out in the countryside and the little villages all this seemed not to belong. Even
the Shell and Standard Oil signs or Coca-Cola ads from years
before were incongruous here.

This was better than living in prison camp. Our marches
were not very long, weather was pleasant, and there were
frequent days of rest. We began to hope that we would not
soon reach Nürnberg, our rumored destination. There some
of our sick had gone by train, and there (we understood)
were the bunch who had been rounded up on the hill near
Hammelburg the same morning that we left.

(Easter)

Easter Sunday (April 1) we spent in a delightful little town, where our barn opened on the main street (the only street, as I recall). That morning we received a Red Cross Parcel for every three of us. A shipment had arrived at Hammelburg, we learned, and the General had sent our share to us on a truck. Most of Easter Sunday we spent around our little fires. The townfolk were generous with food; we bargained with them as before, but often they gave us things. We enjoyed some of their Easter baking and soft-boiled or fried some of their eggs—incredible luxury.

We gathered for Easter worship outside a barn. A rude cross was fashioned of logs and placed behind the communion table. Spread over the table was a beautiful white cloth with words embroidered in gold, "Jesus Christ, the Lamb of God, who takes away the sin of the world." I forget whether the words were Latin or German. It was said to have been made by a local *Hausfrau*. Oberstleutnant Loida joined the worshipers, although he could understand no English. So did a few of our guards. The local Bürgermeister gave a bottle of wine for the communion. Each of us brought his own bread, for there was no extra ration for communion. We prayed very literally, "Give us this day our daily bread." The worship was real. That was the most memorable Easter of my life.

That afternoon half a dozen of us went out, with a guard, to hunt wood for fires. We pulled a cart up a hill outside of town into a woods. The man who owned the land came along to show us which trees we might cut and to help cut some himself. The Bavarian woods are beautifully clean and carefully tended. It was good to stand out here and relax. Before we finished, the German guard gathered us in the woods, pulled out a box of bread, and gave it to us. He didn't try to

trade, but we gave him a few cigarettes. He was middle-aged
—old, as we reckoned soldiers in the American Army. As
we talked, he told us that his wife and child had been killed
in Aachen. With no dreams or hopes left, he went on obeying
his orders and wishing the war would end.

The Germans gave us no news of the war in those days.
We could get rumors from some of the French prisoners we
saw occasionally working on the farms. But the rumors were
always the same; for Frenchmen our armies were always very
close. So we got tired of asking them. But on April 3, I found
a village newspaper with the communique: the Americans had
reached Kassel. That was a big advance from the Rhine. It
meant that things were rolling now.

We kept marching toward Nürnberg. Now we heard that
the camp there was crowded and might not hold us; and we
hoped it would not. This life was better.

At Furth, on the outskirts of Nürnberg, we hung over the
fence of our barnyard trying as usual to swap "Cigaretten
für Brot." An old fellow came along on a bicycle, and stopped
to talk to us. He had lived in New York, he said, and described the German Yorkville district. We tried to get some
news out of him, but he wouldn't give us any. He was the
only German civilian I ever talked to who gave us the
thoroughgoing Nazi spiel. When we asked him when the
war would end, he said, "Not when you think. Of course, in
a military sense it is already over. But we know that if we
give in, you will kill all of us and destroy our country."

We laughed a little at this thought, and started to argue
with him.

"Oh, I don't mean you fellows," he said. "I mean your
Jews and Roosevelt. Why do you come over here anyway?
What do you have against us? Haven't you got everything

you want at home? When I was in New York, it was wealthier than Germany. But I like it here better."

"Why?" we asked.

"Oh, they didn't like me there," he said. "But tell me, why do you come over here? You certainly don't believe that old Wilson stuff about democracy." We had not the slightest desire to argue with this man, and didn't try any more. So he started exercising his mouth again.

"I'll tell you why," he said. "It's because your Jews make you do it." As we started to laugh again, he quickly went on, "Oh, I know you don't realize it. They're too clever for that. But do you know how much of your Supreme Court is Jewish?" He gave an outlandish figure and continued his torrent of canned words from the Nazi propaganda factories. On and on he went. I had not thought that even the Nazis actually believed this stuff they shouted, but this character seemed to.

He finally got on his bicycle and went on his way. The next across-the-fence visitor was a Luftwaffe lieutenant. His English was hesitant, and he was personally very friendly. But his Nazi discipleship was firm. The lieutenant's big talking point was his hatred of Russia. And how, he asked, could we justify our alliance with communism? Someone gave him the usual save-an-argument answer of asking about Tojo and the Japanese. To our surprise, he defended the Japanese. He was the only German I ever heard speak well of Japan. "You see," he said, "they are not Nordic, true, but they belong to a very ancient culture. They are no savages like the Russians."

I was glad to hear these two, because among all the German civilians and soldiers I talked to, these were the only ones who spoke the party line. It served to remind me, not only that Nürnberg was the birthplace of the party, but that the Nazi strength was in the cities. The country was usually nonpolitical. Here in this industrial town, we found two ardent believers. The rest of the people seemed unconcerned. One woman gave a few of the officers a big kettle of boiled potatoes, and many gave bread for soap.

(Nürnberg and Disaster)

On April 5 we marched through Nürnberg. Our routes generally avoided cities, and this was the only large center I had been in since Koblenz so long before. The desolate city was a convincing demonstration of the power of our air force. In street after street we looked at demolished buildings, at city blocks piled high with rubble. There were few people around, but again, as at Koblenz long before, the air breathed hostility. We felt uncomfortable and wanted to get on out of town. For more than an hour, we walked through this city, and never saw a single building without marks of destruction. Everywhere were signs pointing to air raid shelters. People still used the air raid shelters, still lived and worked in this monument of destruction. Stores were open and had a little food in the almost-empty cases. We passed close by the wreckage of one big factory and surveyed the damage the block-busters had done. There was one place that would turn out no more war materials, I thought. We moved close by the remains of the building and heard astonishing noises. It was hard to believe, but machinery was still running in the basement. This demolished building was still a a war factory. As at Koblenz, the aerial destruction of industry was more apparent than real.*

* General Bradley was to comment later on "how extravagantly air had overrated its effectiveness against the German industrial plant" and on "the astonishing recuperative powers of German industry after bombing." As a ground soldier, I heartily concur.

Nürnberg, I remembered, was one of the ancient and picturesque cities of Germany, famous for its history, its toy-factories, its clocks. Nazism had made it a center of party strife and a cog in the vast war machine. War had made it an inferno of destruction and a pile of ruins.

We turned on to a different street and saw a mass of laborers, shovels on their shoulders, walking somewhere. They were Italians, French, and Slavs, hundreds of them going out to clean up the damage from the last air raid. Their clothes were more nondescript and tattered than ours, their bodies more scrawny. Hopelessness stared out of their faces. Here was the worst fate a prisoner could have: to live in a German city where food was always scarce, where incessant bombings tore at nerves and mind, where hostility was suffocating, where work of cleaning up after the bombs was unending.

On the far edge of Nürnberg we stopped under some trees near the road for a short rest. There the Oberstleutnant met the column and said that we would not enter the Nürnberg camp. We were glad and loaded on our packs to march again. Before we lined up on the road, the noise of planes was in the air, and we saw in the distance the formations of American bombers. We never moved on the road when planes were overhead, so we sat down again under the trees. On the other side of the road were a few houses, but here was a thin woods. Sometime every day, sometimes several times a day, we saw the bombers, often by the hundreds, fly over us to targets deeper in Germany. American planes ruled the skies. Rarely we saw a German fighter or one of the swift jet-propelled planes flashing through the sky. But we never saw them challenge our formations. On many a day we heard the rumble of the bombs dropping, but we had never been very close. We used to sometimes wonder, rather ridiculously,

I guess, whether the war might end while we were marching on the road away from every source of news; and there was often the remark, as the bombers went over, that obviously the war must still be going on.

There was something majestic in those huge formations of Flying Fortresses, their streamlined silver forms gleaming in the sun, their movements so precise and perfect. Tremendous controlled power they symbolized—power so great that no one could fight back, so great that they moved unperturbed through their missions and rained destruction on cities without disturbing their beautiful formations. Today, as so often, the flack burst around them, burst close but never hit. Up in the B-17s, we knew, that flack was frightening. Some of those planes were buffeted in the air; the crews were tense and sometimes frightened. But from here we could see only the smooth undisturbed movement, the perfect formation.

Now, as the great planes flew on, a streamer of smoke dropped from one. They must be bombing the center of Nürnberg, and we would see the dramatic sight! The bombardier of the lead plane in each of the small formations dropped the smoke flare at the exact time that his precision sight was on the target. Behind him, each plane, with bombardier's eyes on the lead plane, dropped its bombs accordingly. The smoke flares were easy to see. Sometimes, when they reflected the sun just right, we saw the bombs tumbling from the planes and speeding toward their targets. The planes moved on in Olympian calm. No, even Zeus on Olympus had to lose his calm enough to *hurl* his thunderbolts of destruction; these bombardiers simply made their calculations, pressed a button, and rode on.

On and on the bombers came. Each flight came in from a different direction, moved in an undeviating line until the bomb release point, then curved away to left or right, so that the anti-aircraft gunners below could never get the pattern of the movement. After each smoke flare, we waited, waited, waited, then at last heard the distant rumble and thought again of the sights we had seen that morning.

We lay on the ground or sat leaning against trees, eyes in the air. Now the bombs were dropping a little closer, the targets were nearer our end of the town. Still it was majestic, and we could see even more.

I don't know when I became afraid. First there was the thought, not yet a worry, that the falling flak might strike in our vicinity. Then we heard it. I suppose it was flak I heard, for the sound was something strange and weird, unknown to my ears. It was like the upper range of an organ, playing softly and in jangled disharmonies. It lasted a few seconds, then stopped. Then more. The flak never landed near, but we listened and wondered.

While we listened, the bombings grew close. It happened gradually, I suppose, but it was with startling suddenness that we felt danger. There was a railroad visible only a few hundred yards away. Impulsively we felt that it would be the next target. We were afraid, but it was too late to move. Running would be like trying to escape a tornado. Even as we waited we thought of the strange caprice of fate that had put us here at this time. It was the only time on this trip that we had come through a city, the only time that we had stopped between a highway and a railroad. That one time the American bombers came over.

The flares dropping from the planes had the fascination that music is said to have for a snake. Still the bombers were remote and majestic. But now the bombs came crashing in on the railroad, and the rumbling was terribly close and real. Everyone was lying flat on the ground. I don't know when we moved into that position, but there we were. I lifted my head to look toward the tracks, and saw flames on the other side of them. They could bomb the tracks, I thought, and still not hurt us. It was too close for comfort, but might not be really dangerous.

Now there was another sound in the air, a gentle swish which I had never heard before, but that told me unmistakably to lower my head. It ended in a terrifying explosion, a tremendous violence to earth and air. Body and mind felt the shock, tried to resist, and were helpless. Now trees were falling, rocks flying through the air. For second after second, painfully slow seconds, dust of earth and concrete fell like a silt from the air, settling upon trembling bodies. A little rest. Eyes were afraid to open. Then the swish, and again the awful crash. This time several of them. The body and mind were buffeted from every side. Falling trees and flying rocks. Screams. More noise—not explosions but crashes, like buildings caving in. Air filled with debris. I saw it all, though my eyes never opened. Then again the dust like silt, falling gently and relentlessly as if it aimed to bury this body.

It is strange how swiftly the mind acts when it thinks it is going to die. It is said that a drowning man sees his whole past life go swiftly before his eyes in the moment when he goes down for the last time. I never knew anyone who felt that. Rather it was a whole future life that flashed through our minds. As always in these crises of the mind, recollections and anticipations were fused. But mostly it was the future—the longing to live, the thoughts of home, the tiny irrelevant things like clasping a hand or sitting across the table from someone, that in the human mind mean the great things of life. Electricity cannot act faster than these impressions in the mind, steel cannot be sharper. Imagination becomes more vivid and real than fact.

Dozens of men, perhaps every one there, said that they

prayed, but what they prayed, I don't think they knew. They just prayed. For the mind, so swift in catching the flashing impressions of past and future, is slow in forming thoughts.

Yet one absurd half-thought struck me—something between an impression and a thought. I thought of the moment months before when I lay on the ground and felt helpless as the "screaming meemies" poured in. These explosions were more tremendous. They did more violence to land and air and human bodies. But here any bomb might be the last. It would be pure luck if two bombs landed side by side. There was not that relentless probing for a target, minute after minute, that I had felt in those long artillery barrages. I don't know which was worse, and it does not matter.

The air was clearing, the dust no longer falling. Somewhere there was a jarring infernal racket, but bombs were not crashing. I opened my eyes and lifted my head. I saw other figures pressed against the ground like my own, a few heads cautiously looking around like mine. My nerves were numb, and I didn't know whether my body was all there or whether I could control it. I tried. I could move! Evidently I was not even injured. Now a few men were dashing across the street where there were craters that might be protection if the bombs fell again. I moved over there, then looked around to see what had happened. Two or three houses on this side of the street were ruined. On the other side of the tracks, an ammunition dump was on fire. Flames reached for the sky, bright tracer bullets flew out of the fire, mortar shells exploded. We were probably at a safe distance, but it would be better to keep low. Now some were calling for doctors. The wounded were being collected at the head of the column. The bombers seemed to be gone. A frightened horse ran madly down the street, broken harness hanging on his body. A few civilians walked about in desperate anxiety, their homes destroyed. The racket from the ammunition dump beat on our eardrums. Were there any wounded nearby? I looked and yelled and found none. They were calling for water at the head of the column. I had a canteen—had happened to find it and pick it up when we left Hammelburg. I ran to the head of the column.

Up here destruction was awful. Mangled bodies lay beside the craters. Many were obviously dead. Someone called for help; one wounded man was placing a tourniquet on the thigh of another. The leg below the knee was a mass of blood and muscle, the foot was gone. If the bleeding could be stopped, the man might live. He was conscious, but in such deep shock that he felt no particular pains—only pain. He didn't wince as we moved the leg enough to wrap it. We finished the tourniquet, and wrapped the man in a blanket. I tried to help a couple others. Now the doctors were gradually getting control. The Oberstleutnant was trying to get ambulances.

There was a call for those who could walk to get on the road. The doctors and chaplains and a few designated others would stay. The ammunition dump was still exploding. The mass of torn earth, scattered equipment, water bottles and canteens, mangled human flesh and blood—all were still there. But the dead were now separated, and the doctors could turn to the living. The rest of the crowd milled about the road. No one knew whose orders to follow; the ranking officers had been killed or wounded beyond power to walk. Somehow a column was formed and moved down the road. Several hundred yards and it stopped, while we tried to find out who was in command and how many of us there were.

Twenty-nine were left back, dead or dying. A slightly greater number were wounded enough that they had to be evacuated then or that night. Out of every six men, one had been hit badly. Minor wounds were too many to count.

Sitting in that woods and waiting, I thought. Here were a few hundred army officers, all combat veterans and professional "brave men." They had all passed through an experience which they called the most terrifying, or among the most terrifying, that they had ever known. But this was the experience that the civilians of these cities were facing, not once or twice or three times, but day after day. Some of them could sit them out in bomb shelters, but many could not. And to experience this day after day, week after week, to see it coming and coming through an endless future—that was worse than anything 90 percent of combat soldiers would ever know.

This sort of thing must bring hopelessness and hate. Few people, when bombs were crashing in on them, would ever be able to see beyond those brutal facts to the thoughtful reasoning that might tell them that perhaps this was partly their own fault—the result of total war which their country had brought on the world. For bombs are crushing things, and thought is delicate and tenuous.

But I was surprised that night. A couple hours after we reached the night's barn, a Lt. Colonel straggled in, coughing blood and walking with pain. He had tried to walk with the column, but had fallen behind. He sat down in front of a house. The civilians took him inside, offered him wine and help. They knew about the bombing. They had been through them themselves. Usually people like that are gleeful that Americans are caught in their own bombs, as we thought it only fair when German V-bombs went wrong and landed in Germany. But these people, with no compulsion at all or no reason to fear this lone American, were kind to him, and talked of their hate for Hitler and the Nazi government that was responsible for this. They were, of course, rare people in Germany, as they would be in any country. It was good to know that Germany still had such people.*

(Wanderings)

With Nürnberg past, we had no place to go. Most of the prisoners of war still in Germany were being concentrated in the vicinity of the Moosburg camp, not far northeast of Munich. We headed in that direction. Since it was known that the camp was crowded, and the whole area thronged with PWs, we were in no hurry to get there, and our commandant seemed to feel the same way. So we moved by short marches, often taking a day's layover. Life was leisurely, but boring.

A group of air corps officers joined our column. They had tried to escape from another column somewhere, and when caught were put with us. We were amused by the flyers. They had no idea what ground combat was like and were constantly talking about escape, as though it were the easiest thing in the world. Occasionally they would try it and usually get picked up long before they got to the front or reached any dangerous territory. But it was interesting to get acquainted with them. They had come through Nürnberg the day after we had, and they spoke of the revealing experience of seeing that city. Some of them said that their view of combat from the air was so remote that they never comprehended what it was like on the ground. They knew of course what their

* That April 5 ranks with the battle in Luxembourg and the interrogation at Limburg as one of the three most harrowing days of my military career. For concentrated traumatic experience within five minutes, it was the worst. But it was a far more memorable day in history than I knew. Long afterwards I learned that on that day, by order of Adolf Hitler, Dietrich Bonhoeffer was hanged at Flossenbürg.

bombs accomplished; yet the actual sight of the destruction was shocking.

From some of them, captured very recently, we learned that the crews of fighters were briefed to strafe ground columns only when they were sure of their identity. The air forces were aware of the great number of American prisoners marching the roads of Germany. That relieved us immensely. We had feared strafing. From the air we might look like any bunch of soldiers, and for the fighter pilot speeding over us the mere pressing of a button might mean death for many of us. All our marches in these last days were made early in the morning—starting out at three or four o'clock and ending before the morning haze had cleared. Still we were often frightened by the fighter planes. Their speed was so great that it was useless to try to scatter, so we simply stood on the road when they came over, hoping that our very avoidance of running would make us appear friendly. We carried white panels, but there was never time to put them out on the march. On farms where we stayed, we spread the panels to spell "PW," until a German order stopped that. Some General issued the order, saying that if the Allies could tell the locations of the PWs, they could tell something of German movements and plans. No doubt there was something to that, but we didn't look at it that way.

A few British flyers got into our column, and I enjoyed talking to them. One I got to know rather well. He had flown a Mosquito bomber in the RAF, had taken his training in Canada and spent furloughs in the States. I liked him. He had been in the army for five years, and was still young. Experience had aged him, but he was very youthful in many ways. He was a political radical, convinced that Churchill's usefulness was over and that he would not last beyond the peace. He saw little in the Labor Party, but put his hopes in

Sir Roger Ackland's radical group. He was, he thought, typical of a great many British people, and he was sure that Britain would swing far to the left at the end of the war. I knew of significant active groups of leftists in Britain, but had my doubts as to their strength. He was not sure, but thought that they were large.

He was very cynical about the war and its possible results. Completely secular, he remarked that the British army was much less religious than the American. Knowing the religion of the American army as I did, I thought that a very strong statement. I asked him whether he had ever heard of the late Archbishop Temple or the Malvern Conference. He had not. It seemed to me a sad reflection on the Established Church in England that it had become so linked with British conservatism and complacency that even the vigorous efforts of a great Archbishop of Canterbury had done nothing to change that impression upon this intelligent flyer.

Despite his radical social ideas, the pilot's cynicism extended to human nature, and he had little hope of society getting beyond its present confusion. The best chance, he thought, was in Lin Yutang's idea of contentment. If men could be made biologically happy, by a social order that would feed everyone and take the worst discomfort out of life, people would perhaps be amiable and get along. I told him I thought I was probably more cynical than he there, and suggested that ambition of men caused more unrest and tyranny than hunger. He doubted it.

April 8 and 9 we spent in a huge barn at a place called *Kloster Seligporten*. The name matched our yearnings. It had been a sort of monastic farm in peace time. Now, like all farms, it was part of the government food program and was farmed by slave labor in a very unmonastic way. Here a German General inspected us. We thought that German

Generals should be extremely nervous in the present sad state of their country, but this one was calm and resplendent in his uniform with its insignia in General's red. In a very courteous way he talked to our senior officer and asked about our welfare. Once more I was surprised that when the Nazi state was so obviously tottering in its last days of survival, a General should bother to look at us. Sometimes the German treatment of prisoners had been so inadequate, even cruel, and so often had the Geneva Convention been violated, that it seemed amazing to see this attention to amenities.

I remember for two reasons the village of Zell where we spent April 13 and 14. One reason was the village priest. Like a character out of a storybook, he walked along the streets in a long black coat, a middle-aged man and the picture of friendly piety. Everyone in town greeted him, and all the children when he came near stopped their play and ran out to meet him. He bent over and took their hands, said something and smiled, and they ran back to their play. He greeted every woman, whoever she was, with a sweeping graceful motion of bowing and removing his hat. I saw him do it a dozen times and he never hastened the rhythm of that movement, though the woman might be several steps past him before he got his hat back on.

The other reason was that here we heard of the death of President Roosevelt. Its actual date, though we did not know that, had been April 12. The first news came from the guards. We didn't know whether to believe it. The guards were always so hopelessly ignorant of war news, even when they were friendly enough to tell what they knew, that we were skeptical that they would have the news from America. But everyone in Germany knew when Roosevelt died. And soon we were convinced that the report was true. It was a jolt to us. Here, so far separated from American society and ideas,

I would not have expected it to make so great a difference. In many ways I had been critical of the President, although I had supported him against his electoral opponents. Now I, and many who had opposed him even more than I, felt concerned. We realized more than before how much we expected him to pull us through the postwar arrangements and especially to keep things all right with Stalin. Most of our column could not name his successor, and I enjoyed the instant authority of one who could name Harry Truman and tell a few facts about him.

(Across the Danube)

On April 17 our path led down into the valley of the Danube, where the muddy river flows between steep white cliffs. On that spring day the river valley was beautiful. We walked less than a mile upstream, and crossed the river into the town of Weltenburg, lying on the south bank. An ancient ferry took us over. The current was rather swift, and something had to keep the boat from slipping downstream. An overhead wire stretched across the river. One end of a rope was tied to the ferry boat, and the other end slid along the wire on a little wheel. The woman who ran the ferry poled the boat slowly across the river, and the rope kept it from going with the current. With male gallantry we felt that we should do the work, but none of us knew how.

Across the Danube, we moved in leisurely style. In prewar days this had been tourist country, and even to us it was beautiful. April 20 was Hitler's birthday, the Germans told us. The Allies celebrated it with a tremendous air show. We watched it from the hilltop where our barn was. The day was warm, and we spread out blankets, took off our clothes, and lay on the hillside, soaking up sunshine and picking lice out of our garments. Hour after hour the planes passed over—those same majestic formations that could be so awful.

We were scheduled to spend an extra day and night there. But toward evening we got unexpected orders to move that night. From our hilltop we had looked down that afternoon on the road and watched German squads and half squads moving south. They often moved that way when they retreated. Could it mean that Americans had crossed the Danube? We didn't know whether that might have been the cause of our movement.

As we moved out that night, we saw once more a column of Russian prisoners. They were the same wretched starved sight as before. The Germans showed brutality, rooted in hate and fear, toward their Russian prisoners. And the more brutal the treatment of the Russian prisoners, the more the Germans feared Russian revenge. These Russians barely moved as they walked. They seemed to need all their energy to stand on their feet. Some could not maintain even the snail's pace and straggled far behind the column. One poor old man appeared to be entirely blind. Two comrades led him by the arm as he walked. Their feet without socks rubbed against wooden shoes. Again their guards were brutal. As at one time months before, some Americans gave the Russians cigarettes. This time a guard struck a Russian in the head with his rifle butt, and we gave them no more.

As we marched that night, we saw German troops on the roads, moving by platoons and companies, both north and south. It looked as though they might be preparing for activity, but we could see no pattern in their movement. After midnight we arrived on a farm and moved into a barn in the dark, where we tried to sleep sitting up because there wasn't room to lie down.

It was the first time in Bavaria that we were low on food.

Just a little of the old northern hunger had been coming back. But that day we received two Red Cross parcels each. We had been trying for a week to get parcels. We were in the vicinity of Moosburg, where the main Red Cross depot in Germany was said to be located. After many tentative arrangements had fallen through, the Oberstleutnant found a truck and let one of our officers, with a guard, go to Moosburg for parcels. He brought them back, with information. Germany, he showed us, on a map, was fast collapsing under pressure from east and west. At Moosburg they had told him that the parcels should last us the next two weeks, which would bring the end of the war, they thought.

Probably every officer in our column was thinking of escape in those days. Now that we had food, we might try it. The guards would not stop us any more. With the Americans advancing so fast, it would not be necessary to "cross the lines." It would be rather easy to hide out somewhere, with a couple parcels, and wait for our troops to arrive. Most German civilians would not turn us in any more, it seemed; or so some of our number, who had tried to escape before, thought. Of course there was always the chance of stumbling into some SS troops and getting killed; but that was not a great danger.

But the news made it appear that the war might end soon and that escape was scarcely worth the risk. Our professional courage seemed unimportant now. We wanted to survive. Only two officers of the three or four hundred left that night; perhaps more would have, except for a torrential rain. But most decided it was not worthwhile.

(Sielstettin)

We moved on, still closer to Moosburg, and stopped on a large farm at the edge of the village of Sielstettin. We heard, when we arrived, that we might stay a few days. Perhaps, we thought, the Oberstleutnant is satisfied to sit out the war here. It suited us. We settled down and, with plenty of food, enjoyed ourselves.

The eating situation had generally been good this trip. Throughout the tour of Bavaria we averaged a Red Cross parcel a week, though there was one two-week stretch with none. The local population did well by us, too. When I finally became a free man, I read in *Stars and Stripes* just before V-E Day that the German civilian egg ration had been cut from 24 eggs to 12 eggs a year. As a prisoner of war, I sometimes ate three to five eggs in a day. They were never issued us, of course, but farmers would give us an egg for two cigarettes. Chickens were rigorously controlled by the state in Germany; hens wore a metal tag, and farmers had to keep records of egg production to convince the government that they were not holding out. But a farmer always has a little extra to eat himself, and in Germany he would part with it for some cigarettes. Toward the end, with transportation and communication broken down, the food piled up on the farms and the people no longer worried about government controls. So the worse the general situation got in Germany, the better we ate.

Another source of food was grain. We would pick up in a grain bin a sockfull of wheat or barley, carry it a couple days or so until we slept in a barn that had a grinder, and then turn it into cereal or flour. With flour, eggs, and a Red Cross parcel, culinary possibilities were unlimited. For variety, French prisoners on the farms would trade parts of their parcels for cigarettes. Usually we could build small fires until blackout hour. When we couldn't do that, perhaps the women in the farmhouses would cook something for us. Or sometimes we could just take over the kitchen for a few hours; two or three officers would do the cooking. The rest of us prepared our gourmet dishes and sent them in with a note telling how they should be cooked. It was amusing one day, as we crouched around the fires in a barnyard, to see some of the town women gather around to watch us. One of them offered a few comments as she saw me fry pancakes. I had a time explaining to her, in my faulty German, that I fried them so long because I liked them well done, not because I didn't know better.

When we were receiving parcels regularly, we ate better than our guards. I have to admit a certain generosity in the German Army, allowing us to receive our parcels (whenever the transportation situation let them come through) when those parcels contained such luxuries as cigarettes and chocolate—things that the German soldier couldn't have. It was a requirement of the Geneva Convention, but I can imagine the howl in our country if German PWs had received from home packages of luxuries that our troops did not have.

But the guards, in Bavaria, had the advantage that they were frequently invited into the homes of the people. Sometimes they both ate and slept there, while we were consigned to the barn and the chow line. I didn't envy them their meals —they were nothing to rave about—but I felt an alien in this foreign land. The guards belonged, we did not. And I longed to see my own country again, where I belonged.

It was during this stay at Sielstettin that I went to a mass one day, probably the first time in my life. Both Protestant and Catholic chaplains had daily services when we were not marching. The Catholics usually got permission to use the little Roman churches that dotted the countryside. The Protestants had to be satisfied with a spot inside or outside a barn. I went to the mass to try to see what it meant to these prisoners of war. It was a beautiful little church. On stones set in the walls were carved the names and dates of men killed in the First World War. The building, the priest in his robes, and the established ritual made a very different impression from the Protestant service where a man simply got up and talked to a bunch of other men, who might or might not agree with what he had to say.

The priest started by telling what day it was and what Saints the mass remembered. That didn't seem very relevant to us, and I don't think anybody cared much. The mass itself I did not understand; that, of course, was my ignorance, not the fault of the mass. I think everyone there did pray. Everyone knew that he was worshiping. Everyone left knowing that he had prayed and worshiped. That was more than I could say for some of our Protestant services. The Roman service, with its established ritual, its definite words and acts of worship, and its idea of the grace of God mediated through the sacrament of the mass with no dependence upon the worthiness of the priest who happens to officiate, has something that our often slovenly Protestant service, depending so much on the personality of the man who happens to be preacher, lacks. That, of course, is not the whole story. I could never accept the superstitions of Romanism, its exaltation of itself. The weakness of its service is that it may seem entirely irrelevant to life outside the church. Many men who attended that mass left feeling that they had done their religious duty; there was little sense that this should make a difference in living. There is too much of form and ceremony, too much that jars against the character of Jesus Christ. But there were things that Protestants might think of.*

Our Protestant services were sometimes good, sometimes

* After the rich ecumenical experiences of recent years, these remarks seem naïve. But they belong to the record of past days, and in honesty I let them stand as such.

bad. Much depended on the Chaplain—his choice of scripture and hymns, his remarks. We had something in the hymns that the Catholics lacked. We had a directness and a challenge to life in the words of the Chaplain, if he was a good man with a good talk. Sometimes we had real worship. The services were small. But sometimes, when the Oberstleutnant might come, and both Negro and white Americans were there, there was a real feeling of the community of the church.

No Negroes had been with us in our march out of Poland. At Hammelburg there had been a few, and on this march there were one colored lieutenant and several Negroes in the enlisted men's platoon. Racial friction had been marked in England and France. Here there was none. The Negroes were accepted more completely than in any other army group I had ever seen. One Alabama lieutenant, who in the past had often spoken contemptuously of "niggers," became entirely cordial to the Negro lieutenant. I hunted for a reason. One difference was that these were all combat troops. And combat troops often come to appreciate a man for what he is worth, not for the group he belongs to. I have heard many white soldiers say that after they saw Negroes fight and die, they were convinced that those men deserved well of democracy. But there was something else involved, because combat leaves many prejudices unbroken. I suppose it was the practical comman-sense realization that we were all prisoners of the Germans, all in this mess together, and that as against our captors, we had to stand side by side. Common sense, but strange. Strange that it should take Nazism, with its fanatical racial tyranny, to make Americans democratic.

At Sielstettin we heard that the Russians were fighting on the edge of Berlin, that Hitler had taken personal command in Berlin. It was hard to believe, but the German soldiers did. We had thought that Hitler would leave Berlin for the

Salzburg area when the collapse of northern Germany came. We were glad that he was staying in Berlin. It would make the fall of that city more decisive for the war.

There were visitors at Sielstettin. The white car of the YMCA, painted with the neutral Swedish flag, drove into our farmyard. In the tottering Nazi state of late April, 1945, almost the only transportation and communication left were the white cars and trucks of the Red Cross and YMCA. They crossed and recrossed Southern Germany, doing anything they could for prisoners of war. The Y car found out what we needed and came back the next day. It brought toothbrushes; I had not had one since I was captured. And most important, it brought louse powder. We were all itchy and crawly by this time, and the powder brought blessed relief. In the warm afternoons we could wash and lie naked in the sun, while the powder sent the lice scurrying out of our clothes.

We remained four days at the Sielstettin farm, and hoped that we would stay longer. But on April 27 we moved about eleven miles, south and east. That afternoon and evening the rumors were wild. The Americans, we heard, were near Munich. They were in Landshut. The latter city was northeast of us; if our troops moved south from there, they could cut us off.

Orders came to move at three o'clock in the morning. We did not like that. Our one fear was that the Germans would try to move us south into the Bavarian Alps or east to the region of Salzburg. We hated to think of getting into the center of the so-called "Redoubt" area, of the possibility of being held as hostages in the last desperate guerrilla warfare the Nazis might choose to wage. It was good news that the "Redoubt" was crumbling so fast, that both Americans and

Russians already seemed to be inside its boundaries.* But we didn't like to go south or east.

From the last Red Cross parcels I had been saving the most concentrated food items—particularly the chocolate ration bars. I was ready to escape if that made sense. So far, it was better to stay with a group of Americans, with German guards and officers who were friendly and who felt some obligation to us and perhaps fear of us, than to break loose alone or with a few others and take our chances with SS fanatics.

We moved at 3:00 A.M. The Germans had all got drunk the night before. We tried to see some significance in this; probably it was only because liquor happened to be available there. On that early morning walk the guards with their hangovers were a miserable bunch. For weeks their morale had been gone. They had trudged along, muttering "All' ist kaput in Deutschland" or the German equivalent of "Germany is a dung-heap." From one after another I heard the tale of woe. Homes were gone, farms taken over by Russians, families lost. They had not received mail since they left Oflag 64. They could only hope for the end of the war, and that was not much of a hope. This morning they were just a little extra miserable. It rained as we marched, and at one halt a guard threw his rifle down in the mud and sat on it. Then he passed around his canteen, full of schnapps, to the Americans.

We finished our march late in the morning, tired and soaking wet, and moved into the usual barns. Several men dropped out of the column in the town and traded for food. One was invited in for a meal and listened to the BBC broadcast in English. The Russians had three-quarters of Berlin. The war seemed to be moving to a finale.

* As General Bradley later explained, rumors of the redoubt were greatly exaggerated. But there is no doubt that the rumors influenced the strategy of military leaders and the fears of the PW's in those days.

The Red Cross trucks visited us here with more parcels. It was only a week since we had received two apiece, but Germany was crumbling fast and they might not be able to reach us again. The driver said that at Moosburg the Americans were running the camp. The German Army, he said, had made an agreement with the Americans that prisoners in camps in the path of advancing armies would be left in those camps and not moved. We were not in a camp and could be moved. But maybe Oberstleutnant Loida was ready to give up too. We slept a night here and did not move the next day. In the afternoon we heard demolitions nearby—probably bridges blown up. There were other sounds; we argued over whether they were artillery or tank fire.

Then late in the evening as we were about to go to sleep, we got orders to move at ten o'clock. Our senior officer, Lt. Col. Palmer, went up to argue with the commandant. Loida's explanation was plausible: German artillery was setting up in the town, and American counter-battery fire would endanger us. So Col. Palmer agreed to march.

We moved out in the dark on trails across the hills, keeping away from towns and roads. Artillery echoed through the hills. We could not tell what direction the sounds came from. It is always that way in the hills. But the noises seemed close.

We went only about six miles. The rain had wet us, and no one could find the billeting party which should have picked us a barn. We went into a church where we sat in the pews and waited for morning. Then we marched again, another six miles. We were getting shoved around more than we liked, and this marching in the rain was uncomfortable. But freedom must be near.

Munich has fallen, we heard that day. Peace negotiations are going on, someone else said. And persistently came the rumor that Hitler was dead. No one could prove or deny it. But strangely it always came from the Germans. They believed it, but were never quite sure.

Our column was shrinking. About fifty had left us in the last couple days, attempting escape. The vast majority stuck with Col. Palmer and figured that there was some strength in numbers.

In those few days the German officers and guards led our column but did not control it. In night marches we kept together. But in the daytime the column spread out for miles. After arriving at a barnyard, it would be a couple hours before the stragglers got in. They traded at every farmhouse along the way. There was no discipline left. If a Jerry guard protested, the American simply muttered, "Krieg ist fertig" (War is over). The guard shrugged his shoulders and let it go at that. The German officers were afraid to administer discipline now. They had more to fear than we. Col. Palmer was satisfied to keep the Germans' confidence low and to demand only enough organization to keep the group together.

Next day, May 1, we marched another ten miles. Again the rumors of peace and Hitler's death were strong. (In fact, Hitler's suicide was on April 30. Admiral Karl Dönitz announced it on May 1 at about 9:30 P.M.) It snowed that May Day, though not very much. Why, we wondered, did Oberstleutnant Loida keep marching? The "Redoubt" was obviously crumbling. Every day we heard artillery; it was only a matter of time until it was all over. Most of the American prisoners had been freed by this time, or so we thought. Was he ambitious to be the last German to surrender? There was as much dissatisfaction among his own men as among us.

He ordered us to march on May 2. We started early. There was an unusual commotion and delay as we lined up in the dark. Loida spoke sharply to Hauptmann Menner, the

German adjutant, and asked what the delay was. Menner had been drunk the night before and was in no hurry to move. Anyway, he had his fill of this foolishness. It was has duty to count us each morning as we moved out. Today he stood there counting as if he were still drunk. A couple of his English-speaking NCO's always helped him and tried to get us in a column of threes for the count. "Column of threes, gentlemen, column of threes," they always shouted. (A couple days before, the old boxer-sergeant, as he lined us up, had said, "We know this is a lot of bunk, but we have to do it.") Today as they shouted, Menner said to one of them, "Ach, it doesn't matter," and went on counting mechanically without caring for the result.

We got out of town and on the road. We never saw Menner again, but finally pieced together an amusing story. He always marched at the end of the column, as did one of our medical officers, a Jewish captain. Both decided that morning that this thing had gone too far. They stopped in a German farmhouse together for breakfast and never rejoined the column. Later in France I met an officer who was with them. They had it figured out, he said, that they could take off together and protect each other. So the German captain and the American Jewish captain made their "escape." Hitler must have spun in his grave, if he was buried.

We moved along the road as daylight came. We stopped for a rest period in a heavy woods on a hilltop. Artillery was sounding again, but we were used to that. At the end of the ten-minute break Col. Palmer was not ready to move. The road we were following joined, at the bottom of the hill half a mile away, a column with German military traffic on it. Wagons and troops were moving on that road, retreating. They might become a target for American artillery, and we didn't want to get mixed up with that. Hauptmann Welsh, who led our column, agreed. So we waited in the woods. I got to talking to one of the German sergeants who knew English. He said that Loida had promised his officers and NCO's that morning that this would be the last day of marching. Hauptmann Welsh had told Col. Palmer the same thing. We were skeptical. "Why didn't he decide that yesterday?" someone asked the Sergeant.

"That's what we tried to tell the old booger," he answered. We laughed. The American slang and the contempt for an officer sounded funny from a German mouth.

Artillery still sounded. Some of the noises might have been tanks. The Jerries below were retreating as though Americans were close. Lt. Col. Palmer decided that freedom was near. He was almost ready to declare independence. But we couldn't just sit in the woods with snow on the ground. And the chow truck had gone ahead. We would go on to our destination for the night. Then, we all assumed, we would go no further. Col. Palmer waited until the stragglers had caught up, then ordered the column to stay organized. The road below was almost clear now, and we moved down into the broad valley. We felt a little ticklish walking on that road with hills all around. An American tank might show up on one of those hills and decide to shell the column below. We hoisted our white panels on long sticks and carried them high in the air.

(Gars a. Inn)

About noon we reached the town of Gars a. Inn. The Inn River flowed north from Innsbruck at the Brenner Pass. Farther north it formed the boundary between Germany and Austria, before it emptied into the Danube; but here it was all in Germany. Austria lay not many miles east. It was here we expected to stop.

But here there was word that Loida was on the other side of the river, with the mess truck. The bridge which he had crossed had since been blown by the Germans. We waited for someone to figure out something. While we waited, we talked. We did not like this plan of Loida's to get across the river for supper. Perhaps that river would hold up the American army a day, delay our freedom longer. Gars, we soon learned, was an open city, because of a huge military hospital. This, we figured, would be the ideal place for our armies to find us; they could take us without a fire fight. For a long time we had thought of the possibility of getting caught between German and American fire and didn't like the idea.

A lot of Americans had already found their way into nearby houses, asking for hot water to use with their soluble coffee. I wandered into one crowded house. In the kitchen was a big radio. A BBC news broadcast was on. North of us, we learned, the Americans were already across the Inn. The Russians were racing westward. The redoubt had crumbled! Only in this southern area no armies had penetrated.

The news was carried to Col. Palmer. Now he heard from Hauptmann Welsh that there was another bridge, not yet blown, only one or two kilometers away. We could use it to get to the other side.

But Col. Palmer had no desire to get to the other side. He stood talking to Hauptmann Welsh, with both German and American interpreters helping. The village priest was eager for us to stay, and he insisted that the town people wanted us. (They knew the army was coming, and our presence might be a little security for them.) The priest could find us quarters and food. Someone mentioned barns, and the priest said, "But we cannot put officers in barns." We laughed.

Col. Palmer talked more to Hauptmann Welsh, and the

German officer said that he would not force us to cross the river. That was enough. We would stay.

Barns it was, despite the priest, because Col. Palmer wanted to keep us together. The column stayed in three separate barns that night. We laid out our blankets and ate a little from our parcels. We were nervously excited and wondered what would be next. Loida still had to be heard from. A few anxious hours passed. From our position on the west edge of town near the main road, we could see a few German soldiers, singly or in small groups, walking wearily east, down into the town and toward the river. They looked too puny to suggest an army in retreat, but that is what they were.

In late afternoon, a messenger came from Col. Palmer who was down in the town. Someone kept the guards busy, and we gathered to hear.

A patrol, sent out to hunt for American troops, had met two officers of the 14th Armored Division on the hills overlooking the town. The division planned to take the town at dusk, the officers said, and expected to move in without a fight. It was Col. Palmer's order that we remain quiet where we were and make no demonstration that might upset the plan.

Oberstleutnant Loida had come back to Gars and found Col. Palmer. He made no attempt to force an issue, but asked only for some sort of signed statement from Col. Palmer. I think it said that we refused to cross the river because of danger from American fire; Loida could use it with his superiors to show that he had tried to do his duty. Col. Palmer was glad to get by that easily and gave him a note. Loida even agreed to send us three days' rations.

There would be no food issued that night. The mess truck was still across the river, and the town had not yet collected any for us. But for once eating was a minor concern, and we had enough in our parcels. Since the guards had nothing to eat, it was suggested that we give them a few contributions from our parcels. Odds and ends of cigarettes and food were collected and turned over to the guards, who ate better food that night, if less than they were used to.

Most of the guards were sitting in the yard eating when two jeeps rolled in and the American soldiers jumped out. A few of the Jerries jumped to their feet, held up their hands, and excitedly tried to surrender. Someone told them to go on eating. It was hard, in our intense excitement to follow orders not to demonstrate, but we kept quiet and everything moved smoothly. The weapons from the guards were collected and dumped in a pile, and the guards were sent down to the barn where they were to sleep that night. Most of them were happy that the war was over.

The first soldiers were from the 86th Infantry Division. They were only a few who had advanced out of their sector when they reached us. But soon the 14th Armored Division tanks and half-tracks rolled into the town, and we knew there was plenty of power there to match anything the Jerries had within miles. Now our excitement could let go. We gave greetings to the American soldiers. They showered us with K-rations, candy, pencils and paper, cigarette papers, and all the odds and ends that the American army carries.

The certainty of freedom overwhelmed us. So smoothly had the whole operation gone that it seemed almost unreal. There had been none of the tremendous excitement of the tank battle at Hammelburg with its noise and fire and wild elation. But this time we *knew* we were free. That knowledge was a wonderful thing.

Behind the barn was a tiny Catholic shrine, a place where one or two could kneel. I walked back to it, entered, knelt, and prayed. Then I went into the barn and slept.

11. IN THE
U.S. ARMY AGAIN

Morning came. A convoy of trucks would come for us soon, we learned. Our guards assembled and prepared to march away as a column of prisoners of war. We talked to some of them. I had heard many an American talk about how when he was liberated he would get back at a guard for something. But today we all felt sorry for them. They were glad that they were done with the war, but they had no hope ahead. In our darkest days we Americans had always looked to the hope of the end of the war. But for a defeated nation the end of the war is a sad hope.

I saw the Feldwebel I had known—the boxer. I gave him a package of cigarettes and asked him if he had ever heard from his wife. No, the last he knew she was in a wagon moving out of Poland, about to bear a child. I saw another sergeant, who had been worrying about his family. No, he had heard nothing of them since Poland. I offered Hauptmann Welsh some cigarettes. His pockets were already overflowing, but he thanked me. His home was destroyed, he had no place to go.

I had a little extra food and looked for the guard who had given me bread when I went out to cut wood on the afternoon of Easter Sunday. I gave him something, and told him that I hoped he would soon get to go home. "Home?" he said. "I have no home." I had cruelly forgotten. His home had been in Aachen, his wife and child killed. "I will never go back," he said. He held out his two hands. "I have hands, I will stay here and work."

There were few in that guard company who had not felt the war, few who could not point to a home destroyed, a family evacuated and in some unknown place, a brother or mother or wife or child killed by the war. We knew these men, and today we could only pity them.

We had never expected to feel so friendly to them. The night before, when the Americans had arrived and the Germans had turned over their arms, Hauptmann Welsh came out of the house where he had a bedroom, expecting to turn over the bed to the senior American officer in the barn, and to sleep in the small barn with the German guards. "Tell him to go ahead and keep his bed," our Major told the interpreter. This morning we gave the guards cigarettes and foods until they could hold no more. *Americans are generous,* I thought.

The guards marched out. Soon we loaded on trucks and moved out. As the convoy moved up the hill, out of the valley of the Inn, we passed the guards marching and called out "Weiter marchieren!"—the "March on" that had been so familiar on all our trips.

The American rear area was a tremendous sight. Mile after mile we saw the tanks and trucks and stacks of ammunition. What a contrast to the German rear, where there had been nothing. In those last days when we were never far from whatever defenses Germany had, we had seen no supplies, no weapons except the rifle and panzerfaust, weapons that a single man could carry. If the Nazis had any intention of continuing resistance in areas that we had conquered, this display of military might, so impressive as against German weakness, should be convincing.

Our convoy rolled along, covering swiftly the miles that had been slow and sometimes painful as we walked the other direction. Many miles back we saw a huge wire enclosure, jammed with hundreds of German PWs. Some MPs were looking over a German Lieutenant General, not quite sure what to do with him. Most of us said nothing, as we passed. A few leaned out the trucks and jeered or called to the guards to kick the Germans and feed them nothing. *Americans are vindictive*, I thought.

We got to Moosburg that day, May 3. There in the old prison camp the liberated prisoners were assembled, waiting for transportation out of Germany. Supplies had not quite kept up with the swift advance of the American armies, so for a few days we still ate Red Cross food. The camp was crowded, and our group was installed in an airplane parts factory across the street. We slept on the shelves of the stock room and tore up crates of precision parts, worth thousands of dollars when there were planes to use them in, to get wood to burn or excelsior to sleep on. We wrote our first letters home. We tasted army white bread and couldn't quite believe it was bread; it seemed more like angel-food cake.

I looked over the few sheets of paper that held my diary of life in Germany. The walking tour of Bavaria had covered 240 miles. Altogether I had seen some 600 miles of Germany on foot—and on two pairs of socks.

From Moosburg we moved by truck to the airport at Ingolstadt on May 8. We spent a night in an old stone fortress. The town had been badly bombed and shelled, and there was no electricity or water. I wandered down to the Danube River, where I took off my shirt and washed. There was a battery of anti-aircraft machine guns on the bank, and the crew was listening to a radio. The voice was English. Maybe it was the BBC news. I listened to the words: ". . . and Mr. Churchill told me . . ." I moved over to the radio and heard King George telling the nation that the war would cease that night, at a minute after midnight. Already my mind was in the Pacific. But first would come America and home.

From Ingolstadt we flew on May 9 the next day to Reims. The town was celebrating V-E Day, but it was not until the next day that we learned that Reims was General Eisenhower's advance headquarters and that in a schoolhouse there General Jodl had signed the German surrender at 2:41 A.M. on May 7. At Reims I ate the first "meal" (by which I mean a plate with meat, and vegetables, bread, and a dessert) in months. I had a shower. I saw a chaplain and got a Bible.

On May 11 we flew to Le Havre. On those two flights we passed over many a battlefield and battered town. The towns still looked bad, but in the fields the green of spring was covering the marks of war. From the sky the craters below looked like fast-healing wounds on human flesh. There are wounds of this war, I thought, that will not be healed in my lifetime. I wondered how many generations it would take to heal this war's scars on history. I wondered whether the nations would find a surgery less destructive to the face of the earth and the lives of men.

From Le Havre we moved by truck to Camp Lucky Strike, near Dieppe, where we went through the necessary processing and waited for a ship. We got new clothes, learned again the feel of money, read old issues of *Time* and *Life* and *Newsweek*, rested, and ate. Eating was a strange experience. Each new old American food tasted inexpressibly good. Gradually we controlled our appetites. Gradually we achieved the psychology of free men—of men who can eat a meal and remember that there will be more meals tomorrow and next day, who can walk into a place without their eyes roving about for something to eat or to burn in a fire.

One news item from Lucky Strike should be noted. I read in the *Stars and Stripes* a Swiss news dispatch (which I have not seen confirmed anywhere else) that in his last days Hitler ordered all PWs in Germany killed. The German Army, according to the press, ignored the order. The report, whether true or not, is not inconsistent with what we know of the macabre ending of this dictator who carried his nation to destruction with himself.

On May 20 we moved back to Le Havre and on the 21st boarded the U. S. Army Transport *Sea Owl*. It crossed to Southampton where we picked up some wounded, then on May 24 sailed in convoy for America. The convoy was thought necessary because some German submarines might not know of the end of the war. A convoy moves at the speed of its slowest ship; so it was not until the morning of Sunday, June 3, that we arrived in Boston Harbor. It was foggy enough that it might have been Southampton, but we knew we were home.

My adventure in war was over. It had been harsh in fact, but was rich in memory. I had asked for it and had taken it. I recalled E. M. Forster's *Passage to India*, which I had read in the cold, dim-lit barracks of Oflag 64. Of his heroine, he said, she had left Britain to question India and life. Before she returned, "she was no longer examining life, but being examined by it." If I had gone into the army with perhaps too conscious a desire to question war, I could now say that war had questioned me.

PART II
A QUARTER CENTURY LATER
REFLECTIONS AND
EXPLORATIONS

1. CONSCIENCE
AND HISTORY

"I went to a Catholic Field Mass where all of us were armed. As we knelt in the mud in the slight drizzle, we could distinctly hear the roar of the guns, and the whole sky was filled with airplanes on their missions of destruction . . . quite at variance with the teachings of the religion we were practicing." General George S. Patton, Jr. on his first Sunday in Normandy in World War II.

Now and then the practitioners of war reflect on the deeper meaning of their actions. General Patton, the most flamboyant and aggressive of American generals, was usually convinced that God was on his side. In a famous encounter he ordered a reluctant Army Chaplain to write a prayer, asking for better weather for the destruction of the enemy, then decorated the Chaplain when the clouds broke. But Patton was able on occasion to note the ultimate paradox of war, as he did in the early days after the allied invasion of France in World War II: "An arresting sight were the crucifixes at road intersections; these were used by Signal personnel as supplementary telephone posts. While the crosses were in no way injured, I could not help thinking of the incongruity of the lethal messages passing over the wires."

That incongruity has haunted my life, as it has haunted two millennia of history. Whether men think of Christ as the revelation of God or as a revelation of human possibilities—or with Christian orthodoxy as both—they face the conflict. Armies usually make some appeal to moral idealism, often to specific religious faith; yet their business jars men's moral sensitivities.

Herman Melville made the point when he paused in telling

the story of *Billy Budd* to reflect on the role of the chaplain in military service. "Bluntly put, a chaplain is the minister of the Prince of Peace, serving in the host of the God of War—Mars. As such, he is as incongruous as a musket would be on the altar at Christmas. Why then is he there? Because he indirectly subserves the purpose attested by the cannon; because, too, he lends the sanction of the religion of the meek to that which practically is the abrogation of everything but force." To that comment, Melville added a note: "An irruption of heretic thought hard to suppress."

Whether heretical or profoundly orthodox, Melville's observation puts sharply the problem of war. Twice at the U.S. Army's Chaplains' School, I have read Melville's statement to classes of career chaplains. So far from resenting my statement, the educational officers of the school, concerned that chaplains be genuine men and ministers rather than functionaries, both times invited me to return. The problem of the chaplain is the problem of every person of faith as he thinks about or acts in war.

According to an ancient Roman saying, "It is sweet and fitting to die for one's country." In contemporary America those words can hardly be said without cynicism. The romantic tradition of war that they represent has died, a fatality of wars in the modern style. It is scarcely believable that the saying could once have been persuasive. Yet it had a logic of a kind. Every man must die. What better death could there be than to offer his life for a cause? His country represented such a cause.

Christian faith could never entirely accept such pagan romanticism. The Christian might love his country, yet in Abraham Lincoln's words his allegiance was to "this nation under God." Loyalty to God meant a qualified, though real, loyalty to country.

In a long history Christians have taken diverse attitudes toward war. Sometimes, with appeals to Old Testament precedent, they have fought holy wars in the name of God, their religious beliefs adding intensity to their fanaticism against enemies—as though the prophets and Christ had not transformed that ethic by an awareness of love and forgiveness. Sometimes, appealing to the Sermon on the Mount, they have refused any participation in war or the machinations of the international politics of power. Most often, they have regarded war as sometimes a tragic necessity, justifiable if fought with conscientious restraints to repel a conqueror or resist an intolerable wrong. Such was the reasoning that produced the classic doctrine of the just (or justifiable) war. Taking account of characteristic human prejudices and perceptions, it should not be surprising that most people in most wars, including opponents on both sides of most conflicts, should think their own cause justifiable. The erroneous use of a belief does not *necessarily* discredit the belief itself, but it is a warning to believers.

War in our time might be seen as a tale of two generations. The generation of youth who fought World War II grew up in an ethos of peace; they had to learn that peace may be a rationalization of the comfort and irresponsibility of the uncommitted. The generation of their children grew up in a world that took war for granted; they learned that war can be "the arrogance of power" and the hypocritical betrayal of the idealism it claims to serve. It is possible that both generations learned something true. Certainly it is desirable that they communicate to each other what they experienced.

The earlier generation made its crusade for peace. Not all youth participated, of course; some were hostile and some were indifferent. But the most articulate of youth raised their voices for international concord. They hailed the Kellogg-

Briand Peace Pact of 1928 by which the world's leading nations renounced war "as an instrument of national policy." Since the treaty did not silence threats of war, college youth went further. They organized the Veterans of Future Wars—a parody on conventional veterans' organizations, demanding a prewar rather than postwar bonus, thereby satirizing the whole politics of militarism. In 1937 half a million American students took part in a campus "strike against war," and many signed pledges never to support any war declared by the United States government. The Princeton graduating class of 1939 voted, 247 to 141, their refusal to fight any war on foreign soil.

That generation watched the rise of Hitler, first with unbelief, then with sickening awareness of the age-old "mystery of iniquity," now so contemporary. Many who had pledged themselves to peace marched off to war. They uttered none of the rhetoric of World War I about "a war to end wars." The wiser among them made no claims to perfection for their own cause. As Albert Camus put it, they resolved to fight the lies of others with their half truths. They made choices when no choice was entirely right; they sought some cleansing of the world's filth with no expectation of keeping themselves entirely clean. Some of them entered war with a prayer of repentance for their participation in the sins of a world that made war the best choice they could see. Grim though war was, it appeared to them better than standing by while fierce aggressors conquered ill-prepared nations, exterminated Jews, and indoctrinated children with poisonous ideology.

That generation won its war resoundingly—in whatever sense wars are ever won—but had little success in maintaining a peaceable world. As years went by, it encountered its own children in a new peace movement. Again not all youth demonstrated for peace; again, some were hostile and some were indifferent. But again it was the most idealistic and articulate who rejected war. Some of the once-young saw in the new young a reincarnation of their own high resolves. But they saw also differences—three major differences.

First, war had a new fury. It started with the saturation bombings of cities, mounted to a new scale of destruction with the invention of the atomic bomb, then dwarfed that with thermonuclear weapons that could devastate buildings and people and, even in controlled tests, poison land, air, and sea. The old analogies that had made some sense out of war became more and more strained. There had been a real logic, persuasive to anyone except the moral absolutist, in the claim that there was moral justification in inflicting death upon a warrior and thereby preventing him from killing others. Large-scale warfare always stretched the analogy; the possibility of thermonuclear warfare in an age of overkill—an age when each major power could destroy the other several times over—made the analogy break. If war had sometimes been the lesser of two evils, no one knew how to describe the evil greater than mutual annihilation with uncontrolled consequences of radioactive fallout spreading destruction on peoples far from the fighting.

Second, war became endemic as never before in American history. It is not necessary to maintain the old illusion that war has been rare in American history. Even so, the nation conceived both World Wars as irrational intrusions upon its life. The eager hope of soldiers in both those wars was to get the fighting finished and go home. The American experience in both those wars was, by later standards, short. But today's youth have lived in a constant atmosphere of war. They were born in a world of "cold war," sometimes alleviated but never entirely ended. In early childhood they heard of war in Korea. They grew to see war in Vietnam enter its second decade. The military draft, once an emergency measure, became an intrenched part of a way of life. A great General, turned President of the United States, warned against the domination of a military-industrial complex. Youth heard and agreed.

The third change complicated everything. Despite the widespread rejection of war, the youthful generation rarely cultivated the consistent pacifism of many in the earlier generation. There were, to be sure, impulsive advocates of "flower power" and some individuals and groups who simply "checked out" of the whole world of political conflict and economic competition. What was missing was a widespread movement committed to persuading a nation that war was obsolete. One reason was the frustration many youth felt in trying to find effective political levers and handles. But more important was the awareness of the role of power in the life of every society. Critics of American militarism might justify the use of violence by black militants. Had not history taught the black community that the only defense against oppressive power was the use of counter-power? Occasionally representatives of the New Left used the rhetoric of revolution and guerrilla warfare in romantic ways—sometimes with little awareness of the brutality of real guerrillas. Their logic was a faint echo of traditional Marxism with its rejection of international war and its advocacy of revolution. But the New Left was rarely guided by rigid doctrine or comprehensive theory. It was more frequently moved by a spontaneous revulsion against national policies that led to war and an equally strong objection to injustices that might justify violence.

The result was less a moral system than a moral sensitivity. Young men had great difficulty explaining themselves to draft boards. The law required a conscientious objector to base his stand on "religious training and belief." Then the Supreme

Court liberalized the interpretation of the law to include any fundamental ethical conviction that had the force of religion for the believer. Still Selective Service officials expected the conscientious objector to appeal to some system of belief. Often he could not produce the system. But he could testify to his own conscience. Perhaps in a world of "incongruity" that impressed even a militant General, systems of belief could not encompass the bewildering reality. If so, the lack of system did not negate the belief.

But belief and protest had to assert themselves in a world where madness often reigned. It was the madness of a nation unable to maintain peace and health in its own cities, yet trying to supervise far corners of the world; the madness of a military method that dumped more explosives on a small agrarian land than it had rained on all Europe during World War II; the madness of a war that in many a week killed more allies than enemies. What logic, rhetoric, or art could address itself to such madness? Cinematic art gave one answer. Prior to World War II, cinema might make a somber protest against the horror of war, as in *All Quiet on the Western Front*, based on Erich Maria Remarque's novel by the same title. Or it might make the comic protest of Charlie Chaplin's *Shoulder Arms*, where innocent slapstick confounded all military cleverness. Or it might turn the whole business into sheer spoof, as in Buster Keaton's *The General*.

But no such movies followed World War II. True, there were early attempts at realistic portrayals of war with some affirmation of meaning. But as the insane nature of war burned its mark into human consciousness, the films that protested it did so by mimicking the insanity of war. So people laughed and gasped at the bizarre humor of *Dr. Strangelove*, *M*A*S*H*, and *Catch-22*; or they shuddered at the surrealistic trauma of *Johnny Got His Gun*.

191

All this was remote from the relative innocence of an earlier day. That innocence had always had its moral perplexities. General Omar Bradley, one of America's foremost troop commanders, puzzled over them. The son of a widow who supported him through high school, he was wondering where he would find money for college when his Sunday school superintendent suggested that he go to West Point, where there were no fees. From West Point he went to successive army commands, until he directed the American 12th Army Group. He was known as a humane general, "the G.I.'s General" as Ernie Pyle called him. He could say that "compassion is the measure" of command, that no man untormented by the ordeals of troops is fit to command. Yet by the cruel logic of combat, he had to declare that "war has neither the time nor heart to concern itself with the individual and the dignity of man." To prepare for the breakout of Normandy, he ordered the saturation bombing of the St. Lo carpet without warning to civilians, conscious of "the slaughter of innocents" involved. He saw that war had "little room for the niceties of justice," that it was "a wretched debasement of all the thin pretensions of civilization." All that he could see and say, yet fight on. Only those who fail to recognize the tragedy and agony of moral conflict can look superciliously at the warrior who recognizes that tragedy, yet does his duty as he sees it.

Bradley still belonged in the age of relative innocence. War was then only beginning to reveal itself in the madness the next generation was to know. The later generation, too, was to struggle with moral agonies—agonies so painful that many in it would resort to short-cuts and simplistic moral judgments either endorsing or rejecting all armed force without facing the consequences of their judgments.

In this latter-day world every responsible person—those

who rushed to judgments and those who hesitated to act on any judgments—faced the same question: how do persons act sensibly in an apparently senseless world, how act rationallly in an incomprehensible era, how act morally in demonic conflicts? Those are the questions of conscience in our history.

2. THE MYSTIC CHORDS
OF MEMORY

"The mystic chords of memory, stretching from every battle-field and patriot grave to every living heart and hearthstone all over this broad land, will yet swell the chorus of the Union when again touched, as surely they will be, by the better angels of our nature."
Abraham Lincoln in his First Inaugural Address.

Our age is likely to find Lincoln's language strange, even embarrassing. We rightly are suspicious of sentimentality. Not so rightly, perhaps, we are better at debunking than at commemorating the past. Patriot graves are as remote as hearthstones from our metropolitan consciousness. Yet, I must confess, the mystic chords of memory have been vibrating for me, touched by contemporary persons and events. War today persistently inflicts its presence upon mankind; for some that means the awakening of memories. If nostalgia is the worst of moods for anticipating the future in our world of momentous change, nevertheless memory may become a source of understanding and strength.

✷   ✷   ✷   ✷   ✷

On February 9, 1968, I crossed upper Manhattan from my West Side home to East Harlem. There at the Church of the Ascension, part of the East Harlem Protestant Parish, I went to the memorial service of a young man, killed in action in Vietnam. Inside the door I embraced and kissed his widow of a few months. She had more gallantry and composure than I that day. I was asking myself what responsibility I had for her husband's death.

194

Many months before, in the summer of 1966, Russ Flesher had come to see me for our only meeting and conversation. He was an attractive young man, a graduate of Wooster College, a theological student on intern year. Although white, he found his church home in the multiracial East Harlem Protestant Parish. He held an R.O.T.C. commission—second lieutenant, I think—and he wanted to talk to me about going on active duty.

As a theological student he disbelieved in the legal provision that exempts from the draft ministers and students preparing for the ministry. Many theological students resent that law: if it spares them the burden of their compatriots, it also denies them the privilege of making a profound decision. It seems to say that ministry is a privileged status rather than the calling of a servant who shares the responsibilities of his fellowmen. Russ Flesher was troubled by this situation and uninclined to accept the sanctuary that Congress and the President, by due process of law, had ordained for him.

A friend had told Russ Flesher that, in a similar situation long before, I had chosen to become a soldier. He wanted to bounce his ideas off me. Yes, I answered him, I had once left theological studies to learn the skills of an infantryman and to fight a war. No, I had not had any dramatic yearning for combat. But some of my closest friends, ardent pacifists, had gone to prison rather than cooperate with the Selective Service Act even to the extent of registering for the draft and claiming the status either of divinity students or of conscientious objectors. They made me aware that I, who disagreed with them, had a comparable responsibility to act on the basis of my convictions. Rarely do any of us really accept the cost of our beliefs; but times come—and no man can prescribe for another when such a time has come—that demand accountability.

195

I was giving him no new ideas; he had already gone through all that reasoning. But I was not persuaded that this was the time or the act for him. We exchanged opinions about the war in Vietnam and found that we disagreed. Resistance to the war was not yet the *cause célèbre* that it was soon to become on university campuses. He gave a sober and reasoned argument as to why he thought our nation had a military responsibility in Indochina. I told him, as I had already publicly written and said, that I thought we were making a grave mistake there. But we did not argue long, and neither of us questioned the good faith of the other. His real concern was not enthusiasm for war but a conviction that he should not be spared the ordeal of his generation.

So we talked further, and I gradually guessed that he was in fact about to decide to enter on active duty. Perhaps I could and should have done more to dissuade him of his judgment about the war. But granted the honesty of his judgment, I could not reject his conviction to act. I cannot remember many of our exact words, but I do remember that, almost at the end of our conversation, I told him that I was convinced of his integrity and would honor whatever decision he made. And I said that if I were ever to hear word of his death in battle and were to suspect that our conversation had led to it, I would shed a tear. His reply was light and undramatic, and he left. I sat and wondered for a while.

I did not get to Russ Flesher's wedding. Occasionally I saw his bride and she gave me news of him. She told me of one of his letters from Vietnam. Then came the night when the phone interrupted a conversation with guests in my living room to say that Russ had died. A few days later a congregation gathered in East Harlem to celebrate his life.

People came from far and wide through streets piled high with trash because of a famous strike of New York's sanita-

tion workers. Among them were some seminarians who in
the previous autumn had turned in their draft cards as a protest against war. But most of the congregation were people
of East Harlem, especially young people among whom Russ
had worked. The mimeographed order of worship said on
the cover:

CELEBRATION OF PEACE

in

Time of War

for Russ and all of us

February 9, 1968

Turning the page the worshipers read the words:

> We gather as men must to seek meaning in the midst
> of confusion, to affirm life in the encounter with death,
> and to witness to a peace which passes understanding
> and yet gives purpose and confidence to our lives. May
> each one of us participate fully and personally in this
> hour of celebration.

In unison we prayed:

> God, open us to affirm life and death in such a way
> that we can really be present to each other now. Help
> us to trust you enough to become vulnerable to change
> in ourselves—as we hear it in our own voices and as
> we see it in each other's eyes. Push us to use all our
> senses to experience this event and to be not afraid
> for Christ's sake and our own. Amen.

In the impressive informality of worship in the East Harlem Protestant Parish, anyone who had known Russ was invited to stand and say what was in his heart. Person after person did. I felt compelled to tell of my talk with him, although I could not maintain dry eyes or a steady voice. But the most impressive statements came from the boys and girls who told how they had loved him. Then one of the pastors, George "Bill" Webber, led us as we celebrated the Holy Communion. The service ended with the "passing of the peace" and a prayer of thanksgiving.

* * * * *

More than any other single event, the death of Russ Flesher, a man whom I saw only once, stirred thoughts and emotions that united past and present to shape my ponderings over the future. But before and after that were other events, major and trivial.

There was, among the more important, a trip that was almost a pilgrimage back to Luxembourg in the summer of 1962. With my wife I drove northward from the capital city into the terrain that I had once known so well. We stopped at the Hotel Meyer, where I had been besieged, and found it in good repair—a quiet resort hotel off the main tourist tracks. I introduced us both and apologized to the owner for the damage I had once contributed to the hotel by making it a target for explosives and fire. In response he insisted that we be his guests for dinner. Today the hotel has a picture book about America and President Kennedy as a souvenir from me. We drove on to the battlefields where once I had raced, crawled, and clawed myself as deep into the ground as I could. I blessed nature for the healing powers that had removed the marks of war from woods and soil. We visited the home in the tiny village of Kehlen where I had once been

billeted—the friendly home where I had known two generations and where now there were three.

Then we went to the great military cemetery at Hamm
near Luxembourg City. I looked out on the thousands of
crosses, knowing not how many marked graves of friends.
My wife with a wise intuition walked off and left me alone
for awhile. It would be trite and untrue to say that I cried
like a baby. I cried, more than I could ever remember crying
before, but like a man with overpowering memories. I asked
myself, as so often before, why that war had been and why
wars continue to be.

* * * * *

Army clothes wear well, and I still have a few. I keep
them, not as mementoes, but because they are warm and
durable for the outdoor winter days that are rare in my life
and because—as my family teasingly tells me—I don't like
to discard old clothes. I take a petty pride in my ability to
get into those clothes, although I grant that there is a little
strain in fastening the waist button on the trousers. Only
one item of that clothing has any sentimental meaning: the
boots. They are the boots that I wore to Europe, wore in
England and France, wore in battle and in 600 miles of
marching as a prisoner, then wore in a few months more of
military duty in this country. They are good and comfortable
boots. Until not so long ago I wore them frequently on days
in the country. The soles are still sound, but one little hole
in the uppers has made them unhandy to wear in dust or
mud. So now I have a new pair of boots. On rare occasions,
when the new boots get soaked, I put on the old ones.

Pulling on those boots normally has no more military
meaning than the custom of shaking right hands, which once
was the assurance that no weapon was concealed in the

fighting hand. These are pragmatic boots, especially those durable soles. But once in a long while the boots remind that I was a warrior. Then I wonder (since my children are daughters) whether my sons-in-law and grandsons will be warriors.

* * * * *

In days not long past the professorial life was often known as an ivory-tower existence. In more recent years campuses have sometimes been battlefields, but their militancy has usually been directed against the military establishment. In either case the life of the theologian was likely to be remote from the armed forces. Yet from time to time my career has led me back to army posts. Occasionally I have visited the Army Chaplains' School. In programs arranged by the Chief of Chaplains, I have gone to a number of army camps to counsel with chaplains, line officers, and NCO's on problems of the young soldier. Once or twice I have lectured to an R.O.T.C. class at a state university.

Any man out of his normal milieu is likely to grasp at anything, however trivial, that assures him of a little status and security. So on such occasions I have found one kind of status in the memory that I was once a troop commander and another kind of status in the memory that before that I was a trainee and a private. With the memory has come again the question: how is that former life related to this present life? How is the commitment that once led me into war related to the commitment of faith to seek peace?

* * * * *

In 1969 duties in the Middle East provided the occasion for travel with my wife. In Athens I climbed the slippery rocks of Mars Hill—the hill of the God of War—from which the

Apostle Paul once told the Athenians of the Unknown God and of Christ and his resurrection. I looked in one direction to the nearby Acropolis—the word means fortress—with its Parthenon and other buildings honoring the Greek gods and goddesses and recalling their wars. In the other direction I looked out over the agora where Socrates, both a soldier and philosopher, often talked with his friends and argued with the foes who decreed his death.

We went on to Mycenae, where Schliemann's excavations vindicated much of the historical detail of Homer's *Iliad* and its account of the Trojan wars. There were the ruins of the palace of Agamemnon and his reputed tomb, and we marveled and grieved that so much of human history and epic poetry is the history and poetry of war.

In Lebanon we looked at the cliff at the mouth of the Narh al-Kalb near the Mediterranean Sea. Beginning with Pharaoh Ramses II in the thirteenth century B.C., a series of nineteen conquerors carved on the cliff their pretentious versions of "Kilroy was here." Assyrians, Babylonians, Greeks, Romans and their successors through the centuries made war in that land. The inscriptions communicate less the triumphs they were intended to mark than the futility of man's aggressive pomp and propensity for war. In that valley before that wall the most persuasive words of Scripture are, regrettably, the words of the skeptic in Ecclesiastes: "Vanity of vanities, all is vanity. . . . I have seen everything that is done under the sun; and behold, all is vanity and a striving after wind."

To the south lie Israel and Jerusalem, city of sacred memory for the faiths of Judaism, Christianity, and Islam. These are the faiths that declared that history is not merely vanity, that time is neither unreal nor insignificant, that God is Lord of history and leads it according to his purposes. Every acre of Jerusalem tells of that faith. Yet what does that faith make of Jerusalem, the city whose name combines the words for vision and peace, the city that has been besieged thirty-eight times since David took Mount Zion from the Jebusites, the city over which armies threaten to fight again today and tomorrow? Jerusalem evokes wonder and prayer. But what does the history of war, so overpoweringly evident in all ancient lands and so poignantly characteristic of this biblical land, say about the humanity that prays and the God to whom men pray?

* * * * *

Upon my first return home from war, I marveled every night at the sheer luxury and comfort of a bed with springs and mattress. To lie on that bed in a friendly home with a roof overhead—never interrupting sleep to inspect the guard and never worrying about attack—seemed incredibly good. I made no vows, but the thought occurred to me that I could never again go to bed without a silent prayer of thanksgiving for such a privilege. Often, of course, I have quite forgotten that thought. Man, said Dostoevsky, is "the ungrateful biped," and I can go to bed as matter-of-factly as anybody else. Yet frequently that thought recurs. Perhaps half the time—more or less—I remember it and make that prayer.

* * * * *

The movie *Patton* lured me to see it. I never knew or saw General Patton, but I often lived with his legend. The initial cadres of the Ninth Armored Division, to which I was assigned at its activation, included many officers and NCO's who had served under him. We maneuvered at the California Desert Training Center that he instigated. The film portrays Patton as an enigmatic warrior. It represents him as saying, "God, how I hate the twentieth century." Its German intelligence officer Steiger calls him "a sixteenth century man," "a magnificent anachronism."

The film is itself an anachronism in its accents on the dramatic quality of war. The National Board of Review of Motion Pictures named it the best film of 1970 and it won seven Academy Awards. One must guess that the voters were middle-aged and elderly. Young people, for the most part, were unimpressed with the movie. It was significant to me, because it depicted history I had lived through.

A few weeks after seeing the film in New York, I saw the display advertisements for it in Nairobi, Kenya. I was taken aback. Black Africa had made me sensitive to the image of America in that dynamic continent. I wondered what Kenyans made of the film. I rather hoped that not many saw it. But there could be little doubt that thousands saw the ads spread through the city. Unlike the New York ads, these carried in large type a quotation from one of Patton's speeches in the film: "No bastard ever won a war by dying for his country. He won it by making the other poor dumb bastard die for his country." Did that symbolize the U.S.A. to Kenyans?

As jolting as the film was a long news report in the *East African Standard* for August 26, 1970. It suggested that the film influenced President Nixon's decision to invade Cambodia. Twice, said the dispatch, the President saw the film; a third time he requested a copy, but apparently did not view it. He commended its portrayal of leadership to forty-five business and financial leaders at a meeting in the White House. Although he was a bit nervous about its profanity, he admired its representation of decisive leadership. I recalled a saying about straining at a gnat and swallowing a camel. My impression had been that the film showed Patton as a man of military genius but a diplomatic fool. Then I remembered that a few people in the theater had evidently taken it differently. Perhaps the President was better in tune with them than I.

The film, I recognized, was in some ways a real work of art. It exaggerated the dramatic spectacle that war can be, but the spectacle sometimes is unquestionably there. I remembered the magnificence of the Flying Fortresses just before their bombs hit us on the edge of Nürnberg. The film showed both the gallantry and the brutality of war. I wondered why mankind found it so difficult to separate its own inherent gallantry from its brutality.

* * * * *

There are friends from wartime, comrades in arms now scattered over the country. Our paths rarely cross, and we seldom write. But now and then, mainly at Christmastime, we renew old ties. From Providence, Rhode Island; from Nazareth, Pennsylvania; from Wichita, Kansas; from North Fork, California; from army posts in the United States or overseas come occasional greetings and messages. Most important of them are those from Harmony, Minnesota, where one of my former platoon leaders is the proud father of a college youth who is a conscientious objector to war.

* * * * *

Many other events, shared with the entire American public, call attention to war past and present. One day it may be a secretary's troubled comment about a brother in Vietnam, another day a student's report of his place in the draft lottery. For a time the newspapers, week by week, were commemorating twenty-fifth anniversaries—of Pearl Harbor, of D-Day, of the Battle of the Bulge, of V-E Day, of V-J Day. From time to time they have carried stories, often poignant ones, of prisoners of war—some years ago the prisoners in Korea, then those in Vietnam. Every day they tell of hostilities and combat somewhere.

If some of these pages give the impression that I live in the past, I think that is mistaken. On most days I don't think of World War II. Most of my friends don't know that I fought in it. I told the truth in the Foreword when I said that in twenty-five years I never reread my own war memoirs. It was some students, questioning me in my home one night, who sent me back to them. I was startled at some of the things I found, reminded of events I had totally forgotten, driven to bring a new perspective to some of the current questions on my mind, led eventually to this act of writing.

War will not let us forget it. For the most part it is good that we not forget it. But the reminders of war are not always to our gain. They may embitter us, frighten us, deaden our human sensitivities. But not necessarily. The mystic chords of memory may swell a chorus of courage and hope for mankind.

3. FIVE PATRIOTS

"Civil courage . . . can only grow out of the free responsibility of free men." Dietrich Bonhoeffer, 1942.

The mails of autumn, 1968, carried some correspondence with the Post Commander at Fort Dix, New Jersey—Major General Kenneth W. Collins. In the days when he commanded a battalion in the Bulge, most of us expected that he would someday be a General, if war did not destroy his life or health. He had the competence and confidence of a military leader—the kind that soldiers can trust in battle.

Now he was playing host to a reunion of the old gang. I sent a note of regret—genuine regret—and greeting, because I had long before made a promise to be on the West Coast that weekend. Thinking of the rebellion at Columbia University the past spring, I wrote: "As a veteran of the Battle of Morningside Heights, I'd like to chew the rag with you and learn whether college-age soldiers are anything like the college and university students these days. If so, I wonder how you handle them. If not, I wonder why."

His reply was cordial. He went out of his way to send a set of photographs of the occasion, showing old friends quite recognizable despite changing hairlines and waistlines. Then he added his reply to my afterthought: "Strange as it may seem, we have little difficulty motivating the young men here to serve their country. Unfortunately, the few who do not want to serve get most of the publicity, while the great majority who are loyal, patriotic soldiers doing an outstanding job receive little or no attention."

Not many weeks thereafter, the youthful peace movement reached Fort Dix, and the press reported a number of disturbances in and around the post. The General evidently handled them rather well. By two years later reports from Vietnam told of soldiers who grew skilled in avoiding battle and of some who disobeyed orders to fight. Among them, I have little doubt, were irresponsible men, as there are among any sampling of humanity. But I suspect that they included some "loyal, patriotic soldiers," frustrated by a war that could not evoke their commitments. Certainly among the resisters to war whom I have known in the United States were men whose "civil courage" grew out of "the free responsibility of free men."

Believing that patriotism is not alien to civil courage, I have always wanted to support men whose careful judgment led them to conscientious dissent against national policies, including war. For many years, partly because I had a military record and was less vulnerable to popular attack than some of my colleagues, I sought to help conscientious objectors, even though I disagreed with their pacifism. In the past I could usually take for granted that the conscientious objector was a pacifist, a man who simply found war morally abhorrent and could not, in integrity, fight. The law of the land is written on that assumption; it recognizes only the conscientious objector who is "conscientiously opposed to participation in war in any form." That law, as it has been implemented through administrative procedures, grants no standing to the many young men who, while they might find some wars justifiable, are conscientiously unable to enter into the only war they are called to fight.

That has meant for many youths an irreconcilable conflict between conscience and the state. For some Christians it has been a conflict between Christ and Caesar. The church could not ignore the issue. So with a few friends I undertook a puny crusade. (I say that autobiographically, with no implication that mine was the first or most important voice to raise the question.)

In the religious press, in a sermon widely distributed by the National Student Christian Federation, in a telecast (NBC, April 17, 1966) I tried to make the case. As a representative of the Council for Christian Social Action of the United Church of Christ, I went to Washington on April 14, 1967, in an effort to persuade the Senate Armed Services Committee, in its revisions of the Selective Service Law, to broaden the provisions for conscientous objectors. The committee was far more interested in the testimony, the preceding day, of General Mark Clark, who thought the provisions should be narrowed. To me the logic of "selective conscientious objection" was utterly lucid. Certainly *nobody* of Christian or humane conscience could favor *all* causes in *all* wars. Hence it followed that a responsible person—unless he was a total pacifist—was morally obliged to distinguish between those wars which he could conscientiously support and those he could not. Anything less than that was moral nihilism.

That the legal changes implied would be administratively difficult was obvious. But Great Britain had given some evidences that they were not impossible. More important, the devotion of a nation to freedom meets its test not when freedom is easy to institutionalize but when the difficulties are grave.

In the course of discussions on the issue I found that some members of the German church had given the question more thought than any Americans. They included men of deep faith and judicial experience, men who were not pacifists but who were aghast at the frailty of conscientious protest against Hitler in their own nation's past. To them the real test of any legal protection for conscientious objectors was its provision for the conscience of the objector to particular wars. Elsewhere in the world other people were coming to the same conclusion. Gradually a few Christian denominations in the United States, the National Council of Churches, and the World Council of Churches took their stands. The American Civil Liberties Union decided to take up the cause as an issue of constitutional freedom.

To me the issue of selective conscientious objection was not simply a tactic in opposition to the war in Vietnam. Hence I became suspect to some of the doves, as I had already become suspect to the hawks, because I seemed to be more concerned for persons of integrity than for causes. I believe that causes are momentously important, never more so than today. But integrity can never be made subsidiary to causes. Integrity is never in such abundance that it can be taken casually. Hence, while I have poured some energy into causes, I have admired persons of varied convictions.

I think of five—I could double or triple the number—young men of integrity who have set their resolves against the war they were called to support. I see no less reason to call them patriots than to call Russ Flesher the same.

DALE E. NOYD

On March 6, 1968, I met Captain Dale E. Noyd at Cannon Air Force Base in New Mexico, where I had gone for his court martial. He was already a figure of some national reputation because, from the heart of the Air Force establishment, he had declared his conscientious objection to the war in Vietnam.

Superficially Dale Noyd was the type of the all-American boy who makes a superb military pilot. On the basis of outstanding performance in the R.O.T.C. at the University of Washington he was offered a regular commission in the Air Force. His comrades testified that he was an exceptional flying officer, on one occasion incurring great personal risk to save a disabled plane after he had been authorized to bail out. As part of his military career he undertook three years of graduate study in psychology at the University of Michigan, leading to an appointment to teach psychology at the Air Force Academy. There students and peers recognized him as a superior teacher.

Noyd had left far behind his thin and conventional childhood Protestantism. But as he read widely and deeply, he came under the influence of several great thinkers, most notably Albert Camus and Paul Tillich. He wrote of himself, "Increasingly I find myself in the position of being highly involved and *caring* about many moral, political and social issues—of which the war in Viet Nam is the most important." In a conflict between his convictions and his duties, he declared that his "faith and ultimate loyalty" forbade him to fight in Vietnam, although he was willing to fight in defense of his country. The Senior Protestant Chaplain at the Air Force Academy wrote: "There is absolutely no doubt in my mind but that this officer is completely honest and sincere in taking the action which he has taken. He is deeply concerned with his own integrity and that of the nation."

Dale Noyd's course of action was to take the two steps available. One was to offer his resignation "for the good of the Air Force." The other was to ask recognition as a conscientious objector. Both were denied. Noyd sought help through the federal courts, which refused to accept jurisdiction until he had exhausted all military possibilities. The

Supreme Court refused to intervene after Solicitor General Thurgood Marshall submitted a memorandum stating that "we know of no case where it has ever been suggested that objection to a specific war rather than to war generally qualifies a man as a conscientious objector."

Events moved on to the place where the only possibility was a direct refusal to obey a military order. The point came when Captain Noyd was assigned to the training of fighter pilots. This was not itself an act of warfare, but it was a clear and direct contribution to the war. Both he and his superior officers understood the issue when he "respectfully refused" on grounds of conscience a direct order to instruct a student pilot.

The American Civil Liberties Union offered help in the case. Three of its attorneys (Executive Director John de J. Pemberton and Marvin and Rhoda Karpatkin) worked with the legal counsel assigned by the Air Force. When Jack Pemberton asked me to testify at the trial, I was nonplussed, since I had not even met Noyd. He explained that my role would be that of an "expert" witness. I found that amusing. Socrates had long before persuaded me that there are no experts on ultimate questions, that the greatest human wisdom lies in knowing that one is not wise. Hebrew prophecy had convinced me that there are no experts on the ways of God. But an experienced lawyer convinced me that I qualified as an "expert" scholar in areas of theology and of moral and political philosophy. I studied the records of the case and found them filled with issues on which I had done thinking and research. So I agreed.

But the Trial Officer did not permit me to testify. He rigorously excluded from the trial any discussion of issues of religion, ethics, or constitutional law. In an amusing moment he refused Attorney Pemberton's effort to submit in evidence copies of Paul Tillich's *Courage to Be*. The impressive statements of Noyd's fellow officers, including those who had fought in Vietnam and who rejected his position, were allowed as testimony of character witnesses, but any discussion of the merits of his case beyond the limitations of regulations was excluded.

It was, therefore, no surprise that Noyd was found guilty and sentenced to dismissal from the service and a year of prison. The sentence was not vindictive; civil courts were frequently giving sentences of three years for resistance to the draft. As a result of legal processes during the consequent appeal, the limitations on Noyd's freedom were relatively trivial, and he was soon able to accept a teaching appointment at Earlham College.

Symbolically the court martial brought a clash between irreconcilable moral convictions. On the one side was the whole military system with its reliance on discipline. Under interrogation the President of the Court, a combat veteran with rank of Colonel, said: "Anyone in the Air Force should do what is required of him." Perhaps it is impossible to have an Air Force unless some such belief is almost axiomatic. On the other side was the dignity of the person which requires that nobody can ever surrender to any system ultimate responsibility for his own decisions. I expect that conflict to continue. I see no reason to think that it will ever be ideally resolved in human history. The ultimate naïveté of morality is to expect that mankind can avoid hard decisions and tragic conflicts. But, I am convinced, short of ultimate answers we can do much better than we are now doing.

In one way I found myself reluctantly agreeing with the Trial Officer in the court martial. When I thought through the meaning of his rulings, I realized that I did not really want courts martial to make fundamental decisions on constitutional law. They had no qualification to do the work of the Supreme Court. But, with Dale Noyd and his friends, I was frustrated at a system that kept bouncing the ball of responsibility elsewhere—federal courts shifting the trial to military courts and military courts refusing to face basic issues.

Eventually the issue of conscientious objection to specific wars reached the Supreme Court. In the cases of *Gillette* v. *United States* and *Negre* v. *Larsen* the Court ruled by an eight-to-one decision (March 8, 1971) that the Selective Service Act, in disallowing selective conscientious objection, is constitutional. This means that under present law the man whose conscience forbids him to fight in *some* wars has no legal standing. In the later case overruling the conviction of Muhammad Ali (June 28, 1971) the Court may have seemed to open by a bare crack the door that it closed on March 8, inasmuch as Ali did not take his stand as a total pacifist; but that almost certainly was not the intent of the Court. Congress still has the right to revise and extend the legal definition of conscientious objection. Thus far Congress has shown no inclination to do so. But if ever persuaded that the American people want greater protection for conscience, Congress will probably act.

ROBERT E. PRICE

On July 1, 1968, a gathering of people, mostly young but of various ages, assembled for worship in St. Paul's Chapel of Columbia University at 5:30 A.M. Most of them had at various times in the past months worshiped at one or another services at the same early hour. The time of day was dictated by no ascetic discipline, certainly by no youthful inclination, since contemporary students in general do not love the early-to-bed, early-to-rise philosophy. The predawn schedule was due solely to the time schedule arranged by the Selective Service System for induction into the armed services.

On this occasion the Rev. Robert E. Price, theological student and Methodist minister, had invited his friends to worship with him before he reported to the Armed Forces Induction Station as directed, in order to refuse induction, contrary to direction. He was one of a company of theological students with whose destinies I felt entwined, but rather than summarize many stories, I am here saying something about the group and a little more about one member of it.

During the preceding autumn young men all over the country had considered possible ways of expressing their opposition to the war. In a democratic society citizens can often register and further their convictions through the ballot. But many draftable men were too young to vote. Furthermore, many thought that the nation, in electing President Lyndon Johnson over Barry Goldwater, had registered its desire for peace. So, as American involvement in Vietnam became more intense, they felt betrayed.

The autumn discussions culminated in a series of demonstrations throughout the nation on October 16, when men returned their draft cards to federal authorities as a symbol of their resistance to the military system. In the educational community I know best, Union Theological Seminary, twenty-seven men joined in this act. Not everyone in the community endorsed this tactic; in fact, those who did turn in their draft cards were a small minority. But everyone respected the integrity of those who chose so to act. I think it is fair to say that as the months went on and frustrations mounted, an increasing number agreed with this action.

The Faculty of the Seminary included many shades of opinion about the war and about methods of expression. It took notice of the act of the resisters, saying that while they might be disobeying the law, they might equally be said to be challenging the legality of governmental acts. It continued: "We can affirm, on the basis of our knowledge of and our conversations with our students who are resisting the draft, that they are acting with thoughtfulness, integrity, and willingness to accept the cost of their convictions. We are convinced of the patriotism and the concern for humanity of these men."

After noting that other students in the school were making different decisions, the statement went on: "War imposes special burdens and hazards on youth. We respect our students who are reminding us of the cost of courage and compassion. We seek ways of supporting them, of identifying with them in their moral sensitivity, of helping to bear the burdens they carry, including the financial cost of legal defense. We regard them as valued members of this community, and we will continue to do so if they are separated from us by acts of the government. We trust that in our present experiences, both those which we share and those which must be unique to each of us, we can all discover in greater depth the meaning of responsible citizenship and of Christian faith."

The characteristic response of the Selective Service System in those days was to advise local boards to reclassify men who had returned their draft cards and to call them for induction. Bureaucratic wheels move at various speeds, usually slowly, and nothing happened immediately. Throughout the months one after another of the men received notices to report for induction. Usually our students arranged for the actual reporting to be shifted from local centers in their hometowns to New York. On the appointed day the young man invited his friends to share with him in early morning worship, then went downtown to the designated Selected Service center to refuse induction. Arrest followed, usually with release on the man's own recognizance pending trial.

In the case of Bob Price a special flurry took place between his initial act of resistance and his order to report. He was a graduate of Columbia University, and during his theological studies he worked on the staff of Earl Hall, the center for student religious activities. One morning *The New York Times* disclosed that the Rev. Robert Price, himself a draft resister, was acting as a draft counselor at Columbia. For some people his resistance automatically disqualified him as a draft counselor. Others pointed out that the country is full of draft counselors—some of them war veterans, some of them men liable to the draft, and some of them opposed to the draft.

At the early morning act of worship on July 1, Bob Price had asked several of his friends to share in the service. Some of his contemporaries took part. At his request I commented briefly on a part of Jeremiah 8—the passage including the prophet's complaint against those who say " 'Peace, peace,' when there is no peace." Paul Lehmann, distinguished theologian, commented on the New Testament episode in which Jesus urged men, "Render therefore to Caesar the things that are Caesar's, and to God the things that are God's." John Bennett, a seminary president and leader in many a cause of social justice and peace, led the prayers.

Then Bob Price told us briefly and simply why he was refusing induction. In his explanation he said, "My action is consistent with what I consider to be the best Christian tradition and the purest American patriotism."

The service closed with a benediction by Daniel Berrigan, S.J. Father Dan—priest, poet, activist—later become the subject of the dramatic documentary, *Father Dan Berrigan: the Holy Outlaw*, produced on National Educational Television and elsewhere. He was convicted in court for joining with others to burn draft files in Catonsville, Maryland. Rather than acquiesce, he became for four months a fugitive, dramatizing his protest by occasional public appearances and disappearances. As I write, he and his brother Philip are in Danbury Prison.

It is always possible that those who resist law lack a due sense of the majesty of law and of the necessity that any citizen adjust his personal impulses to the needs of the civil community. But it is equally possible that law has forfeited its majesty by becoming the tool of injustice.

Can draft resisters be patriots? Bob Price has spoken for himself; he understood his resistance as an act of patriotism. In that early morning worship he asked the congregation to sing with him, "America the Beautiful," the hymn whose final stanza begins, "O beautiful for patriot dream/That sees beyond the years."

Did draft resistance accomplish anything? There are no ways of measuring all the consequences of deeds. But more than three years after the acts of the twenty-seven students I have mentioned, only one has been convicted in court. That one, Vincent McGee, whose actions were held to involve some technical legal violations beyond simple refusal to enter the armed forces, has served time in prison. In none of the other cases was prosecution carried through to conviction and sentence. I doubt that this record is the result simply of clever legal counsel. I think it shows that, despite some evidences to the contrary, acts of conscience have some influence on government in this republic. Furthermore, opposition to war of these and many other young people has unquestionably had an effect, immeasurable but real, on federal policies regarding war.

PAUL E. CASWELL

Roman Catholic religious training and belief made a conscientious objector of Paul E. Caswell, First Lieutenant, United States Marine Corps. As a boy he learned Catholic teachings in Sunday school and a "released time" program related to public education. He attended Holy Cross College and found a deeply religious experience in the Catholic Mass. He earned an M.A. degree in rehabilitation counseling, doing his supervised training in a New Hampshire prison and an industrial school. As a volunteer, he put some of his energies into organizing athletic and recreational activities for young people.

For awhile none of this was inconsistent with his career as a Marine. But the information he learned from wide reading about the war in Vietnam disturbed him. The cost of war came home to him when he was assigned duties as a Casualty Assistance Officer. This meant carrying news to parents that their sons had been killed in war, arranging funerals, acting as pall bearer.

Such experiences led him to close study of the traditional Roman Catholic doctrine of the just war. He sought out his priest, who cautioned him against a rash decision. He did not decide hastily; but going over the criteria of the just war, point by point, he came to the judgment that the war in Vietnam did not fit the definition. However, traditional Catholicism did not normally expect the individual layman to come to his own conclusions on issues like that. So Lt. Caswell looked to contemporary ecclesiastical authority. He found that the American Catholic Bishops had issued a statement from Washington in 1966, saying: "No one is free to evade his personal responsibility by leaving it entirely to others to make moral judgments." Behind that statement were insistent themes of Vatican II and of Pope John XXIII's *Pacem in Terris.*

Caswell came to the firm conviction that he could not participate in combat in Vietnam. He was entirely willing "to serve in the Marine Corps in any capacity" other than waging this war. Eventually he went to Vietnam, not in a combat role; there he was wounded and returned to this country for neurosurgery.

In the interim he entered my life on three occasions. First, after I had carefully studied his record and his statements of his beliefs, he came to visit me and engage in a long conversation. I became convinced of his sincerity and offered to be helpful if I could. Second, I went to the Marine Corps Base at Camp Lejeune, North Carolina, to help interpret Lt. Caswell's beliefs and the moral tradition behind them to a Marine Major, who had been instructed to conduct a hearing that might or might not lead to court martial. I found that the Major had once been a Lutheran theological student, taught by a warm friend of mine. Although that may have helped, nothing in his Lutheranism or in his Marine career prepared him for the specific reasoning of the Catholic Lieutenant. Even so, he was determined to be fair, and he succeeded. Third, with Attorney Marvin Karpatkin of the American Civil Liberties Union, Father (later Congressman) Robert Drinan, and Caswell's legal counsel from the Marine Corps, I visited Secretary of the Navy John Chafee at the Pentagon, in an effort to communicate Lt. Caswell's beliefs. We had been warned that the Secretary could give us only half an hour; he himself prolonged the appointment to an hour and showed a remarkable attentiveness and concern for justice to an individual.

The issues in Lt. Caswell's position show the genuine problems involved in moral decisions and the attempt of the legal system to take account of them. Most moral decisions, certainly in the area of public policy, revolve around two focuses, and therein lies the difficulty.

At the one focus, most people recognize that there are moral convictions, deeply rooted in individual integrity, which the state should be extremely reluctant to overrule. Even on such issues, absolutism is hard to maintain; if a man holds a sacred conviction that the gods command him to commit ritual murder, the state will find it advisable to inhibit his conscience. Hence I talk of extreme reluctance rather than absolute refusal of the state to intervene. Human societies recognize this domain of conscience; a liberal society stakes off areas into which it does not intrude. It is, for example, a terrible thing to command a man to kill, if this violates his conscience in its depths. For this reason our society, despite administrative inconvenience and the outright resentment of some people, acknowledges the status of conscientious objector and spares men, for conscience's sake, duties that are required of others. As statecraft goes, in the hurly-burly of history, this is a fairly imaginative and enlightened policy.

The other focus is that of opinion, based on experience and information and personal advantage. In this area the state overrules private judgments constantly and inevitably. After every national election, close to half the people judge the outcome to be mistaken, but most of them abide by the decision. Probably nobody thinks the tax laws are the best that they could be, and many people think they are downright unjust; but few people refuse on grounds of conscience to pay them. To live in a society is to grant that society some rights of judgment over individuals.

The problem with conscientious objection is that it works itself out around both focuses and their interactions. Except in the rare case of the absolutist, who will not take human life under *any* circumstance, conscientious objection requires some interweaving of fundamental convictions and everyday judgments or opinions. Never has this been more obvious than in the hearing of Lt. Caswell at Camp Lejeune.

The Catholic doctrine of the just war is a moral position, but built into it are some quite practical assessments of a situation. For example, one of its criteria—the one that becomes the critical center of debate in most cases—is known as proportionality. The damage done by the war must not outweigh the good to be achieved. The ethical importance of that is clear: it is immoral to destroy a population in order to punish a thief, or to inflict major cruelties in order to correct minor cruelties. But in warfare there are always confusing estimates of achievement and damage, to say nothing of outright lies. Lt. Caswell could make a case, well-researched from reputable sources, that the war in Vietnam was inflicting terrible damage and doing little good. He was countered by some Marine Corps officers who said that their actual experiences in Vietnam showed them the opposite. At this point, the moral argument tended to become a factual argument. And, it might be argued, the Joint Chiefs of Staff and their intelligence sources are duly designated and well paid to assess such matters of fact. Lt. Caswell might come up with documented evidence they had overlooked; but, his interrogators wanted to know, in what way was this a *moral* judgment?

Yet for Paul Caswell to surrender his judgment under such argument would have been to betray his conscience. He was morally and religiously concerned. Among the many conscientious objectors I have talked with, he was probably the most unabashedly religious. He sincerely used language that for many would be pious pretense: "For me to willfully ignore the question of the justness of the killing in Vietnam would most certainly create a wide chasm between me and God. But I need God's closeness and love more than I need anything else. I need Him to be forgiven and to forgive, I need Him to be strengthened and to give strength, I need Him to be understood and to understand, I need Him to be alive and to bring life—I am His alive and I am His when I have no more life."

I can imagine no statecraft so wise and perfect as to distinguish with precision between those moral judgments that it must sacredly refrain from violating and those opinions that it must expect to override. But I am sure that the wrong answer is to restrict morality to abstract judgments insulated from workaday observation and reasoning, because the critical issues are exactly in those realms where root loyalties meet observable situations. To repeat, I expect no entirely satisfactory answer to this issue. But I do believe that our society, in its respect for conscience, can do better than present institutions are doing.

LEROY BEATY

This time the phone call came from a lawyer in Newark whose name I had never heard—Morton Stavis. Weeks later, as I recall, I learned that he was a successful corporation lawyer, helping to form the Law Center for Constitutional Rights, a coalition to give legal services to protesters, mostly from black and radical causes. It was generally considered somewhat to the left of the American Civil Liberties Union, but ACLU Attorney Marvin Karpatkin (whom I have mentioned twice before and whose judgment I value) gave me a good opinion of Stavis. I knew none of this at the time of the call.

Morton Stavis asked whether I would consider giving some help in the trial of a conscientious objector. Or rather, since he didn't expect an immediate commitment, would I read the papers of a young man and talk with him, in order to judge whether I should become a witness for the defense? Life was pressing on me with many demands, and I had little free time and little desire to start another set of associations in the civil rights movement. Certainly I had no intention of becoming a career witness in courts military or civil. But it seemed rudely callous simply to say no. So, more to delay an answer than for any other reason, I asked what good I could possibly do for a man I didn't know. Stavis replied, as I expected, that I was not to be a witness on matters of evidence or character, but that I could testify, if I was so convinced, that the man's position was a valid religious and conscientious objection to war.

Then he added that the young man was a black high-school dropout. He hit me at a sensitive spot. I had protested long and hard against the Selective Service procedures that discriminate so unjustly against the poor, the undereducated, and the black. Stewart Alsop later was to point out in *Newsweek*, June 29, 1970, that in 1969 just over 10 percent of draftees were college men, although well over 40 percent of young people go to college. He further showed that as of that date the total of Harvard, Yale, and Princeton graduates drafted and killed in Vietnam was two men. Other *volunteers* from those schools died in action. Alsop's point was that the Ivy League man seldom gets drafted. No such privilege functions in the ghettoes. When I talked to Morton Stavis, I did not have Alsop's figures. But I had the general idea, and it angered me.

In short, I knew I had to talk to Leroy Beaty. He visited me and surprised me. Although he had failed in more than one attempt to finish high school, it was not for lack of intelligence. He had his hang-ups and emotional blocks; they prevented his defining a goal and going right after it. Such problems, as well as lack of information, had prevented him from filling out the application for classification as a conscientious objector. (It is, I grant, a formidable document for anyone without a college education.) He had even asked for the form, but had never completed it. Then on the day of induction he refused to take the symbolic step forward. After a conversation with an Army Major, he was given a chance to amend his ways and return the next day with no penalty. He still refused.

The story was confused enough that a bureaucracy could be forgiven for thinking that Beaty was not genuinely, consistently a conscientious objector to war. He was indicted, and trial was scheduled.

During our two-hour conversation he told me something of his life history and beliefs, and he showed me some of his writings. He had grown up in a home with a Baptist father and a Methodist mother. From about the ninth or tenth grade he had been attracted by the Church of God (Worldwide). In common jargon it would be called a black Pentecostalist sect. He could not accept some of its biblical literalism and beliefs about the future, but he found its ethic convincing.

In his own written statements of beliefs he included a quotation from the Constitution and By-Laws of his church: "It is the conviction and firm belief of this Church and its membership that Christian disciples of Christ are forbidden by Him and the commandments of God to kill, or in any manner directly or indirectly to take human life; by whatsoever means; we believe that bearing arms is directly contrary to this fundamental doctrine of our belief; we therefore conscientiously refuse to bear arms or to come under the military authority." That statement plainly ruled out any military service, including non-combatant duties.

Leroy Beaty had also done his own thinking. He could quote the Nuremberg tribunals and Vatican II, the documents of several churches, the Bible. Within his thinking was a black man's resentment of the white man's authority that has inflicted monstrous racial injustices; yet his reasoning was consistently pacifist. He could not delegate the exercise of his conscience to the military system: "Once you take that step forward," he said, "your will and conscience is subordinated to that of the officers who command your body."

He knew and I knew that the situation was stacked against him, so we agreed that I would give him as hard an interrogation as I knew how, though without any personal hostility. I took notes on the conversation. I turned to some of his statements about the current war and asked him whether they were not political rather than moral judgments. He answered, "I am not involved in politics. My church frowns on worldly politics."

I asked whether he was really opposed, as he claimed to be, to all wars. He said, "I believe life is sacred. It is wrong for men to take the lives of men. Only God who gives life can take it. I am opposed to war. Men have a higher calling than to kill each other."

I pushed him on the issue of civil authority. Was it not necessary, I asked, that in society we give up some rights of private judgment? "The army," he said, "is a form of slavery. I'm against it with all my being."

I tried a question so trite that I was ashamed to use it, but it seemed inevitable. Suppose, I inquired, he were in South Africa and the great black majority should rise up in revolution against the white racist tyranny. He smiled gently and answered; "I know which side I'd favor. But I would not take a human life."

I decided that he was authentic. That is, insofar as it is

given to men to know authenticity, I believed I had found it in him. Since I can never know for certain how authentic I am, since I cannot always detect my own hypocrisies and rationalizations, I cannot make the judgments on other men that only God can make. But by all the standards of normal social life and of courts of law, he was a genuine conscientious objector, moved by religious faith and not by fear.

The trial was in the Federal Courthouse in Newark at 10:00 A.M. on June 3, 1969. The Judge was a man known for integrity and fairness, and Leroy Beauty, on the advice of Attorney Stavis, waived the right of trial by jury. The prosecutor was an attractive young woman. I quickly guessed that her heart was not in this prosecution, that she had no desire to be the white, middle-class persecutor of a black youth. But her oath of office and whatever personal pride and ambition she had forbade her to do a slipshod job. She easily established the facts, showing that Beaty was guilty of violating the law or at least the administrative regulations promulgated to implement the law.

Morton Stavis conducted the defense with dignity. He sought to demonstrate that Beaty was a genuine conscientious objector in the meaning of the law and that his mistakes had been slip-ups in relation to administrative regulations, not crimes. A psychiatrist testified that Beaty was not clever in intricate maneuvers but had genuine convictions. I testified that by all recognized standards of religion and law, Beaty was a genuine conscientious objector. Beaty came through beautifully on the witness stand. The cross-examination simply reinforced the impression of genuine religious and moral conviction, combined with some clumsiness in negotiation of legal mazes.

The Judge did not announce the verdict that day. Later I got the information in two stages: first the verdict of guilty, second the sentence. Although I had hoped for an acquittal, I decided the decision had a kind of Solomonic wisdom. The Judge, in finding Leroy Beaty guilty, upheld the law and its administration. But he gave a suspended sentence, conditioned on Beaty's performing some work in the national interest. Since classification as a conscientious objector would have had the same stipulation, this meant in effect a judicial assignment of the status of conscious objector. In a tangled world where rational patterns rarely fit the mixed stuff of history, such an outcome is not bad.

CORNELIUS M. COOPER, JR.

West Pointers are not expected to become conscientious objectors, but some do. One who did was Louis P. Font, a Methodist in the class of 1968, who less than two years later asked for release from the army as a selective objector to the war in Vietnam. Another was Cornelius McNiel Cooper, Jr., a black cadet in the class of 1969, who became as thoroughgoing a pacifist as I have ever known.

The class of 1969 at West Point was noted for unconventional activities. One of its number, since released from military service, is on the staff of the *Village Voice*. Another, a Southern Baptist who agitated against compulsory chapel on the grounds of religious liberty, writes occasionally about country music for the same paper. The contribution of the United States Military Academy to the *Village Voice* has never given due credit and I am glad to point it out.

Cornelius Cooper was born into an army family and had part of his boyhood education in an American school in Germany, more of it in California. During high school he was president of several student organizations, active in the YMCA, and "Chief Justice of the State Supreme Court" in the annual "California Boys State." During one summer he was a laboratory assistant at the Medical Center of the University of Southern California. Some of his supervisors predicted a brilliant future for him in medicine, but he chose to go to West Point.

His transformation from committed cadet to radical pacifist came from the interaction of two lines of development, one connected with external events, the other an internal religious movement. The external stimuli began at West Point. He felt a revulsion against boxing, because the aim seemed to be "to strip my opponent of his personality, to view him as an object to be physically abused." A summer as a volunteer for the Los Angeles Urban League, working with underprivileged children, led him to question the social usefulness of a military career. The month of that summer spent in a Ft. Hood orientation program as an armored platoon leader seemed far less constructive than the work with children. Several incidents at West Point impressed him with the horror of war and the inner brutality of some of his instructors. By the time of graduation he was doubtful about his chosen career, doubtful also about the war in Vietnam, but prepared to give military life a trial.

In the Artillery School at Ft. Sill, then in the Airborne course at Ft. Benning he found opportunities for thought and discussion. He was angered at some of the Airborne chants:

> I want to be an Airborne Ranger,
> I want to live a life of blood and danger,
> I want to go to Vietnam
> I want to kill ol' Charlie Cong.

The spirit he found in that chant he was to find again in the Ranger course, where he sensed a racial contempt for the

Laotian officers in the program, even though they were there as allies. Much of the training he felt to be degrading, dishonest, and dehumanizing in its inculcation of hatred toward enemies.

This sequence of events interacted with an inner pilgrimage that had started in childhood. Several of his ancestors and relatives were Christian ministers. During public school years he enjoyed released time religious instruction, both Baptist and Catholic. He was a leader in a Lutheran youth organization and took his catechetical training so seriously that he quit the school basketball team for its sake. But eventually he found this belief personally unconvincing and, when he went on to West Point, maintained no church life apart from compulsory attendance at chapel. In one or two elective courses at the Military Academy he found his mind approaching questions of the ultimate meaning of war and human relations, but in the intensity of training these questions got no discussion. Perhaps, he began to suspect, they were deliberately pushed out of the consciousness of cadets. Nevertheless, an occasional incident—a photograph on an infantry adviser's desk of "an old, wizened Asian lady, her naked breasts pierced by a green dart from someone's dart board"; an evening at the theater watching *The Man in the Glass Booth*—made him wonder about war and personal human responsibility for it.

At Ft. Sill he discovered Martin Buber's *I and Thou*. Buber's imaginative, poetic mood spoke to a similar strain in Cornelius Cooper—who himself was writing poetry. The idea of human relationships described by Buber, of life as meeting and as dialogue, became "a beacon of sorts." How was he to relate *I-Thou* to the killing that went on in war? Without the slightest doubt Cooper's sensitivity to racism in society and in the army, his intensified belief in the misplacement of

229

national resources, and his judgments about the horrors of Vietnam influenced his convictions. But, he said, "it was Buber who was to put into focus for me what I was seeing."

Lt. Cooper was feeling the conflict that any soldier of sensitive conscience feels between the ideals of his society and the requirements of war. Soldiers do some things as acts of war that they would not do as citizens in a civil society— above all, killing other people. For most of them, insofar as they stop to think, these acts are justified by military necessity. Cooper turned the argument around; if military necessity requires such acts, something must be wrong with military necessity. From that point his convictions moved rather quickly through three stages. First, he decided that he could do military service only in non-combatant role, and he wrote to the Secretary of the Army initiating a request for transfer to another branch of the service. Second, he moved closer to pacifism by deciding that, although he might conceivably have fought in World War II, he "would not fight in this war and could not anticipate a war" in which he would fight. The third stage came in conversations with the pacifist writer and activist, David McReynolds, who led him to the conviction that "non-violent resistance was a viable alternative" to war.

When he wrote out his thoughts, Lt. Cooper came up with aphorisms like these:

> I cannot participate in war in any form and retain my humanity.
> It is impossible to kill a man in war without first denying his humanity. . . . Wars cannot take place unless the enemy is first robbed of his humanity in order for the war to proceed.
> War unlike any other form of conflict is utterly without dialogue.

I cannot conceive, conjure or otherwise reduce from
the vast realm of possibilities, circumstances in which
the benefits of war are to the advantage of humanity.

In long conversations with Corny Cooper, I became convinced that he was a rare human being. In a few of his ideas
I saw the influence of my old friend, the late A. J. Muste—
not because Cooper had read Muste but because Muste's ideas
had influenced pacifists who had talked with Cooper. Repeatedly I saw the traces of Martin Buber, and Cooper sent
me back to writings of Buber that had already stirred me
deeply. (It is true that Buber, though a prophet of peace,
was not quite a pacifist; Cooper never claimed that he was,
but only that Buber's dialogic faith led Cooper to pacifism.)
I also found in Cooper signs of what Charles Reich in *The
Greening of America* calls Consciousness III—the consciousness of those youth who have seen through the foolishness of
the competitive goals and extravagant consumption that
characterize our society. But unlike Reich's examples, he did
not come from the white affluent society. He was more concerned about injustice, more interested in political action than
the representatives of Consciousness III.

Corny Cooper impressed me as remarkably immune to
many of the incentives that characterize our society. He was
so atypical of army officers that he did not even know the
location of a liquor store in the town adjacent to Ft. Bragg
where he lived. He was indifferent to military and capitalistic
folderol. His goal, following army service (and prison, if
necessary) was to become a physician; then, instead of climbing the status ladder of the profession, to engage in medical
service.

Lt. Cooper's father was present at the hearing at Ft. Bragg
on November 25, 1970. So were others who testified to his

231

integrity and sensitivity. The officer in charge had once studied in a Roman Catholic theological seminary. He was genuinely interested in the moral issues at stake. I spent nearly two hours in testimony, under questioning first from Marvin Karpatkin, Cooper's legal counsel, then from the hearing officer. The questions were so interesting that I felt less in a legal situation than in a seminar on ethics and theology. But something was at stake that is missing in most seminars: the fate of a man. Lt. Cooper spoke well in his own behalf. I think the hearing officer respected him. But the talk was between a conscientious officer in the military system and a unique civilian, by mistake wearing a uniform. So there were limitations on the possibilities for communication, and I could not guess how well it was going.

A curious thought puzzled me. Had Corny Cooper been a somewhat different person, I might have wished that he had advanced through the ranks and become a Colonel, as most West Pointers do, or a General, as some do. In an army so overpopulated with black men in the lower ranks and underpopulated in the higher ranks, he might have made a powerful contribution to democracy. But he could not be a career officer without warping what was most precious in himself. So I stifled my tentative wish.

Eleven and a half weeks later—on February 13, 1971, to be exact—the front page of the *New York Times* headlined: "West Point Alumnus Released Honorably as a War Objector." My eye, racing down the column, found the name of Cornelius McNeil Cooper, Jr.—"the first graduate of the academy to be discharged as a conscientious objector." Later in the day he telephoned, and I congratulated him. The paper quoted the recommendation to the Department of the Army from Major General George S. Blanchard, the Post Commander at Fort Bragg: "I am completely convinced that this officer should be released from active duty as soon as possible. He is quite sincere and is of no benefit to this division or the Army as a result of the beliefs he holds." The language made me smile faintly. The General was right in his major emphasis: Cornelius Cooper could be "of no benefit" to the Army. He was equally right on his lesser emphasis: this man was sincere.

* * * * *

The five men I have described were all unique individuals, all markedly different from one another. I became involved with them, not because I was trying to prove something about war, but because I was concerned for persons in a system that (like all systems) has trouble doing justice to persons. I could not possibly agree with all of them on all their major convictions; the differences among them were too great. I did not totally agree with any, yet I shared some of the convictions of all, as I did with the very different young man, Russell Flesher. By personal commitment and professional role I am concerned about the truth of men's beliefs. But there come times when the issue, as the Supreme Court said in the Seeger case of 1964, is not the "truth" of moral belief but whether the belief is "truly held." Kierkegaard understood that distinction, and it is good that the law of the land takes it into account. All these men "truly held" their convictions.

I have called these men patriots. In the words of Daniel Bell, "one can be a critic of one's country without being an enemy of its promise." These men lived with a critical love of country and a love of humanity.

All of them at some time thanked me for some role I played in their lives. Although I appreciated their gratitude,

I felt it more appropriate that I should thank them. We human beings rest too easily in dogmatic slumbers and skeptical indecision. They stirred me—at least a little bit—out of mine and required me to interrogate once again my own faith and actions.

4. THE INSTRUMENTAL
MEANING OF WAR

Woodrow Wilson: *"But don't you believe in the
brotherhood of man?"*
Georges Clemenceau: *"Yes, I believe in the brotherhood
of man. Cain and Abel! Cain and Abel!"*

War and violence are old in human history. The ancient
biblical record suggests that, just as the first sibling rivalry
was between the first siblings, so the first murder was between brothers.

Progress in the arts of civilization has been accompanied
by, sometimes anticipated by progress in the arts of war.
Winston Churchill in *The Birth of Britain*, describing the
coming of the iron age, wrote: "At this point we can plainly
recognize across the vanished millenniums a fellow-being. A
biped capable of slaying another with iron is evidently to
modern eyes a man and a brother. It cannot be doubted that
for smashing skulls, whether long-headed or round, iron is
best."

Contemporary man has maintained the sense of priorities.
The first uses of atomic energy were the atomic bomb.

War is the most massive and organized practice of violence.
It takes many forms: international wars big and small; civil
wars between territorial regions or between races, classes, and
factions in the same territory; wars of conquest and wars of
revolution; gang wars and riots; wars between professional
armies and guerrilla wars; spontaneous wars and intricately
planned wars; quick, climactic wars and wars that smolder

over the years and sometimes fiercely flame; hot wars and cold wars that even in the absence of combat reach outcomes determined by potential powers of destruction. War is not a single, isolable problem. Any understanding of war is an understanding of man and society.

One major reason for violence and war—the reason that is the subject of this chapter—is that they are effective for some purposes. Men need not love war in order to fight; they need only love something else that they think they can get by war. It is often said that a war-weary world craves peace—as though war were somehow an accident or the connivance of a few against the ardent wish of mankind. But that is surely deceptive. Men crave peace on their own terms, and they will often fight for their own terms. Some, craving peace and freedom, will fight for freedom. Some crave peace and their neighbors' land, or peace and their own land that has been taken by a neighbor. Some crave peace and the destruction of the rival who threatens peace. It is not rare for men to fight for, or to persuade themselves that they fight for, peace.

To say that war and violence are effective for some purposes is not to say that they are effective for all purposes. Bismarck made the point by saying that you can do anything with bayonets except sit on them. Sometimes men wanting to sit—to relax, to enjoy concord, to dream and to love—have destroyed their own goals by their propensity to use bayonets. Mankind in its folly has often practiced violence in the pursuit of goals that are unattainable by violence. The habit is very much with us today.

It would be comforting if we could then say that war never accomplishes anything and is therefore useless. But that judgment, however well meant, is surely illusory. Wars have brought about revolutions and have crushed revolutions. The arts of war in the history of the United States enabled this country to win independence from foreign government. War seized territory from the Indians and decimated their population; war and allied forms of violence captured black people in Africa and held them in slavery here. There are few free nations that did not use some violence—often immense violence—in gaining their freedom and maintaining it. Few, when they had sufficient potential for violence, did not use it to expand their territories or victimize others.

Violence is functional to the extent that it contributes to achieving some human purposes. It is dysfunctional to the extent that it fails to achieve and even destroys the possibility of achieving other purposes. The practitioners of violence usually overestimate its functionality, sometimes to the extent of destroying themselves in the process. Advocates of peace usually underestimate the functionality of violence. They are likely, if they hold privileged status in society, to enjoy the advantages of violence without even seeing its evidences. They are likely, if underprivileged, to suffer injustices interminably because they do not know how to unseat violence from its thrones.

VIOLENCE AND SOCIAL ORDER

One problem in talking about war and violence is the difficulty in saying with any precision what they are or where their boundaries lie. Violence is one form—certainly not the only form, but a form—of power. Violence, when sufficiently massive, is war. There are immensely important differences between the power that unifies and sustains a peaceable society, the violence that even such a society occasionally uses to suppress criminal actions, and uninhibited war. Any social morality depends on such distinctions. Hence I cannot agree with Jacques Ellul, who in *Violence* writes: "Condoning violence means condoning every kind of violence. . . . Violence is a single thing, and it is always the same." Yet the distinctions are rarely so clear as they seem to be. The peaceable society incorporates certain structures of power which are likely to exercise violence if their operators consider it necessary. When conservatives appeal for "law and order" and peace, radicals are quick to point out that "the establishment" maintains itself through a capacity for violence that is invoked in emergencies but need not even be invoked if its potentialities are sufficiently strong.

In a conventional definition (*The Random House Dictionary of the English Language*) violence is "rough or injurious physical force, action, or treatment." That is a useful definition, not loaded with moral or emotional weight. It is reasonably clear. Yet its difficulties become obvious in borderline cases. Some examples may make the point.

Assume that a policeman lawfully arrests me for cause. I make a move to resist, and he hits me with his billy club. Moral judgments aside, his action fits the definition of violence; it is rough, injurious, and physical. But suppose he does not hit me; instead he draws his gun. I settle down and obey him. Technically there has been no violence, but the threatened violence is greater than in the first case, and I have responded to potential violence. But suppose, to take the most likely case, I simply obey him, and he does not make a motion toward club or gun. It is possible that I am responding to the moral power of the community represented by its agent of law-enforcement; it is also possible that I am responding to the threat of violence as much as in either of the first two cases. Probably I do not even know how much the knowledge of a lurking potentiality of violence influences me.

To take another example, imagine a small community in

which one man has a storehouse of food and others are starving. To make the point, we might assume that he got it by sharp dealing, but without any physical coercion. He keeps it locked up. Is he violent? Only in an indirect sense, we might say; he is not beating or even touching anybody. If the starving people attack him in order to get the key and seize the food, are they violent? Definitely yes; they use rough, injurious physical action against him. Yet it may well be that the hoarder, if he keeps possession of the food, is directly responsible for more physical injury by starvation than his assailants by their muscles and weapons.

A final example requires no imagination. The maternity death rate of nonwhite mothers in the United States in 1965 was four times as high (in relation to live births) as the rate among white mothers. And the mortality rate of nonwhite infants was nearly three times as high as the rate of white infants. That is not usually regarded as a matter of violence, but if a ghetto riots over inadequate hospitals, everybody recognizes violence. However the deaths of mothers and infants are surely injurious and are physical. The violence that kills them is not direct assault; it is the violence "built into" educational, economic, social, and medical systems. It is sometimes called *systemic* violence, because it is inherent in the system.

These cases show why violence is not always highly visible and why its boundaries are not precisely definable. Elements of violence, overt or potential, are part of all social systems. Hannah Arendt in her book *On Violence* is right in refusing to identify power with violence; power comes in many forms. There is the power of intelligence, of oratory, of common motivation, of loyalties and shared symbols, of respect for justice, of yearnings for peace. These are of utmost importance. They may reduce violence to a minimal level. But

Dr. Arendt overstates her case when she says that "power and violence are opposites." Violence is one form of power, and in most social systems it cannot be isolated from other forms of power. Although it can destroy some other forms of power (by destroying human life and social institutions), it is in practice often welded to other forms of power so intimately that it is not recognized until it is provoked.

Societies try to control violence through government. At its best, government rests on some kind of agreement, explicit or tacit, providing means of resolving conflicts without violence. The ancient social contract theory of government provided a mythological statement of this aspect of government. (The fact that it ignored other aspects need not concern us here.) The assumption was that people, to save themselves from chaos and insecurity, transferred some powers from themselves to government. For example, the individual in a trade-off gave up the right of retaliation for the sake of a governmental system that restrained and punished crime. Men in conflict, instead of slugging it out in the streets, contested with each other in courts and legislatures. Government provided a framework for adjustment of differences.

Such a theory made considerable sense, not of all governments, but of any government that existed by consent or participation of the governed. Good government, although it has never yet eliminated power or violence, does moderate and regulate them.

In doing so, government itself may become an instrument of violence. Even the best government has a capacity for violence. It must *enforce* law. That is the characteristic of government, in contrast to voluntary social groups that may persuade people to adopt the goals of the group but cannot enforce. The ability to use violence is so characteristic of government that many social scientists regard it as the defining characteristic of the state. In his famous essay on "Politics as a Vocation," Max Weber defines the state as "a relation of men dominating men, a relation supported by means of legitimate (i.e. considered to be legitimate) violence." By Weber's own logic that definition exaggerates. It follows by two paragraphs a better statement: "Of course, force is certainly not the normal or the only means of the state—nobody says that—but force is a means specific to the state." Without the capacity for enforcement, he indicates, the state is not a state.

We might well reason that the higher the morale of a society, the less the need for coercive enforcement. Loyalty, more effectively than compulsion, leads to acceptance of the burdens of citizenship. The prevalence of violence in contemporary society is rightly seen as a sign of failure of morale. The overuse of violence in enforcement is as much an evidence of weakness in a society as the failure to enforce law. Even so, the power to enforce is inherent in the nature of government. And the power to enforce includes a final possibility—too often, as an early possibility—the use of violent power: of financial penalties or imprisonment, which are themselves enforced, against any who resist, by physical coercion.

Once the reality of violence in society is recognized, most moral generalizations about it prove too glib. Such was the case in the Report of the President's Commission on Campus Unrest (1970), chaired by Governor Scranton. The report was a good enough one and the agreement among its diverse members was remarkable enough that I have no desire to discredit it by nit-picking. I use it only to show the difficulty that able men have in reasoning about violence. At one point the text reads, "We utterly condemn violence." A reader must wonder, "Always? By everyone?" The statement is unqualified. But a later, more complicated sentence reads: "The use

241

of force by police is sometimes necessary and legal, but every unnecessary resort to violence is wrong, criminal, and feeds the hostility of the disaffected." I find that sentence quite convincing—even though it states rather than solves the problem by the phrase "unnecessary resort to violence."

It may be that the two statements can be joined consistently in some such way as this: "We utterly condemn violence *except* in the necessary enforcement of law by police, and even there every unnecessary resort to violence is wrong." That is a persuasive position—*if* it can be assumed that law represents justice. It is unpersuasive to any who believe that law represents coercive injustice imposed upon victims.

Actual governments sometimes do use violence in ways that are vicious and criminal. This is the most obvious in the case of tyrannical dictatorships, past and present. Mankind's heroes of liberty were in their own time usually resisters— often violent resisters—of government. The criminal use of violence by democratic or representative governments may be less obvious than in the case of monarchies, oligarchies, and dictatorships for the simple reason that the majority of people are involved in the violence. But if the majority employ violence to impose slavery or repression on minorities—a not unfamiliar pattern in the history of the United States and most nations—the criminality of their action is as real as in nonrepresentative societies.

In an efficient democratic or republican form of government repression may be so skillfully executed that its violence is not obvious. Or, to state it another way, systemic violence may remove the need for conspicuous episodic violence. In the American system of slavery, the slave-owner (if he was not a sadist) might not make much use of the lash; he didn't have to if everyone realized that he could. In the inheritance from slavery, institutions of discrimination might function so smoothly that violent enforcement was rarely necessary. Those who resisted the system were likely to be the ones who used obvious violence. But they were able to understand what was happening. The characteristic response of the Black Panthers to charges of violence has not been to pretend innocence; it has been to point to the massive violence built into racist institutions.

To the extent that a society's institutions embody justice and provide for all people access to justice, the society has a moral right to object to violence against its institutions and—judged by the workaday standards of political ethics—a right to use whatever minimum of violence may be necessary to enforce law. A society, however, is hypocritical if its power blocs use violence without qualms to enforce their own will, then judge resisters by some higher standard of nonviolence. The world is filled with people who can quote the Sermon on the Mount against their opponents without the slightest intention of governing themselves by that Sermon.

In the midst of the contradictions that haunt human societies some warnings are appropriate to all of us. Those inclined toward violence might well realize how vicious it can be, how capricious a mode of decision-making it is. They might compare the destructive certainties of its means with the uncertainties of the ends that purport to justify it. They who take the sword are likely to perish by the sword along with their victims. The ultimate logic of violence is chaos or tyranny—the chaos of competing acts of violence or the tyranny of a dominating violence that rises to suppress chaotic violence. The reign of violence means the end of rationality and community; it means disaster.

Those who condemn violence might well realize how much violence there is in all societies. They might ask themselves whether they unconsciously enjoy privileges enforced by violence, overt or potential. They might take notice that the unjust rarely yield their status without compulsion, that the oppressed rarely win freedom without exercising violent power. The ultimate logic of total renunciation of violence is that the functions of violence are left to those who are less inhibited than the renouncers of violence—unless there is an effective social alternative to violence.

POSSIBILITIES OF NONVIOLENCE

But what about such an alternative? What about the possibility of transforming the world by nonviolent means? Eloquent and courageous leaders have called their followers to that mode of life. And, though the world has not been convinced, a few people have believed and many more have had to take notice.

It is probably true that violence-prone societies have barely begun to exercise their imaginations as to the possibilities of nonviolent social organization and change. That nonviolent methods sometimes fail to achieve their goals is no refutation of them; violent methods also frequently fail to realize their aims. In intricate technological societies a nonviolent refusal to cooperate with the system may so frustrate the system as to become an effective technique for modifying the system. The fact of technical nonviolence does not necessarily make the act moral. Refusal to cooperate may be a means of extortion as easily as a means of justice; furthermore, its effectiveness (as in the case of a strike) may have more to do with the strategic position of the protestors than with the merits of their cause. For this reason it is foolish to equate nonviolent action with good and violence with evil. Nevertheless, innovative use of nonviolent techniques may be a major breakthrough in times to come.

However, the unrealized potentialities of nonviolence do not remove the fact of violence from the world or the necessity of dealing with its complexity. This is evident in the careers of the two twentieth-century leaders who have most dramatically caught the world's imagination in their use of nonviolence: Mohandas Gandhi and Martin Luther King, Jr.

Martin Luther King was a Christian pastor. Gandhi, a Hindu, was "overwhelmed" by Tolstoy's *The Kingdom of God Is Within You* and was powerfully impressed by Christ's Sermon on the Mount. Both men are thus witnesses to the influence upon mankind of Christ's message of the kingdom of God with its reversal of many alluring human values and its embodiment of forgiveness and love. To any Christian and to any human being who has been moved by Christ's teaching and his death on the cross, war and violence constitute a major ethical problem. It is not only men like Tolstoy, Gandhi, and King who establish the point; we have seen it (Chapter 1 above) in Melville and Patton.

Jesus Christ, the Prince of Peace, has attracted men even when they could not or would not obey him. To accept the calling of a Suffering Servant, to ask men to forgive seventy times seven times, to bid his followers to resist not evil, to win nothing by violence and to die a victim of violence with a prayer for the forgiveness of his killers—these are sayings and deeds that throw a mighty question mark against the warlike ways of men. If we do not know what to do with them, we cannot easily forget them.

It may be that from such convictions and example, any who profess to follow Christ must reason their way to a consistent rejection of violence and war. It may be that any other alternative is evasion and hypocrisy. Yet Jesus does not easily fit into any moral system. The same records that record the saying, "Do not resist one who is evil" (Mt. 5:39), record another saying, "I have not come to bring peace, but a sword" (Mt. 10:34). If, as I believe, that statement is metaphorical, the metaphor is one of conflict, and Jesus has often introduced conflict into human affairs. Some recent scholarship has argued that Jesus was more closely associated with the militantly anti-Roman Zealots than traditional teaching has recognized. The case is less than convincing. Jesus' association with the Zealots is as remarkable as, but no more remarkable than, his association with "tax collectors and sinners." The attempt to capture Jesus for any partisan cause has through twenty centuries generally ended in the embarrassment of the partisans. If we cannot and should not try to excise conflict from the ministry of Jesus, neither can we excise his blessings on the peacemakers who shall be called sons of God.

The sayings of Jesus are parabolic, situational, metaphorical, dramatic. They do not constitute a system of ethics or a social policy. They disturb men, awaken new styles of human awareness, shatter rigid preconceptions, lure men with unrealized possibilities of justice and peace.

The accomplishment of Mohandas Gandhi and Martin Luther King was to combine the vision of peace, derived largely though not solely from Jesus, with programmatic tactics for nonviolent social change. Modern society does not yet know the possibilities inherent in such goals and tactics. It would be foolish, or at least premature, to set limits to the possibilities of nonviolence.

The other side of the case is that nonviolence, whatever its potentialities, gives no signs of eliminating the reality and the continuous possibilities of violence. It does not discredit Mahatma Gandhi or Dr. King that both died by violence, any more than it discredits warriors that they die in battle. Yet the deaths of both men show the constantly latent, sometimes patent power of violence. Gandhi, seeking to restore peace between his Hindus and Muslims, was killed by a fanatical fellow-Hindu. King, once stabbed by a black man in Harlem, later died from a bullet fired by a white man. Both deaths demonstrate the unpredictable possibilities of violence at any time. Both may suggest that one function of government is to do what it can to prevent such deaths.

Again, it does not lessen the amazing discipline and the heroic achievement of movements led by Gandhi and King to point out some factors that helped both men in their struggles. Along with many others, Hannah Arendt has pointed out: "If Gandhi's enormously powerful and successful strategy of nonviolent resistance had met with a different enemy—Stalin's Russia, Hitler's Germany, even prewar Japan, instead of England—the outcome would not have been decolonization, but massacre and submission." The reasoning depends not upon an assumption of unique English virtue, but only on an awareness that a fading imperialism would not perpetrate the deeds of strident Nazism or Stalinism. It has also been noted often that Gandhi's nonviolent fasts carried the possibility of his death, which would have unloosed violence—as the British well knew.

But we need not conjecture. We can turn to Gandhi's own recognition that his methods had limitations. Erik Erikson, in his admiring *Gandhi's Truth*, has shown from Gandhi's letters that the Mahatma, without renouncing his own convictions, did not think them universally efficacious. He suspected that only through fighting might India achieve nonviolence, that the whole effort might prove too difficult, that carnage might be necessary to India.

Martin Luther King too wondered, especially toward the end of his career, whether he could justify his hopes that nonviolence would penetrate the hearts of his stubborn foes or whether nonviolent pressures could make them yield. He also knew that the very real achievements of his movement took place within a framework of what he often called "the law of the land." It does not diminish his achievement to point out the role of the Supreme Court in breaking the legal power of segregation—a role that eventually led a reluctant President to order federal marshalls and federal troops to enforce this law.

These observations do not diminish two affirmations. First, the commitment of some persons of integrity to nonviolence has its own validity, independent of their success or failure in achieving their aims. Second, twentieth-century man has not exhausted the potentialities of nonviolence and does not know the extent of its possibilities or limitations.

One counter-affirmation is equally important. The achievements of nonviolence have not changed the fact that social structure is shaped by power and that violent power remains effective for some purposes. Violence, organized or sporadic, can erupt and does erupt. Such violence has consequences. One task of any society remains that of finding governmental structures for restraining violence and holding it accountable.

THE PECULIAR PROBLEM OF WAR

The peculiarity of war is not its violence. The seemingly normal society embodies more violence than is usually apparent. The peculiar problem of war is that it represents magnified violence between states or factions unrestrained by government. War takes place where there is no government or where government has broken down. Violence can be moderated where it is held accountable to legislatures and courts. No legislatures or courts adjudicate international disputes and enforce their decisions.

Hence it is not surprising that men have often proposed world government as a method of achieving world peace. The ancient Roman Empire, though achieved by conquest, was something welcomed by its subjects because it brought the *Pax Romana*. A world, weary of social disintegration and warfare, was inclined to settle for a trade-off, giving up freedom for peace. But the Roman peace was enforced by violence and it was far from enduring. As Augustine pointed out in *The City of God*, its peace was not to be despised, but it was always an insecure peace.

The modern world has often dreamed of world government, achieved not through imperial conquest but through voluntary federation of nations. The Enlightenment, with its confidence —a rather touching confidence—in human rationality was the great age of such projections. Immanuel Kant's essay on *Perpetual Peace*, 1795, was neither the first nor the last but was the most impressive of such proposals. In the next century Tennyson's "Locksley Hall," 1842, foretold an age of aerial warfare ending in world peace:

> Till the war-drums throbb'd no longer, and the battle-flags
> were furl'd
> In the Parliament of man, the Federation of the world.

Since Tennyson was so prescient in his picture of "airy navies" raining their "ghastly dew," dare we hope that he was equally discerning in his hope that "the kindly earth" would someday "slumber, lapt in universal law"?

In mankind's haunted contemporary existence the vision of world government, as an answer to present conflicts, is an alluring illusion. Amid the unpredictabilities of history, there is no point in denying that someday some form of world government may in fact develop. If so, its form is probably as unforeseen today as our present state of affairs was unforeseen to Immanuel Kant. I see no value in arguing against the possibility or against imaginative efforts to sketch out possibilities. But I do maintain that world government is a deceptive illusion *if* it is seen as the answer to our present agonies. I say this for two reasons.

First, it is so remote from the existing situation that it offers no answer to persons, like the "five patriots" I have described, who are struggling with moral decisions that they must make day in and day out. It does not help the congressman who is asking whether a specific proposal on armaments (like the anti-ballistic missile) or a delegation of presidential powers will increase the likelihood of war or peace. It does not help the citizen who wonders whether to increase military expenditures in order to attract a volunteer army and end the draft or to decrease expenditures as a step in revising national priorities. The hope that someday such decisions might not be necessary does not in any way change the fact that *right now* destinies of men and nations hang on decisions like these.

Second, the possibility of a future world government does not eliminate the problem of violence and war; it simply recasts that problem. The reason is that one essential characteristic of government, recently mentioned above, is the power to enforce law. Unenforceable declarations may be righteous and moral, but they are exhortations rather than law, like pronouncements of the Vatican or resolutions of the World Council of Churches, or—to take a closer approximation to government—some of the unenforced resolutions of the General Assembly of the United Nations.

Enforcement of law, I have already argued, is relatively

easy if the law represents the common morale of a society; to the extent that this common morale is nonexistent or weak, enforcement requires coercion, including violent coercion. Every city and every nation must live with this problem. In the case of the world, the common consensus and common morale are lacking on most issues—especially on those issues that provoke the world's frequent wars. Consider the major recent situations of war: Israel and its foes (whether nations or guerrillas), Nigeria, the Sudan, the United States in Vietnam, the Soviet invasion of Czechoslovakia, Pakistan. In each case the violence expressed a disagreement in which there was little or no common consensus and little shared morale between the contenders; that is why they fought. Likewise in each of these cases the conflicting parties were not ready to turn over their power of decision-making to any international agency that might decide against them.

A world government without powers of enforcement is only a fictional government. A world government with powers of enforcement—given the conflicts presently in the world—would require immense powers. That is, it would require powers sufficient to enforce its decrees against the strongest centers of power within it. If, for example, it should choose to remove the United States from Vietnam or the Soviet Union from Czechoslovakia, it would need sufficient power to do so. (Moral suasion has already been tried rather extensively.) The result would be war. It would not be the first time in history that peace-keeping forces found themselves waging war.

In the nature of the case an effective world government must have power (including among other kinds of power the capacity for violence) greater than the power (including capacity for violence) of any center of opposition within it.

It need not have the desire or capacity to stifle all opposition, but without dominant power it ceases to be government. The lack of such power makes the United Nations far less than a government, even though it can perform many important functions. Yet to conceive a world government so powerful that it can take on any existing nation or any likely coalition of nations is itself a frightening thought.

It might be argued that some day nations and peoples, under the influence of a more mature morality or fear of destruction, might transfer much of their present power to a world organization. If that should happen, the concentration of power in the central authority would not have to be so great. Nobody knows whether or when that might happen. To work for it is a legitimate enterprise. But present trends are not moving in that direction. Few nations so trust other nations as to surrender power to any combination of nations. This fact about our world is relatively independent of ideological differences. The United States, the Soviet Union, China, the young nations of Africa, Latin American and Asiatic countries—all these are about equally unready to turn over their control of their destinies to any organization that they do not dominate and do not trust. China, for example, is determined not to surrender its rights of decision-making to any power structure dominated by the United States and the Soviet Union, as shown by its total uninterest in the nuclear non-proliferation pact. Nor is the United States Senate likely to make any major surrender of power to a world body in which the Chinese and Indians, if they should agree on a point, would outnumber the U.S.A. population by seven or eight to one. Nor are the young African nations, recently liberated from colonialism and exultant in their nationalism, ready to give control over their decisions to a remote authority that claims to work for their best interests.

The same conflicts of interest and lack of trust that make war a reality work equally to make international government an unreality.

A city is more cohesive, more obviously dependent upon cooperation for its functioning, than a world. Yet violence, both systemic and eruptive, is evident in our cities. To project a world without violence when mankind does not know how to maintain cities without violence is an expectation as unlikely as it is beautiful.

In this reasoning I am not setting any dogmatic limits on human possibilities. In the present age of social upheaval many institutions with long histories are disappearing or changing drastically. Familiar forms of the nation-state and of warfare may become obsolete. My assertion is a relatively modest one that comes in two propositions. First, no international institution is now in sight that will combine the cohesive morale and the power to eliminate war. Second, no such institution that makes violence impossible or its control unnecessary has yet been conceived.

THE NUCLEAR DILEMMA

The new fact that makes war a problem as it has never been before is the reality of nuclear and thermonuclear weapons. The first uses of atomic weapons, traumatic though they were, did not make the point fully evident. The destruction at Hiroshima and Nagasaki may have been no more cruel than the fire-bombing of Dresden. But Dresden represented the top rung on an old ladder of destruction and Hiroshima was the bottom rung on a quite new ladder. It has now become plain that man has invented a new style of warfare that does not fit the old categories.

Other styles of war, I have argued, are functional for some

purposes. Their purposes—to win freedom and independence, to subdue insurrection, to seize or defend territory—have varying moral validity. But war is effective for attaining some goals, as it is ineffective for attaining other goals. That is why war has an instrumental meaning that raises human and moral questions.

The new fact is a mode of warfare that ceases to be functional. Its destructiveness is so encompassing that it destroys any possible goals that it might seek to attain. Experts may argue whether or not there is a present capacity to annihilate the human race; they have little doubt that the annihilation of civilization is possible and that the unleashing of nuclear warfare means self-destruction as well as destruction of any enemy.

The consequence is that the waging of a general nuclear war can no longer be a rational, purposive act—even in terms of a strategy that ignores moral restraints. Old-style wars are aimed at the achievement of some gain. Their critics may point out that the gains are often unrealized and they may challenge the morality of both ends and means; yet fighting armies have intended and have sometimes achieved some purposes. Now nuclear war has become possible on a scale of destruction of both foes and initiator that makes impossible the attainment of any sane and identifiable purpose.

President Eisenhower, in Rio de Janeiro in 1960, put the issue as follows: "Nations now possess power so terrible that mutual annihilation would be the only result of general physical conflict. War is now utterly preposterous. In nearly every generation the fields of earth have been stained with blood. Now, war would not yield blood—only a great emptiness of the combatants, and the threat of death from the skies for all who inhabit the earth." Secretary Khrushchev in 1964 said: "Only a child or an idiot does not fear war."

President Johnson the same year said: "General war is impossible and some alternatives are essential." President Nixon, in an interview by C. L. Sulzberger (*New York Times*, March 10, 1971) said: "I seriously doubt if we will ever have another war. This is probably the very last one."

Probably nobody is so naïve as to assume that such talk assures peace. But it would be naïve to forget why leaders of nations, who did not formerly talk that way, do so now. Furthermore, the realization that prompts such statements has made a difference in world history. No nuclear weapon has been used in war since August 9, 1945. The reason was not lack of conflict and hostility. It was understanding of the enormity of the threat of destruction.

But that understanding has in no sense solved the problem of war. War has continued: every year since 1945 has seen revolution or suppression, aggression or defense, major war or brush-fire war, guerrilla war or police action. Several of the wars would have been called major wars in any historical epoch except our own. One of them has been the longest war in the history of the United States. The human race and the leaders of the nation may have decided, on the basis of incontrovertible evidence, that large-scale nuclear war is nonfunctional. Most social groups (nations, revolutionary groups, or established systems) have not decided the same about other forms of war. Hence the instrumental uses of war continue to operate, excepting the one major case of nuclear war.

The resultant situation almost turns world history into a gigantic theater of the absurd. At preposterous expense to their citizens and at the sacrifice of social gains deeply wanted by peoples, major nations maintain and continuously enhance their nuclear arsenals, even though their leaders insist that they must not be used. Can any reasoning justify such madness?

Yes, there is a strain of impressive logic within the absurdity. It is the logic of deterrence. A major world power wants a second-strike capability—the capacity to retaliate against an enemy, no matter how great the damage the enemy might inflict in a first strike. Some say that no morality or rationality can justify a civilization, wrecked in smoldering ruins, in retaliating against a foe whom it cannot defeat. Yet the power to do just that may be the power that deters the foe from initiating a strike.

Is this an unduly cynical view of mankind and the ways of nations? Would a more generous estimate be better—a judgment that relies less on deterrence and more on the removal of fear as a way to peace? One great fact stands in the way of the more generous judgment. When only one nation had the atomic bomb and could use it without fear of deterrence, it did use it. It is no paranoia, no evil judgment of enemies to say that other nations in the same situation might have done the same. The arrival of deterrence made the difference.

The logic of deterrence is grim and bizarre. The one thing to be said for it is that it has worked—thus far. I return to the fact that no nation has used an atomic weapon in an act of war since August of 1945. That statement maintains its validity only on a day-by-day basis. It may cease to be true before this book is published—in which case the book will probably not be published and I shall not be available to retract the statement. Yet the result of deterrence has been no mean achievement: the interval of time since the end of World War II is already greater than the interval between World Wars I and II. That is some cause for gratitude. Does anybody think that the United States would have observed nuclear restraint for these years if it had maintained a nuclear monopoly? Correspondingly, does anybody think that the

Soviet Union would have observed restraint if it had possessed a nuclear monopoly?

Certainly nobody thinks that a system of massive deterrents is a satisfactory system. It has its absurdity, its terror, its risks, its enslavement of men and their resources. Each country with nuclear weapons believes and wants its rivals to believe—as the quoted statements from Eisenhower, Khrushchev, and Johnson show—that nuclear weapons must not be used. Yet each nation knows that if its rivals had an *absolute* guarantee against use of the weapons, the deterrent value of the weapons would be lost. So nations maintain their systems—maintain them poised for instant action, targeted, and yearly made more fantastically complex. And each nation tries to persuade its rivals to believe, yet not quite absolutely to believe, that it will never use those weapons.

Meanwhile under the umbrella of terror lesser conflicts continue. The nations rage, and the peoples imagine vain things. The major nations marshall their resources and bleed themselves of young men and prosperity to fight their foes, short of using their ultimate weapons, then fret in frustration because relatively tiny nations can fight them to a standstill. The relative powerlessness of the most powerful nations becomes the sick joke of the century. And the risk remains. For the world to live without nuclear warfare from August 9, 1945 until today—perhaps whatever today anyone may be reading these words—is, I have suggested, no mean achievement. But neither is it any assurance of security. The risk is oppressive. If nuclear war is no longer functional, bluff remains functional (or men think it does, and that amounts to the same thing operationally); and accidents remain possible. Hannah Arendt rightly observes, "To the question how shall we ever be able to extricate ourselves from the obvious insanity of this position, there is no answer."

The lack of an answer does not doom the world to destruction by fate or caprice. It is possible to work away at fragments of answers that may someday fit into a pattern. We start with the fact that the umbrella of terror demonstrably has some deterrent effect. Such an umbrella is no roof for an edifice of peace. At best it buys precious time during which men may strive for the conditions of peace. Will it buy enough time? Who knows? What are the conditions of peace? Who knows that? What we know is that limited agreements (for example, on nuclear testing, on non-proliferation, on economic cooperation, on mediation of disputes) are possible, even though too rare. We know that, along with vicious circles of mounting distrust, there can be beneficent circles of growing trust. We know of possibilities, real even when pursued faint-heartedly, of feeding the hungry and liberating the oppressed. By such laborious yet genuine processes, more likely than by any dramatic breakthrough to assured peace, the world may grope its way toward a better day.

My conclusion is no doctrine of historical inevitability, either of progress or disaster. It is a conclusion that the world is insecure and that its insecurity will continue. Violence and war on less than maximum scale still have instrumental meaning; that is, men and groups still use them effectively to attain some ends, good or bad. War on the grand scale has ceased to have instrumental value; but that fact is no guarantee that it will not happen. Thus history remains precarious. But opportunities are real if men will exercise ingenuity and daring in peace, as they so often have in war.

It may seem grotesque that anyone should claim to think with any moral sensibility about such subjects as nuclear deterrents, second strikes, and the instrumental uses of war. It may seem maddeningly hypocritical to move in a few pages from the teachings of Jesus Christ to an assertion, no matter how qualified, of some merits in a balance of terror. If moral sensitivity leads some people to turn with revulsion from these pages, I do not resent their hostility. I find it hard enough to think and write these ideas, and I would prefer that people throw this book on the trash heap rather than lose their sensitivity. Yet it is our burden to think through and live out the meaning of ethical responsibility in this world, rather than in another world—not that we must acquiesce in the world as it is, but that we cannot disdain it or leap out of it. I choose to believe—or am compelled to believe—that our burden is our opportunity.

5. THE EXPRESSIVE
MEANING OF WAR

"It is well that war is so terrible—we would grow too fond of it." Attributed to Robert E. Lee.

War is not always the grim means chosen unhappily to win a desired end. There are mountains of evidence that it has its attractions. Men may wage war because fighting expresses something in themselves. They may even exult in it.

Reading my own war memoirs, I am sometimes astonished. If anyone ever entered war with a burdened conscience and a sense of tragic necessity deliberately chosen, I think I did. But there in the record I cannot change is the exhilaration of battle—of firing a carbine out of the window of the Hotel Meyer and dropping to the floor before the answering machine-gun burst came back through the same window, of matching wits and skill against an opponent with life itself at stake. There is the fascination of the awesome spectacle of the Flying Fortresses over Nürnberg—until like a vindictive nemesis they sent their bombs on my comrades and me. All that is so distant I can scarcely understand it, so distant from the experiences of my students today that I wonder whether they can ever understand that their strange teacher once felt that way. Yet, as I aim to show soon, the distance between their now and my then is not so great as at first it seems.

In a quite different spirit men may find release from desperation in war. Kenneth Boulding in *Conflict and De-*

fense uses the language of game theory to explain: "There is a world of difference, for instance, between what might be called rational aggression, in which a party deliberately plans a movement into the field of another, or even plans a game of ruin against him, in the sober expectation of being better off as a result, and irrational aggressiveness, in which the party thrashes around wildly without any real hope of planned gains but simply as an expression of an otherwise intolerable frustration." Some of my students understand that. They have been told that their tactics of protest may be "counterproductive," but the charge has seemed irrelevant. They appropriate, at least a little bit, the feelings of rioters in a ghetto, who are uninterested in cool arguments about the effectiveness of their tactics when their violence releases something long repressed in themselves.

Such cases—whether in war or campus rebellion or ghetto riots—show that it is not enough to reason about the instrumental meaning of war. Such meaning it often has. But equally important is its expressive meaning. A moral judgment may criticize or reject this expressive meaning, as it may the instrumental meaning. But both meanings are there. Until we recognize and scrutinize them, we are unlikely to know how to deal with them in ourselves or in others.

AGGRESSION

General George S. Patton, Jr., taking command of the Third Army in England in 1944, addressed his troops: "The third reason we are fighting [the first was to preserve liberties; the second, to defeat the Nazis] is because men like to fight. They always have and they always will. Some sophists and other crackpots deny that. They don't know what they're talking about. They are either goddamned fools or cowards, or both. Men like to fight, and if they don't, they're not real men."

Sharply though I disagree with that statement, nonsensical though I believe it to be, I must ask why men can talk that way and others hear and agree. Beyond question, there is aggressiveness in man. This is not to say that it is the only trait in man or the most meaningful. It is to say that aggressiveness is one human experience and a source of many human activities.

In recent years it has become popular, even faddish to seek the clue to human hostility in man's animal instincts of aggression or territoriality. The arguments that swirl about such theories are often incredibly simplistic. Margaret Mead in *Culture and Commitment* wisely states that "theories about human aggression, like those of Lorenz, and the speculations of a dramatist interpreter like Ardrey," as well as "reactions to such interpretations, like those of Ashley Montagu, which present man as inherently good," serve to confuse our understanding of humanity.

The reality is far more complex than either argument shows. Granted, man's behavior shows evidences of his kinship with animals. The more remarkable fact is that human freedom and imagination transform the patterned behavior of animals—whether in the direction of creativity or of destruction. In a dialogue on "The Identity and Dignity of Man" (Boston, 1969) the distinguished biologist, Hudson Hoagland, said: "I believe that we are animals and that we are a special kind of animal. . . . We are imaginative animals. When we want to be cruel, we can be cruel in a thoroughly imaginative way. I do not think you can find any animals that could have produced the genocide of 6,000,000 Jews or any other group of people the way Hitler's Nazis did. This is a human performance. I do not think you could find a concentration camp developed by animals; it takes a lot of imagination to do it; that Stalin had. . . . Genocide is characteristic of the human animal, and so is war."

Animals, with extremely rare exceptions, do not fight wars or seek mass destruction of rival groups within their own species. Nor do animals—as Hoagland also understands—project visions of peace and organize rational efforts to realize them. To me Glenn Gray (*On Understanding Violence Philosophically*) is utterly convincing: "I have become profoundly convinced that man is never on the level of animals. Either he falls below them, as so often in his mad rages, or he rises above them when he achieves humanity." Human aggression is *human* aggression; human concord is *human* concord.

Yet human aggression can have dehumanizing consequences. It may take expression in resentment, furious hostility, and hatred. Even so, hatred is perhaps not its worst expression. Martin Buber's magnificent book, *I and Thou*, says profoundly: "Hate is by nature blind. Only a part of a being can be hated. . . . Yet the man who straightforwardly hates is nearer to relation than the man without hate and love." Aggression is most inhuman when its outlet is not hatred but blind destructiveness that ignores the humanity in an enemy.

In war that destructiveness is as typical of the home front as of the battlefront. War can be furious and cruel; it arouses passions of rage and revenge. Yet it is sometimes relieved by a cameraderie among men at arms, even among men trying to kill one another, a cameraderie that is lacking back home where the enemy is only statistical. I return to that other reported speech of General Patton—the one that disturbed me less in the film than in the display ads in Nairobi: "No bastard ever won a war by dying for his country. He won it by making the other poor dumb bastard die for his country." There is a noteworthy ambivalence in that speech. It can be understood as brutal and insolent. Yet perhaps there is in it a strangely disguised compassion that with no evident malice sees all warriors as "poor dumb bastards" thrown by history into conflict with each other. Men at war feel that ambivalence in their deepest selves.

Even so, war is an expression of aggression that almost defies understanding. Sometimes it is functional; that is, it is a deliberately chosen means to attain certain ends. The ends may be good or bad, and the means may be chosen shrewdly or stupidly; but in either case there is some kind of rationality in the choice. At other times it is not functional; it does not lead toward an end so much as it follows from an inner drive of individuals and groups. In such warfare men are saying inchoately, "We know not what we are achieving, but in doing this we are being ourselves." In such aggression men are finding, for better or worse, some kind of identity.

Sometimes it is argued that man is still in an early age of evolution and that his descendants will be less aggressive than present generations. It is occasionally proposed that genetic manipulation or drugs may program man to be more peaceable. Herman J. Muller, famed geneticist and Nobel Laureate, proposed genetic programs aimed at increasing "brotherly love" and "deep and broad warmheartedness." Yet he recognized the values of aggressiveness in the sense of "independence of judgment and moral courage." In that conflict of values lies the dilemma. Presumably an elite, taking charge of genetic processes, might eventually breed a more passive race of men. Given the world's conflicts and the quality of the world's leadership, it is perhaps just as probable that they would breed a more frenetic race. Humanity's need is not for a race more aggressive or more acquiescent in any simple glandular way. The need is for qualities of character by which free men direct their biological and psychic potentialities to creative and redemptive rather than to destructive or lethargic goals. The reply of many a geneticist to Muller is that we know little or nothing about the relation of genes to the subtler meanings of human character.

Suppose, for the moment, that scientific advance should make possible the programming of a society, whether by genetic devices, drugs, or electrodes, so that the leaders in control might manipulate the actions and even feelings of populations. Suppose also the dubious assumption that the leaders would choose to make men more amiable rather than more militant. Would the result be gain or loss? It might depend partly on the aims of the leaders—on whether they sought to enhance their own status by thwarting racial liberation, the ambitions of the poor, and the vitalities of youth. But let us grant them the most idealistic of aims—a world of cooperation and concord in which men would find their identities in nonaggressive ways. Such a world might lose the hazards and the grandeur of our world. To the extent that freedom remained a reality, some men would protest against being manipulated for their own good.

Humanity with its powers of imagination and of freedom has capacities both for war and for peace. So long as imagination and freedom are real, it remains possible that some men will seek self-expression and identity in violent acts of war.

IDENTITY

No eternal decrees, no immutable nature determine that men must find their identity through violence. Sometimes society very nearly decrees that there will be no other way.

Richard Wright made the point in a prophetic novel of 1940, *Native Son*. Bigger Thomas, the twenty-year-old black youth, resentful of racist oppression, killed a wealthy white girl by accident rather than by intention. Almost inevitably a bigoted white world regarded him as her murderer. But even more important, Bigger Thomas chose to accept the role of murderer. For in that role he found for the first time an identity that society had previously denied him. "He had murdered and had created a new life for himself. It was something that was all his own, and it was the first time in his life he had anything that others could not take from him." He moved around the city, even though a haunted fugitive, with the confidence that he had done something, that police were seeking him, that he mattered. His acceptance of "the moral guilt and responsibility" for the murder "made him feel free for the first time in his life."

I have called the novel prophetic because it anticipated what was to happen on a larger scale in riots of the 1960's. In Harlem, in Detroit, in Watts, and elsewhere black people rioted, sometimes with little or no expectation that the riot would bring economic or political gain for themselves. It says something about our society that such riots did in fact, sometimes, bring economic and political changes that years of cries for justice had not brought. But the rioting was not primarily instrumental in purpose. Repeated testimonies from the communities tell how people felt that for the first time they had put themselves on the map, had required an indifferent society to take notice, had found an identity.

Rollo May's *Love and Will* says psychiatrically what Richard Wright's *Native Son* said fictionally. Apathy, says Dr. May, leads to violence. "For no human being can stand the perpetually numbing experience of his own powerlessness. . . .

Violence is the ultimate destructive substitute which surges in to fill the vacuum where there is no relatedness."

Another psychoanalyst, Frantz Fanon, has become one of the chief theorists of revolutionary violence in our time. Writing out of the experience of the Algerian struggle for independence from France, in a racial as well as an imperial context, he makes a double case for the necessity of violent revolutionary war. The first part of the case is the familiar instrumental argument, considered earlier in this book, that ruling nations or factions rarely if ever give up their power except under compulsion. The second part of the case, which is the concern of this chapter, is the necessity for violence as an expressive act through which a dominated people find their identity.

In the most important of his books, *The Wretched of the Earth*, Dr. Fanon said: "The colonised man finds his freedom in and through violence. . . . Violence alone, violence committed by the people, violence organised and educated by its leaders, makes it possible for the masses to understand social truths and gives the key to them." The argument includes a noble aspiration. Fanon did not seek simply to reverse the pattern of oppression so that former subjects became conquerors; he proclaimed his crusade for the sake of "humanity" and "a new man." But that idealism in no way undercut his insistence that violence is a necessity in social revolution.

Jean-Paul Sartre outshouted Fanon in a preface to the latter's book. "Irrepressible violence," wrote Sartre, "is neither sound and fury, nor the resurrection of savage instincts, nor even the effect of resentment: it is man re-creating himself." And he continued: "The rebel's weapon is the proof of his humanity." That latter sentence requires scrutiny. It says something about the nature of humanity—a topic on which Sartre has said many different things in many situations.

Once, in a famous lecture, "Existentialism Is a Humanism," he said: "As soon as there is a commitment, I am obliged to will the liberty of others at the same time as my own. I cannot make liberty my aim unless I make that of others equally my aim." He might have remembered that when he later argued that the killing of others is the proof of the rebel's humanity. He might have asked whether the killing of others does not destroy something precious in the killer.

Martin Luther King in his last published book, *Where Do We Go from Here?* gave his answer to Frantz Fanon. I have already expressed both my admiration for and my perplexities about King's beliefs on the instrumental meaning of violence. Now I consult his wisdom on its expressive meaning. After citing Fanon on the "new man," King replied: "These are brave and challenging words; I am happy that young black men and women are quoting them. But the problem is that Fanon and those who quote his words are seeking 'to work out new concepts' and 'set afoot a new man' with a willing-ness to imitate old concepts of violence. Is there not a basic contradiction here? Violence has been the inseparable twin of materialism, the hallmark of its grandeur and misery. This is the one thing about modern civilization that I do not care to imitate."

Put King's words, for the moment, beside those quoted early in this chapter from Patton. By Patton's logic King is a fool or a coward or both—and in any case is not a "real man." But what is a real man? Might it be that Patton's glori-fication of war is not real manhood but a truncated manliness or a fixated adolescent insecurity?

Bertrand Russell, writing *A History of Western Philosophy*, came to his consideration of Nietzsche's attack upon the de-generative "slave morality" of Christianity. In a host of other writings Russell made clear that he was not a Christian but that he admired Christian love. Looking at Nietzsche's accusations, Russell immediately granted that certain types of humility and pretended love come from the fear of those who are not strong enough to exercise power. But he replied to Nietzsche that lust for power "is itself an outcome of fear," that "those who do not fear their neighbours see no necessity to tyrannize over them," that "spontaneous love of mankind" may flow from strength rather than from fear. (I note, for the record, that there is more to Nietzsche than Russell recognizes or than I can mention here, but Nietzsche's own rhetoric sometimes confounded his best insights, and the deposit of his worst rhetoric is still with us.)

Violence and war, I maintain, are sometimes expressions of identity. But to establish one's identity by the destruction of others is morally questionable, if not downright unjust. Perhaps, as I believe, such an act does not even establish an authentic identity of the actor. If one need of men is for love, the identity found in violence and war is a truncated identity involving some self-destruction. It may be in some cases of radical injustice better for an individual and for society than persistence in non-identity or nonentity. But it is neither good nor adequate.

I am not here saying that violent rebellion or defensive warfare is never justifiable. I have earlier made the case that the eruptive violence of the rebel may be morally superior to the systemic violence of the oppressor. As against the absolutists of violence and nonviolence alike, I have said that war —not including total war—may at some times be a tragic necessity. But now the question at issue is the expressive, not the instrumental, meaning of war. Here, as in the earlier case, I see no monopolistic truths. Dogmas that avoid moral perplexity are in all times, and especially in confusing times like our own, a deceptive temptation. So I agree that individual acts of violence and communal acts of war may liberate something that has been violently repressed in men—but only at the risk of destroying something of humanity in the executors of violence and in their human objects.

If there is moral condemnation in such a statement, it is not necessarily or chiefly directed against the violent rebel. It may be directed against the society that evokes the rebel. A society that enables persons to claim dignity and identity in harmony with others removes some of the pressure that leads to violence. It does not remove all causes of violence, since men may employ violence for the sake of conquest as well as for the sake of liberation. But such a society contributes to the possibility of meaningful community.

COMRADESHIP

An individual is never solely an individual, and his identity is never exclusively individual identity. He participates in groups and finds his identity in relation to those groups. One of the many paradoxes of war is that this form of conflict, which is the most extravagant of all destroyers of human community on the grand scale, is a powerful creator of community on the small scale. Therein lies one of its fatal attractions.

In combat men are knit together as in few other experiences of life. At first glance the unity of the fighting squad may seem to be artificial. The men, usually from diverse backgrounds and worlds of discourse, have been thrown together by accident. They may share few memories or few common interests apart from their role in war. They usually have divergent values, religions, superstitions, ethical standards, and goals. Whether or not they like one another, as human likes and dislikes usually go, is relatively unimportant. They are embattled together, and that does matter.

Social theory recognizes this phenomenon. Karl Mannheim, the eminent sociologist, has written (in *Ideology and Utopia*): "We belong to a group not only because we are born into it, not merely because we profess to belong to it, nor finally because we give it our loyalty and allegiance, but primarily because we see the world the way it does (i.e. in terms of the meanings of the group in question). In every concept, in every concrete meaning, there is contained a crystallization of the experiences of a certain group." The army squad, in certain limited but utterly important ways, sees the world in terms of common meanings. It shares a problem of survival, of a common enemy, of mingled loyalty and resistance to the same system. Studies of army morale repeatedly show that the most important loyalty of soldiers is not to the grand ideological cause but to the small combat unit.

The mutuality of the military unit contrasts starkly with most of the promptings of a competitive society. I recall the efforts of a career Sergeant to motivate reluctant recruits in my first weeks of military training. In early weapons training the motivation was individual survival. "The better you can shoot, the better your chances of killing the other guy before he kills you." The reasoning, abstractly plausible, was actually specious. The individual rifleman is about as likely to find himself firing at the one man who is firing at him as he is to see an opposing General in his rifle sight. But the motivation was consistent with the ideology of a competitive world. Then in the first days of training in squad tactics the motivational world swirled and landed upside down. The Sergeant explained that some men would deliberately expose themselves and draw enemy fire in order that others might make a concealed move. At the phrase, "draw enemy fire," we recruits laughed nervously. The moment was not traumatic: we were far from the seriousness of combat. But the grim humor came from the way that the Sergeant's words threw askew all normal motivations, including those this same Sergeant had used over past days.

Combat requires and builds trust. Men who read the fine print before signing purchase orders, who hire lawyers to draw up foolproof contracts on relatively trivial issues, who bargain incessantly over an automobile trade-in, when they engage in combat are likely to make hasty agreements, "You cover me while I make this move, then I'll cover you." The soldier may say that to someone whom he knows to be a cheater at dice (usually outside the squad), a lying seducer of women, and a chiseler on income tax; but the two count on trust in an instantaneous and unenforceable agreement concerning life and death. In such trust they count on each other and perhaps catch a glimpse of what human relations on a more enduring basis might be.

Philosopher Glenn Gray's superb book, *The Warriors*, describes profoundly such intimacy and interdependence. "This confraternity of danger and exposure is unequaled in forging links among people of unlike desire and temperament, links that are utilitarian and narrow but no less passionate because of their accidental and general character." When all the larger purposes of war are obscured or lost, he points out, "the fighter is often sustained solely by the determination not to let down his comrades." This sense of community produces "an ecstasy" and "a consciousness of power that is supra-individual." Major Bill, interrogating me in the forbidding castle at Diesz, though he was no philosopher, understood the raw data behind Glenn Gray's conclusion. His most powerful intimidating tactic was not to beat me; it was to remind me of my absolute loneliness, thereby throwing into question whatever courage I might have known in battle.

A little more than three years after the end of World War

II, the Army and Air Force Recruiting Service made an effort to persuade veterans to re-enlist. The main pitch was to the veteran's nostalgia for a lost "feeling of security," sense of belonging, and "warmth of comradeship." Many years thereafter, during the second decade of war in Vietnam, the old recruiting ad looks somewhat ridiculous. It is a sign of the changed morale of a society and the changed military situation that the recruiting services would not use anything remotely similar now. But the feelings to which the ad appealed have often been real.

Lost Something, Vet?

Lost that feeling of security you had when you were in the Army or Air Force? The knowledge that you could always count on that generous, free retirement policy down the road, and that in the meantime you'd be given a helping hand someway, somehow, when the going was a little tough, because you *belonged*? Lost all that?

Lost the warmth of comradeship you had when you were in the Army or Air Force? The good times you had with a bunch of square-shooting buddies? The horseplay and standing jokes among real friends, that shortened the toughest assignment and made Yesterday a pleasant memory? Lost all that?

Excerpts from ad of Army and Air Force Recruiting Service, from *AVC Bulletin*, December, 1948.

More surprising, there are evidences that even now they are not totally unreal. An article by William G. Pelfrey, "No Laurels for Legionnaires," in the *New Republic* for November 21, 1970, tells how this one young man entered the army rather cynical and opposed to the war in Vietnam, and how he finished his term of service even more cynical and opposed to the war. Yet he comments: "In those wandering first weeks after the return I perceived that the only time in my life I had had an identity other than my vague personal goals had been as a member of a combat unit in Vietnam."

Experiences of contemporary youth show many analogies. On occasion the peace movement has discovered the power of a morale more often known in war. Numberless accounts of students, embattled against university officials or police, in sit-ins or seizures of buildings, tell of the exhilaration and comradeship awakened by such events. The normal life of this generation has deprived its youths of any intense awareness of community. Then in a crisis, where there is some slight perception of actual danger, they recognize the "ecstasy" and "consciousness of power that is supra-individual" that Glenn Gray described in war. If we ask why modern society is so sterile in enabling people to find in peace a gratification that is common in war, we may have begun a profound interrogation of our culture.

HEROISM

War asks ordinary people to be heroic. Often they respond. They discover in themselves powers previously unknown. When all the brutality, stupidity, and tawdry glamor of war have been debunked—as indeed they should be debunked—the facts of heroism remain. And something in mankind answers to calls to heroism.

Heroism is not limited to war. There may be a more mature and creative heroism in the life of a modest mother, a social worker, a public school teacher in the ghetto than in the life of many a swashbuckling warrior. But most of the common images of civil life mute the heroic possibilities. The press and the public expect soldiers to be brave; that is their business even in dreary and unpopular wars. The same press and public expect people in civil life to respond to the profit motive and hopefully show a peripheral generosity toward friends and the public interest. In many jobs the expectation is, in inelegant language, that an employee will get to work on time, keep his nose clean, and do a little extra hustling if he's on tips or commissions. Government assumes that capital and labor will respond to the incentives of self-interest, possibly with a little restraint for the sake of the public welfare. The church in its doctrine emphasizes sacrifice; actually it apologizes if it asks of its members inconvenience.

Peter S. Prescott of *Newsweek*, reviewing Barbara Tuchman's book on General "Vinegar Joe" Stilwell, says: "Something in the American character flourishes in wartime, and we need to know what it is." War, though it brings out the worst in men, sometimes brings out the best. It asks commitment. It asks willingness to accept risk. It asks for subordination of self-interest. And, I say again, men and women respond. They give themselves, often for no reward save "the red badge of courage." They cultivate no illusions that hanging on to life and comfort are adequate motives. "Morale," said General Eisenhower, "is the greatest single factor in successful war." Such a sentence may be discounted as the thing that a General is expected to say. But exactly that is the interesting point. A General is not expected to say that time-and-motion studies or quick amortization of investments or

275

fast capital gains are the greatest factor in success. War creates a different mythology.

William James in 1910 published his essay "The Moral Equivalent of War." The title lends itself to spoofing, and people who know only the title sometimes spoof it. Those who read it have to think. True, it is old-fashioned in some ways. In the relatively short interval of history since the essay war has become less dramatic, more wasteful and dreary. The songs of war seldom pour from people's throats any more. Increasingly we try to make matériel do the work of men. In another way James seems old-fashioned; he wrote before the twentieth century had shown men's cruelty and nihilism. He had less anxious apprehension than contemporary mankind has, more confidence in the ability of humanity to order its destiny. Even so, some of his reasoning speaks to the present condition.

Suppose, he suggests, that our nation were to take a vote on a proposal to repeat the Civil War; we could assume unanimous rejection of the idea. But suppose we could—to conceive a fantasy—vote on expunging the war from our history; few, he thinks, would vote yes. Why? "Those ancestors, those efforts, those memories and legends, are the most ideal part of what we now own together, a sacred spiritual possession worth more than all the blood poured out." We might today modify that judgment; we are more aware than James of the bitter legacy of that war and its roots in slavery. Yet he is right that the past we commemorate is usually the past of sacrifice and heroism. Myth, epic, and saga generally tell of arms and heroes.

"War is the *strong* life; it is life *in extremis*," said James, although he called himself a pacifist. "It is a sort of sacrament." People are reluctant "to see the supreme theatre of human strenuousness closed." They don't want to substitute "mawkish and dishwatery" utopias for "life's more bitter flavors."

James's proposed answer involved both an act of imagination and a reorganization of society. The imaginative act asked mankind to redirect pride and passion toward worthier goals than conquest. The social reorganization called for some redistribution of life's comfortable securities and harsh pains so that all might share in life's toughness and its rewards. Today the Peace Corps and Vista mean for a few something like what James advocated for the many. He did not assume that the transformation he proposed would be easy. But he did not reckon adequately with its difficulties, either imaginative or organizational.

William James would be pleased with some things taking place among youth today. He would understand the phraseology that calls those who believe in a cause to put their bodies on the line. He would understand the patriotism that risks reputation and liberty in opposition to war. He would understand the young men and women who renounce the prestigious careers of corporation lawyers in order to practice law as a community service, or who pass by more comfortable jobs to do service as policemen with the aim of uniting human compassion with enforcement of law.

For two millennia men influenced by Christ have puzzled over the relationship between the pagan virtues and the Christian graces. What have Homeric valor and pride to do with faith, hope, and love? Although Augustine described the pagan virtues as merely splendid vices, he could not entirely hide some admiration for them. Yet he gave impetus to a tradition that separated too much the virtues of earth and the virtues of heaven.

Paul, although he exulted in the foolishness of God that confounded the wisdom and aspirations of men, nevertheless committed no *faux pas* when he occasionally described the Christian life in military metaphors. Believing that man's highest possibilities were gifts of grace, not results of striving, he could still ask: "If the bugle gives an indistinct sound, who will get ready for battle?" (I Cor. 14:8). It was not sheer accident, I have suggested earlier, that Jesus described his mission with the metaphor of the sword.

Heroism is one of the expressive meanings of violence and war. Those who cherish peace cannot deny those expressive meanings, any more than pragmatists can dissolve all the expressive meanings into instrumental meanings. What peacemakers can do is show that the noblest human meanings often expressed in war can find other expressions. A humanity without valor and gallantry would be a poor humanity indeed. But perhaps valor and gallantry can be enhanced if they are transferred from destruction to reconstruction. We are in no position either to guarantee the transfer or to deny its possibility.

6. THE QUEST
OF A KINGDOM

*"Grace to you and peace from God our Father and
the Lord Jesus Christ."* Saint Paul, Romans 1:7.

*"May their peace be their disquiet, and their
disquiet be their peace! This is beginning, theme, and
end of the Epistle to the Romans."* Karl Barth.

A peace without disquiet is as much the enemy of man as
disquiet without peace. An unthreatened life is as unreal as
a totally insecure life is undesirable. Meaning in human striving is as precarious as unmeaning is destructive. Man, craving life, dies.

Of such paradoxes is human existence made. Man needs
no war to tell him so. Yet war, more than most experiences,
does tell man so.

Where are courage and folly, comradeship and annihilation, aspiration and terror so intimately linked? William
James was right in calling war "a sort of sacrament." If that
seems sacrilegious in an epoch that is sick of war, let us say
that war is a parable of the condition of mankind. When
we have analyzed it, moralized about it, paid our taxes for
it, and protested against it—all of which are at one time or
another important to do—we will still be wise to seek its
parabolic illumination of our human existence. War tells us
something about contingency, gratitude, community, and
hope.

Everyone must think personally about such subjects, and I
do not pretend to be authoritative or objective. This book
started with a memoir. It continued through mingled rem-

iniscence and more generalized philosophical and theological reflections. It ends in personal affirmations.

CONTINGENCY

Contingency is natural to life. Daily man encounters the unpredictable, the indeterminate, the unnecessary, the unforeseen. Yet nobody likes to acknowledge dependence on uncertainties, so man constructs institutions and edifices to rationalize his life. He imposes his designs and purposeful constructions on a nonsymmetrical landscape. The most common maps of modern civilization are road maps on which the marks of human planning almost obscure the unpatterned variety of nature. We like to think of our lives and little achievements as the results of our efforts. But "the best laid schemes o' mice and men/ Gang aft a-gley," sometimes for better and sometimes for worse. An earthquake in Pakistan or California, an air flight canceled because of storms, an unpredicted heart attack, a blind date that leads to marriage, the doctor's "It's a boy" or "It's a girl"—such events tell us that our intentions work themselves out within a context of the unknown that we do not order.

It was the genius of Blaise Pascal, superlative scientist and theologian, to see more deeply than most men the contingency that human designing does its best to obscure. As a mathematician, Pascal knew how to establish certainties and predictabilities. As an empiricist, he knew how to observe and detect the uncertain and unforeseeable. As a mystic he pondered his relation to the unknowable. "When I consider the short duration of my life, swallowed up in the eternity that went before me and the eternity that comes after, the small extent of space I fill, the narrow limits of my field of view, swallowed up as I am in the infinite immensities of space, which I do not know, and which know not me, I am terrified and astonished to find myself here rather than there. For there is no reason whatever why I should be here rather than there, why now rather than then."

Three centuries of scientific progress since Pascal have, if anything, heightened this awareness of contingency. Scientists are more likely than in Pascal's time to acknowledge a contingency in the inmost nature of things. Anyone of us can think through the accidents of his own heredity. Through the centuries an uncountable succession of improbable matings, each with its fortuitous causes, led to the one unprecedented and unrepeatable relationship from which each of us was born. And out of the infinite genetic combinations possible to that one mating, came the unique inheritance (duplicated by no one unless by an identical twin) of each of us. Pascal is more impressive now than when he wrote: "For there is no reason whatever why I should be here rather than there, why now rather than then. Who put me here? By whose order and direction have this place and this time been assigned to me?"

A generation or two of logical positivists once conspired to convince mankind by their unanimous decree that such assertions are "nonsensical" and "meaningless." They came and went, persuading nobody. The reason is that nobody can regard himself as an accident. Men and women, not wise enough to answer Pascal's questions with anything remotely like scientific certainty, are yet wise enough to ask them. To ask them is to insist that life has meanings, both hidden and revealed. It is to affirm meaning against the threat of chaos without denying the reality of contingency. It is to recognize that, while the world would have gone right on its way if any one of us had not entered it, the world is different because of us. At a minimum, it would not be *our world* without us; and an important feature of the world is that it is our world.

The awareness of death, as Heidegger has shown so impressively, is the forceful and irrefutable evidence to each of us that he is contingent, not necessary. To face directly the reality and certainty of death, rather than hide it with the intricate death-concealing devices conjured up by a nervous society, is a decisive event in self-discovery. Death can strangely bring a heightened self-awareness and hence a sharpened perception of the world.

Psychologist Abraham Maslow, in a letter written while recovering from a heart attack and quoted in Rollo May's *Love and Will*, describes an experience familiar to many: "The confrontation with death—and the reprieve from it—makes everything look so precious, so sacred, so beautiful that I feel more strongly than ever the impulse to love it, to embrace it, and to let myself be overwhelmed by it. My river has never looked so beautiful. . . . Death, and its ever present possibility makes love, passionate love, more possible. I wonder if we could love passionately, if ecstasy would be possible at all, if we knew we'd never die."

Man has no need for war to make possible such discoveries. But war, with its insistent confrontation with death, may become a parable of such experience. Perhaps something like Pascal's amazement at and Maslow's embracing of the world and human existence enter into all lives. War has thrust them into some lives, including my own. Perhaps I should be ashamed that some insights had to come to me by such a method; I am glad that they did come.

There are moments when I am utterly amazed that I am alive. Once in battle, once under interrogation, and once under American bombardment I made my peace with death. Thereafter everything was a gracious gift, what our forefathers called an uncovenanted mercy. Sometimes I wonder, like Maslow, whether ecstasy would be possible without the awareness of death. I must quickly add that past confrontations with death cannot be deposited in a bank account as accumulated principle, paying automatic dividends month by month. I can cling to life and status as desperately as anyone else, can stake out plans as possessively, can make decisions and reckon consequences as nervously as the next person. I can endure prosaic days and can resent responsibilities that intrude on my carefully hoarded privacy. The past confrontation with death means nothing except as it repeatedly becomes contemporary. In precious moments it does become contemporary and it means a heightened awareness of the world. To give up all claims on life is perhaps the condition for learning to appreciate life.

There are hours when I exult in the sheer unutterable delight of this world. I marvel at the taste of a fresh apple or of cold water . . . at the loveliness of a crescent moon or a snowflake . . . at the awesome power of a thunderstorm . . . at the tingling sting of sleet on the face and the warmth of a fireplace afterwards . . . at the extravagance of nature scattering beauties unnoticed by man . . . at the zest of rising at dawn and the lazy luxury of sleeping late . . . at friendly faces and gestures of trust . . . at the joy of conjugal embrace. There are times when I am overwhelmed with wonder that the world can be so entrancing.

The poets know how to describe such experiences. The rest of us, hearing their descriptions, can sometimes answer, "Yes, that's what we felt and didn't know how to say." Sometimes, because they have said it, we can discover our own perceptions, previously hidden from us. So I feel when William Blake says something that my more prosaic self could never have said but can thank him for saying: " 'What,' it will be Question'd, 'When the Sun rises, do you not see a round disk of fire somewhat like a Guinea?' O no, no, I see an Innumerable company of the Heavenly host crying, 'Holy, Holy is the Lord God Almighty.' "

In so glorious and enticing a world I can easily see why John Calvin worried that the earth might attract "our immoderate love." Hence Calvin in his *Institutes* warned: "Since the present life has numerous blandishments to attract us, and much pleasure, beauty, and sweetness to delight us,—it is very necessary to our highest interests, that we should be frequently called off, that we may not be fascinated with such allurements." God has so provided for our "pleasure and delight" that we need deliberately to cultivate "contempt of the present life."

I dislike the word contempt, used by Calvin as by Augustine before him; I reject part of what Calvin meant by the word. Yet I see his point. For I am as aware as Calvin that this earth, sometimes so entrancing, is also "unquiet, turbulent, miserable." Nature's ravages and men's injustices inflict frustration and cruelty on people. Lurking within any "immoderate love" of the world are two moral dangers: first, an indifference to the plight of those who suffer, often because of the very social structures that bring pleasure to others; second, an attachment to life that makes men unwilling to risk their comforts or to throw life away if courage asks them to sacrifice.

No more than anyone else do I know how to put together in a comprehensive picture those perceptions that persuade me that basically life is good and those that tell me both nature and man are flawed and cry out for transformation. The nearest I can come to an answer is to use the words that Dostoevsky gives to Alyosha Karamazov who, after sharing the agony of his brothers and of others, says to the boys who love him: "Ah, dear friends, don't be afraid of life! How good life is when one does something good and just!"

That answer is far from complete. It leaves many questions unanswered. But to anyone impressed by the radical contingency of existence, many questions are bound to go unanswered. Nevertheless, within the contingencies, not all is chaos. Acts of courage and trust are still real. One of those acts is the trust that some meaning, barely intimated in human experience, not only guides our decisions but even encompasses somehow the contingency. Stated otherwise, it is the trust that throughout all life every man, knowingly or unwittingly, is responding to a mysterious Thou.

GRATITUDE

No man ever made himself or decided to be born. Nor did the human race decide or plan to be. No one can by taking thought add a cubit to his stature, though by failing to take thought he may add to his girth. All this should be obvious. Yet we human beings are so possessive that we lay hold on the gift of life as though we had earned it and could not let it be pried away. Confrontation with death may tell us that life is not really ours to hoard and that we know how to live only if we know how to give away ourselves and our being.

In the winter of 1942 Dietrich Bonhoeffer wrote a meditation, called "After Ten Years," as a Christmas gift for the German resisters closest to him. He already knew that the Central Bureau for the Security of the Reich was getting evidence against him. On March 31, 1943, five days before his arrest, he gave a copy of this bit of writing to his father on his seventy-fifth birthday. Near the end of it Dietrich Bonhoeffer had written: "We cannot hate death as we used to, for we have discovered some good in it after all, and have almost come to terms with it. Fundamentally we feel that we really belong to death already, and that every new day is a miracle. . . . We still love life, but I do not think that death can take us by surprise now."

That love of life, in which every new day is a miracle and no day can be clutched as a possession, means profound gratitude. Yet gratitude is simultaneously one of the most wonderful and one of the most dubious attitudes. Too often gratitude is complacent and self-centered—as in those Presidential Thanksgiving Proclamations that congratulate the nation because God has given us deserved blessings. The prayer of the self-righteous Pharisee in Jesus's parable was a prayer of *thanks* that he was not like other men, especially not like extortioners, adulterers, and tax collectors. To be thankful can be almost as graceless as to be thankless. How dare I be thankful for life when I can give no reason why, after so many friends have died, I should be alive? Yet how can I refuse to be thankful for his gift not of my doing?

Perhaps the only answer is thanks for life as an opportunity. The answer has been put by Laurens van der Post, a career army officer and a literary artist, as I could be neither. Thinking of his own wartime experience in a Japanese prison camp in Indonesia, he wrote in his *Venture to the Interior*: "I had promised myself then that if I survived, which at that moment seemed most unlikely, I would never again return to a life of nothing but private profit and personal gain. I would try never again to say 'NO' to life in its full, complete sense, no matter in how humble or perplexed a guise it presented itself."

If men could live by such a promise, whether verbalized or inarticulate, affirming life without laying claim upon it, they might learn to live out the gratitude that most of them feel sporadically. It is the kind of gratitude—or rejoicing—that led the Apostle Paul to say: "I know how to be abased, and I know how to abound; in any and all circumstances I have learned the secret of facing plenty and hunger, abundance and want" (Philippians 4:12).

Paul puts together those words in curious patterns. Is it harder to know how to face plenty and abundance or hunger and want? I don't know. I know which I would rather face; hunger has no charms for me. Yet, after trying both abundance and want in modest ways, I suspect that abundance is the more severe test. Everyone knows the virtues that go with hunger and want: courage, endurance, resolution. What comparable virtues go with abundance? Generosity, perhaps. But can the generosity of the comfortable rival the generosity of the needy? Can the rich man or the rich nation pass through the eye of the needle? The only biblical answer is that with God all things are possible. Perhaps with God it is possible to be grateful and not grasping, to realize that the life that is a gift is thereby a glorious responsibility.

COMMUNITY

War, I said in the last chapter, generates an amazing comradeship that unites diverse men, who may not greatly like each other or share many convictions, into a unity that transcends their isolated beings. That unity is evanescent; the fumbling attempts to recover it in later years are likely to get lost in reminiscence and strained conviviality. Yet such comradeship—I use Glenn Gray's word—is a token of the human need and capacity for community.

Human community, too, comes out of intimate association. But because of the gift of imagination, community can transcend formidable barriers of space. Once again war is the enigmatic witness to the meaning of such community.

The soldier's hunger for mail rivals his hunger for food. The ancient invention of paper and written language is as important to the spirit of an army as any ingenious modern morale-building device. The written word spans continents and oceans; it maintains community despite the vast spaces and organizations that disrupt it.

Mail from family and friends sustains clearly significant communities against the fragmentation that is yoked with the fortunes of war. Sometimes it sustains stranger communities also. Again I yield to the temptation of recollection. Among my school friends, as I mentioned earlier, was a group who refused to register for the draft in 1940. We argued with one another long into many nights, convicting one another of errors in logic and heresies in faith, all the while building bonds stronger than those among men who easily agree. These many years afterward some of us maintain our affection and on occasion stand by one another in civil strife.

They went off to prison, and I to military encampment and war. They were a gallant few, who brought the prison new glory on the athletic field and took on the warden in a campaign for racial reform within the prison. Each of them was permitted to name one or two correspondents outside his own family. I was profoundly pleased when one of them named me. He was George Houser, a man of enthusiastic and refreshing commitment, now director of the American Committee on Africa. From Danbury Prison to Camp Wolters, Texas, our letters went back and forth. A journalistic friend (now Professor Richard T. Baker of the Columbia University School of Journalism) assembled a few and had them published in *motive*. The prison warden soon put a stop to that, on the grounds that his job was not to provide a sounding board for a convict—somewhat as a later warden was to deny a platform to more famous prisoners, Fathers Dan and Phil Berrigan.

The point of this last excursion into the past is to ferret out, if possible, some of the secrets of community. In some ways I was closer to those prisoners than to the men I trained with on the Texas sands. Later, when I was a prisoner and they (having served their time) were free, I still knew that we shared in the life of a community.

Although time is a more formidable, more irrevocable separator than space, community in some ways can transcend time. Finite and contingent though we are, there are marks of eternity in our humanity. Although no modern miracles of transportation can leap boundaries of time as jet planes leap boundaries of space, although men can never return to a time as they can return to a place, imagination and memory mean that human persons can in some ways incorporate into themselves the time that marks limits to their lives. Most races of men and most faiths have had some vivid sense of the community that includes both a cloud of witnesses from the past and generations yet unborn to whom the present has a responsibility.

HOPE

"While there's life, there's hope," goes the old saying. It can be reversed. While there's hope, there's life. Without hope there may still be a continuing pulse and nerve action, conceivably even some kind of society in a virtual social coma, but these are hardly what we mean by human living. The inscription over the gate to hell in Dante's *Inferno* carried the words, "Abandon hope, all ye who enter here." In that hopeless state men could anticipate neither the glow of life nor the surcease of death.

But what is hope? Surely it is one of the most complex of four-letter words. Sometimes it means only a wish. ("Are you getting well?" "I hope I am, but I don't think so.") Sometimes it means expectation. ("I'm more hopeful than I was yesterday." That means not that I'm wishing harder, but that my expectations are higher.) Sometimes it means confidence. (People talk of invincible hope, unconquerable hope. Nobody talks of invincible wishes or expectations.)

In all its meanings hope reaches into the future and the unknown. As the Apostle Paul puts it, in a matter-of-fact comment within an ecstatic confession of faith, "Hope that is seen is not hope. For who hopes for what he sees?" (Romans 8:24). It is that peering toward the unseeable, that grasping for the intangible which constitute hope. They can also make it deceptive. Nowhere is this more the case than in the life of nations.

It was Thomas Jefferson's "hope and belief" that the American achievement would "ameliorate the condition of man over a great portion of the globe." Abraham Lincoln in his Message to Congress of December 1, 1862, saw this nation as "the last, best hope of earth." As late as 1935 Thomas Wolfe (*Of Time and the River*) described the sea voyage to America as a "drunken and magnificent hope which, against reason and knowledge, soars into a heaven of fabulous conviction, which believes in the miracle and sees it invariably achieved." But by the second half of the century, there is a sickness abroad in the land. Miracles are not invariably achieved. Many wonder, looking at Wolfe's extravagant language, whether the hope was not always more "drunken" than "magnificent."

But the chastening of exaggerated hopes does not refute hope. There is health and strength in a society that can produce the young patriots I have described, along with many another person quietly or dramatically committed to a better world. To my most idealistic young friends, when they make their angry criticisms of my generation, I occasionally reply, "If we produced you, we must have done something right." This society is worth our strivings, as it is worth our criticisms.

However, the balancing of evidence that makes for optimism and for pessimism is not the real basis for hope or despair. "For who hopes for what he sees?" Hope, and the valor and commitment that depend upon hope, have a non-empirical—that is, a non-measurable, non-quantifiable—basis. Hope lives in the world of "in spite of" as well as the world of "because of." In traditional Jewish and Christian faith, the kingship of God has never been demonstrable, never identifiable with any social institutions. This is not to say that the kingdom of God is in some other, some distant world. It is a power—from the origin of things, presently active, yet continuously hoped for—that irradiates all present life and society. Humanity does not always discern it. It is known by revelation rather than calculation in those moments of perception that I have tried to describe by such words as contingency, gratitude, and community.

Yet perhaps everyone has intimations of this kingdom. Surely nobody would say that the meanings of a noble act are exhausted by its practical consequences. Suppose a man or woman sacrifices life for the sake of justice, but justice is not achieved. The act is not therefore worthless. It takes its place in a deeper, more encompassing context than any we see and measure. Thus meaning implies transcendence. The rationalizing and clarifying of that transcendence have concerned some of the best of minds for centuries; perhaps men will never succeed in the task of stating the ineffable.

But usually they know better than to limit their hope to their verbalizations.

Mankind, living by hope, engages in the quest of a kingdom. It will not do to call the kingdom simply an ideal or a vision. In its way its reality and power are as inescapable as and are more enduring than the institutions and causes for which we struggle—though it is not utterly separable from them.

It does not negate the contingency in which we live, or remove the moral confusion. Our quest continues in the midst of the confusion. We must still make perplexing decisions in a disorderly world. Rarely are courses of action marked by the clarity for which men yearn. Hence I must continue to believe in my troubled way that the responsible act combines a trace of skepticism and irony with commitment. In practical terms that means living, as John Kenneth Galbraith has occasionally put it, "between those who want the catharsis of total violence and those who want the comforts of total escape." Skepticism need not, though it sometimes does, cut the nerve of commitment. It is the nature of moral activity that men must pledge their fidelity beyond their theoretical certainty. The word skeptical originally referred to inquirers and seekers. A skeptic, too, may seek a kingdom.

Throughout this book I have been skeptical of any social plan or ideal that promised to remove violence from life. That does not mean that I think war in its particularly institutionalized forms of recent experience is destined to go on forever; rather I have said that if total nuclear war happens again, it is likely to happen only once. Likewise I have not minimized the unrealized possibilities of innovative nonviolent methods of social change. However, I have said that violence is a constant possibility, that there is more of it is normal life than men like to admit, that it may erupt again and again. If mankind is to find security, that security is in the quest of a kingdom that both is and is not yet.

I say this because of what I know of myself and what I think I know of others. Glenn Gray in *The Warriors* (1959) wrote: "Every nation, I believe, conceals in itself violent criminal forces, waiting only for an opportunity to appear in daylight." He was then writing primarily about the behavior of soldiers. Two decades later (*On Understanding Violence Philosophically*, 1970) he decided that the violence of war did not differ so much from ordinary life as he had once thought. So he wrote: "As I study the faces of students in my college classes, I am sometimes greatly tempted to warn them that they have not the slightest idea of what they are capable. This rational dialogue we are carrying on together is likely to seem to some of the sheltered ones the dependable face of reality. . . . Yet I need only close my eyes to imagine those faces contorted with hatred, those hands, feminine or masculine, clenched or clawlike, those bodies tensed and ready to spring, in order to realize that all of us conceal, half-knowing, powers that are at the furthest remove from the present setting." I am sure I do not misrepresent Gray when I say that our conventional intercourse conceals also possibilities of courage and love of which we are only dimly aware most of the time.

Albert Camus at the end of *The Plague* described the experience of Dr. Rieux, who had struggled gallantly as a physician through the desperation of an epidemic disease, which in its multiple symbolizations represented war, tyranny, and man's inner failures. Looking out over the town in its celebration of the end of the plague, he came to his own conclusion: that he had learned in pestilence "that there are more things to admire in men than to despise." Yet his final words were a warning that "joy is always imperiled." "He knew what those jubilant crowds did not know but could have learned from books: that the plague bacillus never dies or disappears for good; that it can lie dormant for years and years in furniture and linen-chests; that it bides its time in bedrooms, cellars, trunks, and bookshelves; and that perhaps the day would come when, for the bane and the enlightening of men, it would rouse up its rats again and send them forth to die in a happy city."

I agree with Camus both in his affirmation that there is more to admire than to despise in men and in his warning that joy is always imperiled. I expect conflict to continue in the history of mankind. I expect that it will sometimes be violent—in the many forms of revolutionary violence, aggressive violence, defensive violence, and the violence that seeks to restore peace. I see no way of knowing when such violence will spill over into what we call war, as it has repeatedly in the days of our years. But men and women will continue to hope. They may achieve new ways of creative conflict, new ways of moderating violence. I set no limits on the possibilities, except that I suspect they will not bring a security unthreatened by violence. Hope will win triumphs, as it has before, yet will reach forward to a kingdom not seen.

That kingdom is not utterly remote. Out of his life of mingled agony and ecstasy, Francis Thompson wrote in his poem, "The Kingdom of God":

> Does the fish soar to find the ocean,
> The eagle plunge to find the air—
> That we ask of the stars in motion
> If they have rumour of thee there?
>
> Not where the wheeling systems darken,
> And our benumbed conceiving soars!—

The drift of pinions, would we hearken,
Beats at our own clay-shuttered doors.

And what does that kingdom tell us of war? The New Testament reports that Jesus said, "And when you hear of wars and rumors of wars, do not be alarmed; this must take place, but the end is not yet" (Mark 13:7). The double affirmation is significant. First, "this must take place." That, I take it, is not a doctrine that any particular war or form of war is inevitable; it is a warning that conflict is part of life, that hidden in all the institutionalizations of peace are threats to peace, that those who count most certainly on carefully contrived security are most vulnerable to threats of insecurity. But second, "the end is not yet." Wars and rumors of wars are not the end. Literally the possibility of a "war to end war" by ending human history is today more likely than when Jesus spoke. I would rather think that will not happen. But whether it does or not, the end is not yet. Destruction is not the last word on human existence. Hope, courage, compassion, trust, and love have their ultimate meaning in a kingdom that has no end.

President John F. Kennedy in his Inaugural Address paraphrased a phrase from Paul's Letter to the Romans (12:15): "rejoicing in hope, patient in tribulation." Those are good words for all people and communities who seek a kingdom.

I put beside them the still older words (Mt. 7:7): "Seek and you will find."

AN INFORMAL

GLOSSARY

Military Terms and Abbreviations—
American, British, and German

Able, Baker, Charlie — A, B, C in the phonetic alphabet; used, for example, to refer to Companies A, B, and C.

AT — anti-tank (guns, vehicles, tactics, or organizations); in this book, the anti-tank platoon of Company C.

C.O. — Commanding Officer; ironically the same abbreviation often means Conscientious Objector, but is not so used in this book.

C.P. — Command Post, for anything from a platoon to a division.

Feldwebel — German Field Sergeant, one grade above what Americans called a Platoon Sergeant or "Buck Sergeant."

4-F-ers — men physically incapable of military duty; derived from the classification 4-F in the U.S. Selective Service System.

H.Q. — headquarters.

Hauptmann — German Captain.

Hommes 40, Cheveaux 8 — sign on aged French boxcars, indicating a capacity of 40 men or 8 horses.

K.P. — kitchen police, as almost everybody knows.

Kriegie — American slang for prisoners of war in Germany; derived from *Kriegsgefangener*.

Luftwaffe — the German Air Force.

NCO — noncommissioned officer.

90-day wonder — disrespectful slang for American officers commissioned at end of three-month Officer Candidate School. The Infantry School was at Ft. Benning, Georgia. Major "Bill's" use of the slang and his reference to Ft. Benning were intended to impress me with his knowledge of American military life. They succeeded.

Oberst — German Colonel.

Oberstleutnant — German Lieutenant Colonel.

Oflag — German term for officers' prison camp; a contraction of *Offizier* and *Stalag*, the terms for prison camp. A *Stalag* might also be called a *Lager*, a more general term.

PW — prisoner of war.

RAF — British Royal Air Force.

Recon — reconnaissance.

SS — German Stormtroopers, an elite military organization, usually strongly indoctrinated with Nazi ideology.

Volksturm — the German People's Army, often a rag-tag collection of civilians too decrepit to be drafted but trained for home defense.